RAISING THE BAR

Creating Value with the United Nations Global Compact

Edited by **Claude Fussler,**
Aron Cramer and **Sebastian van der Vegt**

Greenleaf
PUBLISHING
2 0 0 4

© 2004 Greenleaf Publishing Limited

Published by Greenleaf Publishing Limited
Aizlewood's Mill
Nursery Street
Sheffield S3 8GG
UK

Printed on paper made from at least 75% post-consumer waste
using TCF and ECF bleaching.
Printed and bound by William Clowes, UK.
Cover by LaliAbril.com.

British Library Cataloguing in Publication Data:
   A catalogue record for this book is available from the British Library.

ISBN 1874719829

CONTENTS

FROM THE SECRETARY-GENERAL

The Global Compact is expanding rapidly across the globe, with currently more than 1,400 participants from business, labour and civil society in over 70 countries. With that growth comes an increasing need for practical tools, information, resources and case studies to enable companies and others to give practical meaning to the universal principles — in the areas of human rights, labour and the environment — that are the core of the Compact.

This comprehensive reference guide seeks to organise that material in an accessible way. I hope it will prove a valuable resource for corporate leaders, scholars and others looking to promote — and practise — effective, responsible, globally minded management.

Kofi A. Annan
New York, June 2004

PREFACE

IN 2002 A NUMBER OF PRACTITIONERS FROM business met with experts from civil society and UN programmes and agencies to share their experience in putting universal principles in practice. The principles in question formed the basis of the Global Compact that UN Secretary-General Kofi Annan called business leaders to join, at the start of 1999.

So, three years later, these early adopters met to reflect on what enabled them to make human rights, labour standards and environmental responsibility part of the business agenda while maintaining their competitive drive. They also discussed how their approach could in turn stimulate other companies to increase performance while supporting the Global Compact.

Soon, they realised that they often applied the same methods and even the same terminology as in approaches generally referred to as 'total quality management' or 'managing excellence'. However, although they used specific statistical tools, surveys, training and decision protocols to achieve ever-lower rates of quality failure and ever-higher customer satisfaction, the response to the Global Compact demanded a different set of tools and practices. The early participants all spoke about their experimentation with new tools and practices to bring the Global Compact alive through business action. They also reflected on the problems of confusion and overlap with so many corporate citizenship initiatives demanding their attention. It seemed therefore valuable and timely to take stock of these new tools and organise them into a book. This book would be organised around a robust and familiar framework for managing quality and excellence. It should aim to encourage and help businesses of all sectors and sizes to align successfully with the Global Compact principles.

To do this we constituted an international editorial team to include a combination of management expertise and all the dimensions of the Global Compact. We set out to screen and catalogue resources produced in the burgeoning field of corporate citizenship. It was particularly important to cast the nets wide and to try to test the catch for evidence of performance in real business cases. Many other contributors proposed input and comments.

The title, *Raising the Bar: Creating Value with the UN Global Compact*, reflects what we learned in the process of producing it:

- Business people will continue to face ever-higher expectations from stakeholders who 'raise the bar' of performance in alignment with universal principles.

- When they embrace corporate citizenship, in ways that draw on the same human qualities and practices described as business excellence, companies actually enhance their competitiveness and financial value creation.

- The synergy between responsibility and excellence is not automatic; it presents business people with a number of dilemmas and it also demands a readiness to 'raise the bar' and innovate.

For many companies, the journey is just starting. How can they align themselves with the Global Compact in ways that continue to reward their other business objectives? How should they embrace and capitalise on the Global Compact's potential for bringing together business, the public sector, trade unions and civil society in new partnerships?

Raising the Bar provides practical guidance with an inventory of knowledge, tools, case studies and information sources, all organised around a basic performance model that embraces concepts familiar to most business people.

As an editorial team we have not tried to 'rewrite the book' on business excellence. Many are available. However, we did want to position the classic elements of business excellence in the context of the challenges of sustainable development. For that we deconstructed business excellence into ten elements, from 'vision' to 'reporting'. We found many interesting tools and cases that cover more than one of those elements. What matters is that, within all ten integrated elements, responsible excellence is brought to life.

We are grateful for the input of the large number of contributors who brought the richness of this book together in record time. We are also indebted to David Ballard, Barbara Dubach, Jonathon Hanks, Hans Hofmeijer, François Kaisin, Andrew Kinmont, Malou Lasquite and Sune Skadegaard Thorsen who took the time to review the draft manuscript and who suggested numerous improvements.

John Stuart, our editor at Greenleaf Publishing, provided sound advice at the critical time when we struggled with too much material, too much text and too many questions.

Above all, we now look forward to the comments from those front-line managers, whom we continuously had in mind and whom we wanted to help with clear information and practical support to make the principles of the Global Compact a living reality that is rewarding for society and business alike.

The editorial team
June 2004

Acknowledgements

The following organisations enabled the production of this book through material and financial support. Staff time and guidance on content was provided by:

- UN Global Compact Office, New York
- Office of the High Commissioner for Human Rights (OHCHR), Geneva
- The International Labour Organisation (ILO), Geneva
- The United Nations Environment Programme (UNEP), Paris office
- Amnesty International UK, London
- Business for Social Responsibility (BSR), San Francisco
- European Foundation for Quality Management (EFQM), Brussels
- Instituto Ethos, São Paolo, Brazil
- World Business Council for Sustainable Development (WBCSD), Geneva

Financial support was provided by:

- Calvert, Washington
- Deutsche Bank, Frankfurt
- Electricité de France, Paris
- Hewlett-Packard, Palo Alto
- Holcim, Zürich
- Novartis, Basel
- Pfizer, New York
- Renault, Paris
- Shell, London
- Skanska AB, Stockholm
- Suez, Paris
- Unilever, London

Disclaimer

This book is the work of many people in many organisations. It was produced with an open review process that engaged a number of specialists and practitioners in order to ensure quality and usefulness for its readers. This does not mean, however, that everyone involved in this collaborative effort endorses every statement in the book.

The featured case studies, tools and resources reflect the perspectives of the contributors who supplied material. They do not necessarily represent the views of the editorial team or of their organisations. Nor are the case studies intended to serve as an endorsement of the companies featured.

WHY THIS BOOK MATTERS

THIS BOOK FILLS A CRITICAL VOID. IT OUTLINES how the Global Compact and its principles can stimulate organisational change and provides an essential framework for the credibility and effectiveness of the Global Compact. The significance of this book is best appreciated in the context of the overall mission of the Global Compact.

As a voluntary initiative, the Global Compact has two operational objectives: making the Compact and its principles part of business strategy and operations everywhere and offering an effective platform for multi-stakeholder solution finding.

Since the formal launch of the Compact in July 2000 there has been much experimentation with learning and dialogue at the global and national levels to give practical meaning to the second objective. This has inspired many initiatives and projects.

But the viability of the Compact can be established only if the first objective is met both with regard to its quantitative *and* its qualitative aspirations. Certainly, the commitment to the Compact around the world has progressed well. Today, over 1,000 companies and dozens of labour and civil society organisations from over 70 countries constitute the network.

However, the qualitative aspects (i.e. the degree to which participating companies internalise the idea of responsible corporate citizenship and the Compact's principles) remain a central critical challenge.

The leadership model of the Compact — involving CEOs being backed by company boards to put their commitment in writing to the UN Secretary-General — has proven effective. Change must start at the top, and change requires the support of leaders. But a commitment alone is not sufficient. Such a commitment must be honoured, and change must be reflected in tangible performance improvements.

But what does it mean to implement the Compact and its principles? What expectations can be established? And isn't it true that the strength of the Compact — the simplicity and broad nature of the principles — is also its weakness? Are not the principles too broad as a basis for management change? How can one establish benchmarks and performance indicators for implementation? Is it possible to establish a framework that is broad enough for a global, cross-sectoral initiative, relevant to front-runners and newcomers alike? And is it true that for issues such as human rights there

are hardly any tools available to guide effective implementation?

When Claude Fussler first proposed working on a 'performance model' for the Compact we knew that, if successful, it could provide answers to these critical questions. A Global Compact Policy Dialogue on Business and Sustainable Development, in January 2002, set into motion an ambitious project under Claude's competent and creative leadership. Nearly two years later, this project has concluded its work.

Raising the Bar offers a comprehensive framework for translating the Compact into business practices that create value and progress towards sustainable development. It has exceeded our expectations. The book not only establishes how a leadership commitment can be implemented but also offers a wealth of practical guidance and information. In addition, it shows that improved social and environmental performance is, above all, a question of a commitment to deep process changes that require sustained efforts, and that these changes bring clear rewards.

Hundreds of people from many countries have contributed to this book, bringing together the best material available at this juncture. A truly international editorial team deserves credit for having produced *Raising the Bar* with few resources but much dedication:

- Claude Fussler of the World Business Council for Sustainable Development, the intellectual and operational team leader
- Aron Cramer, Business for Social Responsibility, co-editor
- Sebastian van der Vegt, International Labour Organisation, co-editor
- Peter Frankental, Amnesty International
- Shelley Hayes, World Business Council for Sustainable Development
- Marcelo Linguitte, Instituto Ethos
- Patrick Margaria, European Foundation for Quality Management

- Cornis van der Lugt, United Nations Environment Programme
- Ursula Wynhoven, Global Compact Office
- Ellen Kallinowsky of Gesellschaft für Technische Zusammenarbeit (GTZ) also provided wise support from the Compact Office

Raising the Bar leverages a proven performance dynamic — it shares benchmarks, tools and learning from business leaders. It will be a living asset to help us all realise the full potential of the Global Compact.

Georg Kell
Executive Head, Global Compact Office
New York, June 2004

THE UN GLOBAL COMPACT'S PRINCIPLES

Principle 1

Businesses should support and respect the protection of internationally proclaimed human rights within their sphere of influence.

Principle 2

Businesses should ensure that their own operations are not complicit in human rights abuses.

Principle 3

Businesses should uphold the freedom of association and the effective recognition of the right to collective bargaining.

Principle 4

Businesses should uphold the elimination of all forms of forced and compulsory labour.

Principle 5

Businesses should uphold the effective abolition of child labour.

Principle 6

Businesses should eliminate discrimination in respect of employment and occupation.

Principle 7

Businesses should support a precautionary approach to environmental challenges.

Principle 8

Businesses should undertake initiatives to promote greater environmental responsibility.

Principle 9

Businesses should encourage the development and diffusion of environmentally friendly technologies.

The Tenth Principle on corruption is expected to be introduced in the latter half of 2004:

Principle 10

Businesses should work against corruption in all its forms, including extortion and bribery.

SUMMARY OF TOOLS, CASE STUDIES, AND INFORMATION AND RESOURCES

Tools	Case studies	Information and resources
HUMAN RIGHTS		
Business and Human Rights: A Geography of Corporate Risk *Amnesty International/IBLF* ch. 8 p. 106	The BTC Pipeline: Following through with Global Compact Commitments — BP *UK* ch. 8 p. 109	Global Compact Primer *United Nations* ch. 1 p. 38
Human Rights: Is It Any of Your Business? *Amnesty International/IBLF* ch. 8 p. 108	Shell Pilots the Human Rights Compliance Assessment *Netherlands/UK* ch. 8 p. 112	Universal Declaration of Human Rights *United Nations* ch. 1 p. 38
Human Rights Compliance Assessment *Danish Institute for Human Rights* ch. 8 p. 111	Hewlett-Packard Develops a Supplier's Code of Conduct *USA* ch. 12 p. 178	Norms on the Responsibilities of Transnational Corporations and Other Business Enterprises with Regard to Human Rights *UN Sub-Commission on the Promotion and Protection of Human Rights* ch. 1 p. 38
Conflict Impact Assessment and Risk Management *UN Global Compact Office* ch. 13 p. 195	No Immunity for Business: Fighting Back HIV/AIDS at Eskom *South Africa* ch. 13 p. 186	Human Rights Principles for Companies *Amnesty International* ch. 8 p. 117
	Aventis: Partnerships for Health *Switzerland* ch. 13 p. 187	Transnational Corporations in Conflict-Prone Zones: Public Policy Responses and a Framework for Action *International Alert* ch. 8 p. 117
	A Forum against Human Trafficking in the Manila Ports: WG&A *Philippines* ch. 13 p. 192	Corporate Actors in Zones of Conflict: Responsible Engagement *Confederation of Norwegian Business and Industry* ch. 8 p. 118
	Strengthening Local Institutions for the Rights of Children: Telemig Celular *Brazil* ch. 13 p. 194	Business and Human Rights Resource Centre ch. 8 p. 119
		Human Rights Matrix *Business Leaders Initiative on Human Rights* ch. 8 p. 119
		Voluntary Principles on Security and Human Rights ch. 8 p. 119
		The Business of Peace: The Private Sector as a Partner in Conflict Prevention and Resolution *The Prince of Wales International Business Leaders Forum and International Alert* ch. 13 p. 196
		Measuring and Reporting on Company Human Rights Performance *CSR Europe and BSR* ch. 14 p. 216
LABOUR		
Global Compact Training Material on the Four Labour Principles *ILO* ch. 7 p. 96	Footsteps to Worker Health and Safety: Vietnam Footwear Industry Business Links Initiative ch. 4 p. 70	Global Compact Primer *United Nations* ch. 1 p. 38
Improve Your Business. Basics: People and Productivity *ILO* ch. 7 p. 97	SA8000 Triggers a Quality Process at Beauty Essential *Thailand* ch. 10 p. 138	ILO Tripartite Declaration of Principles Concerning Multinational Enterprises and Social Policy ch. 1 p. 39
Supply Chain Training *BSR* ch. 7 p. 100	SA8000 to Managing Change in Partnership: Switcher *Switzerland* ch. 10 p. 139	ILO Declaration of Fundamental Principles and Rights at Work ch. 1 p. 39
Social Accountability 8000 Standard System *Social Accountability International* ch. 10 p. 136		ILO International Labour Standards ch. 1 p. 39
		ILO Codes of Practice in Safety and Health ch. 1 p. 40

Tools	Case studies	Information and resources
LABOUR (cont.)		
Monitoring Guidance and Compliance Benchmarks *FLA* — ch. 10 p. 152	Dealing with Layoffs at Floreal *Mauritius* — ch. 11 p. 165	ILO Code of Practice on HIV/AIDS — ch. 1 p. 40
Socially Sensitive Enterprise Restructuring *ILO* — ch. 11 p. 164	Unionisation for a Better Working Climate: Delta Electronics *Thailand* — ch. 11 p. 166	Self-regulation in the Workplace *ILO* — ch. 5 p. 84
Labour Rights Self-assessment *BSR* — ch. 11 p. 167	Capitalising on Experience: The Grey Revolution at B&Q *UK* — ch. 11 p. 168	Boosting Employment Through Small Enterprise Development *ILO* — ch. 7 p. 102
Ethical Trading Initiative Workbook and CD-ROM *Ethical Trading Initiative* — ch. 12 p. 177	Working with Disabled People: Alimco *India* — ch. 11 p. 169	The Tripartite Declaration of Principles Concerning Multinational Enterprises and Social Policy: A User's Guide *ILO* — ch. 7 p. 102
Child Labour Monitoring System *ILO* — ch. 13 p. 190	Carrefour Initiates a Partnership against Child Labour *France* — ch. 12 p. 176	Corporate Success through People: Making International Labour Standards Work For You *ILO* — ch. 11 p. 170
	From the Plantation to School: Abolition of Child Labour at Sotik Tea Company *Kenya* — ch. 13 p. 191	As One Employer to Another . . . What's All This About Equality? *ILO, Bureau for Employers' Activities* — ch. 11 p. 170
		Business and Code of Conduct Implementation: How Firms Use Management Systems for Social Performance *ILO* ch. 12 p. 180
		Yardsticks for Workers' Rights: Learning from Experience *Human Rights First* — ch. 14 p. 217
ENVIRONMENT		
Environmental Management Systems: Training Resource Kit *UNEP/FIDIC/ICC* — ch. 7 p. 98	Cleaner Production Makes Cleaner Bicycles: Atlas Cycles *India* — ch. 8 p. 114	Global Compact Primer *United Nations* — ch. 1 p. 38
Environmental Management Navigator for SMEs *Wuppertal Institute/InWEnt/UNEP/UNIDO* — ch. 7 p. 99	Wired for Efficiency: Resource Efficiency Accounting at Muckenhaupt & Nusselt *Germany* — ch. 9 p. 128	The Stockholm, Rio and Johannesburg Declarations, Agenda 21 and the Johannesburg Plan of Implementation *United Nations* — ch. 1 p. 40
International Declaration on Cleaner Production *UNEP* — ch. 8 p. 113	A Smaller Fingerprint for the Moroccan Dyeing Industry: BASF — ch. 10 p. 148	ISO 14000 Series — ch. 1 p. 41
CARE: Computer Aided Resource Efficiency *Wuppertal Institute* — ch. 9 p. 126	Brewing Environmental Quality at Moritz Fiege *Germany* — ch. 10 p. 151	Factor 4/Factor 10 and Eco-efficiency — ch. 5 p. 78
ISO 14001: Environmental Management System *ISO* — ch. 10 p. 140	A Strategic Integration of Environmental Management: Samarco *Brazil* — ch. 10 p. 154	Integrated Environmental and Economic Accounting: An Operational Manual *UNEP/UNSD* — ch. 9 p. 129
Ecodesign and Product Service Systems *UNEP* — ch. 10 p. 145	BAA: British Airports Launch into Supply Chain Review *UK* — ch. 12 p. 175	Contemporary Environmental Accounting: Issues, Concepts and Practice *Schaltegger and Burritt* — ch. 9 p. 129
Environmental Assessment Tools — ch. 10 p. 147	APELL In São Sebastião: Petrobras *Brazil* — ch. 13 p. 189	Environmental Management Accounting Research and Information Centre (EMARIC) — ch. 9 p. 129
SAFE: Sustainability Assessment for SMEs *Wuppertal Institute* — ch. 10 p. 150	The Ciba Experience *Switzerland* — ch. 14 p. 213	Eco-efficiency: Creating More Value with Less Impact *WBCSD* — ch. 10 p. 155
Awareness and Preparedness for Emergencies at Local Level (APELL) *UNEP* — ch. 13 p. 188		Measuring Eco-efficiency: A Guide to Reporting Company Performance *WBCSD* — ch. 10 p. 156
Manual on Eco-efficiency Initiatives *UNCTAD* — ch. 14 p. 212		Environmental Consumer Information for Products and Services *UNEP* — ch. 10 p. 156

Tools	Case studies	Information and resources
ENVIRONMENT (cont.)		
• SME Efficient Entrepreneur Calendar *Wuppertal Institute/UNEP* ch. 14 p. 214		• Analytical Tools for Environmental Design and Management *Wrisberg and Udo de Haes* ch. 10 p. 157
		• Suppliers' Perspectives on Greening the Supply Chain *BSR* ch. 12 p. 179
OTHER ASPECTS OF CORPORATE CITIZENSHIP		
• The SME Key *CSR Europe* ch. 2 p. 48	• The Leverage of a Small Designer Group: Designworks *USA* ch. 2 p. 47	• OECD Guidelines for Multinational Enterprises ch. 1 p. 41
• European Foundation for Quality Management (EFQM) Model and Guidelines ch. 3 p. 55	• Dexia Goes 'Six Sigma' with the Global Compact *France* ch. 3 p. 56	• OECD Principles of Corporate Governance ch. 1 p. 42
• Guide to Engaging with NGOs *BSR* ch. 4 p. 67	• Suez: How Public–Private Partnerships Contribute to Social Inclusion *Argentina* ch. 4 p. 68	• Corporate Social Responsibility: Implications for Small and Medium Enterprises in Developing Countries *UNIDO* ch. 2 p. 51
• The SIGMA Management Framework *BSR/Forum for the Future/AccountAbility* ch. 5 p. 79	• From Tension to Corporate Dialogue: Holcim's Community Advisory Panel Approach *Switzerland* ch. 4 p. 69	• Global Compact Self-assessment Tool *BSR* ch. 2 p. 51
• The Compass *Wuppertal Institute* ch. 5 p. 82	• Think 2020 at Northumbrian Water *UK* ch. 5 p. 80	• The Employers' Guide to the Global Compact *International Organisation of Employers* ch. 2 p. 51
• The Business Case Matrix *SustainAbility/UNEP/IFC/Instituto Ethos* ch. 6 p. 87	• Rethinking Business: From Building Materials to Resource Management — RMC Group *UK* ch. 5 p. 81	• Seven-Step Model for Turning CSR into Corporate Social Opportunity *Grayson and Hodges* ch. 2 p. 52
• Corporate Responsibility Assessment Tool *Conference Board of Canada* ch. 6 p. 90	• A Stakeholder Radar for the European Aluminium Industry ch. 5 p. 83	• Partnership Guide *UNIDO* ch. 4 p. 71
• CHRONOS e-learning tutorial *WBCSD* ch. 7 p. 95	• Developing a Business Case at Natura, Brazil ch. 6 p. 89	• A Guide to Working with Multilaterals *BSR/AccountAbility* ch. 4 p. 71
• The SIGMA Project Accounting Tool *BSI/Forum for the Future/AccountAbility* ch. 9 p. 124	• Leaders into Action: Unilever *Netherlands/UK* ch. 6 p. 91	• Stakeholder Dialogues: The WBCSD's Approach to Engagement ch. 4 p. 71
• Sustainability Framework for Private-Sector Investments *IFC* ch. 10 p. 142	• Dialogue, Motivation and a Clothes Line . . . at Palavra Mágica *Brazil* ch. 7 p. 101	• Putting Partnerships to Work: Strategic Alliances for Development between Government, the Private Sector and Civil Society *Warner and Sullivan* ch. 4 p. 71
• Ethos Indicators on Corporate Social Responsibility *Instituto Ethos* ch. 13 p. 185	• Sustainability Counts at Wessex Water: Working with Full-Cost Accounting *UK* ch. 9 p. 125	• The Millennium Development Goals ch. 5 p. 76
• The 2002 Sustainability Reporting Guidelines *Global Reporting Initiative* ch. 14 p. 202	• Level 3 Bananas for Favorita Fruit Company *Ecuador* ch. 10 p. 144	• Fact Sheet: World Economic Forum Global Governance Initiative: From Aspiration to Action ch. 5 p. 77
• AA1000 Framework *AccountAbility* ch. 14 p. 208	• Basing Supplier Relationships on the UN Global Compact at Bayer *Germany* ch. 10 p. 153	• Business and the Millennium Development Goals *UNIDO/IBLF* ch. 5 p. 77
• AA1000 Assurance Standard *AccountAbility* ch. 14 p. 210	• Giving Street Children a Future: An Employee Initiative at Volkswagen *Germany* ch. 11 p. 163	• Route Map *WWF* ch. 5 p. 84
	• Corporate Social Responsibility and Customer Satisfaction: BT Has Numbers! *UK* ch. 12 p. 173	• Values in Action: Formalising Your Company's Values *BSR* ch. 5 p. 85
		• Sustainable Development Opportunity and Risk Guide *The SIGMA Project* ch. 5 p. 85

Tools	Case studies	Information and resources
OTHER ASPECTS OF CORPORATE CITIZENSHIP (cont.)		
	• Performance beyond the Walls at VanCity *Canada* ch. 14 p. 211	• SIGMA Sustainability Scorecard *The SIGMA Project* ch. 5 p. 85
		• Tomorrow's Markets: Global Trends and their Implications for Business *WRI/WBCSD/UNEP* ch. 6 p. 92
		• Corporate Social Responsibility: A Guide to Better Business Practices *BSR* ch. 8 p. 120
		• The Corporate Responsibility Code Book *Leipziger* ch. 8 p. 120
		• Designing a CSR Structure *BSR* ch. 10 p. 155
		• Sustainability Trend Guide *Sept ou 8* ch. 10 p. 155
		• Developing Countries and Technology Cooperation, Volumes 1 and 2 *UNIDO/WBCSD* ch. 10 p. 157
		• Integrating SMEs in Global Value Chains: Towards Partnerships for Development *UNIDO* ch. 12 p. 179
		• SIGMA Supply Chain Strategy and Evaluation *The SIGMA Project* ch. 12 p. 179
		• Strengthening Implementation of Corporate Social Responsibility in Global Supply Chains *BSR/PricewaterhouseCoopers/ Danish Institute for Human Rights* ch. 12 p. 180
		• Business and Social Initiatives Database *ILO* ch. 13 p. 196
		• AA1000 Conversations: Lessons from the Early Years (1999–2001) *AccountAbility* ch. 14 p. 216
		• The State of Sustainability Assurance *AccountAbility* ch. 14 p. 216
		• Sustainable Development Reporting Portal *WBCSD* ch. 14 p. 217
		• Sustainable Development Reporting: Striking the Balance *WBCSD* ch. 14 p. 217
CORRUPTION		
• Business Principles for Countering Bribery *Transparency International* ch. 8 p. 115	• SAP Enables the Convention on Business Integrity in Nigeria *Germany* ch. 8 p. 116	• United Nations Convention Against Corruption ch. 1 p. 42
		• Rules of Conduct to Combat Extortion and Bribery *ICC* ch. 8 p. 118
		• Fighting Corruption: A Corporate Practice Manual *ICC* ch. 8 p. 118
		• Corruption Perception Index *Transparency International* ch. 13 p. 196

ABBREVIATIONS OF ORGANISATIONS

AA ....AccountAbility ....www.accountability.org.uk
AI ....Amnesty International ....www.amnesty.org
BSR ....Business for Social Responsibility ....www.bsr.org
BLIHR .....Business Leaders Initiative on Human Rights ....www.respecttable.com
CSR ....Corporate Social Responsibility Europe ....www.csreurope.org
DIHR ......Danish Institute for Human Rights ....www.humanrights.dk, www.humanrightsbusiness.org
EFQM ......European Foundation for Quality Management ....www.efqm.org
Ethos .....Instituto Ethos ....www.ethos.com.br
ETI ....Ethical Trading Initiative ....www.ethicaltrade.org
FIDIC .....International Federation of Consulting Engineers ....www.fidic.org
FLA ....Fair Labor Association ....www.fairlabor.org
GRI ....Global Reporting Initiative ....www.globalreporting.org
HRF ....Human Rights First (ex Lawyers Committee for Human Rights) ..www.humanrightsfirst.org
IBLF ......The Prince of Wales International Business Leaders Forum ....www.iblf.org
ICC ....International Chamber of Commerce ....www.iccwbo.org
IFC ....International Finance Corporation ....www.ifc.org
ILO ....International Labour Office ....www.ilo.org
Imagine ...Canadian Centre for Philanthropy and the Conference Board of Canada ....www.imagine.ca
I-A ....International Alert ....www.international-alert.org
IOE ....International Organisation of Employers ....www.ioe-emp.org
ISO ....International Organisation for Standardisation ....www.iso.org
NHO ....Confederation of Norwegian Business and Industry ....www.nho.no/csr
OECD ......Organisation for Economic Cooperation and Development ...www.oecd.org
OHCHR .....Office of the High Commissioner for Human Rights ....www.unhchr.org
SAI ....Social Accountability International ....www.sa-intl.org
SIGMA .....The SIGMA Project ....www.projectsigma.com, www.forumforthefuture.org.uk
TI ....Transparency International ....www.transparency.org
UNCTAD ....United Nations Conference on Trade and Development ......www.unctad.org
UNDP ......United Nations Development Programme ....www.undp.org
UNEP ......United Nations Environment Programme ....www.uneptie.org
UNDESA ....Department of Economic and Social Affairs, Division for Sustainable Development ..www.un.org/esa/sustdev
UN GC .....United Nations Global Compact Office ....www.unglobalcompact.org
UNIDO .....United Nations Industrial Development Organisation ......www.unido.org
UNODC .....United Nations Office on Drugs and Crime ....www.unodc.org
WB ....World Bank ....www.worldbank.org/privatesector/csr
WBCSD .....World Business Council for Sustainable Development ......www.wbcsd.org
WRI ....World Resources Institute ....www.wri.org
WI ....Wuppertal Institute for Climate, Environment and Energy ..www.wupperinst.org
WWF-UK ....formerly Worldwide Fund for Nature ....www.wwf-uk.org

THE GLOBAL COMPACT: AN EXTRAORDINARY JOURNEY

John G. Ruggie
Harvard University, USA

IN PRESCIENT REMARKS SOME TEN MONTHS before the disastrous 'Battle of Seattle', UN Secretary-General Kofi Annan urged business leaders at the Davos World Economic Forum, in January 1999, to join the UN and other global actors in an effort to help provide the social pillars that a sustainable global economy requires:[1]

> National markets are held together by shared values. In the face of economic transition and insecurity, people know that if the worst comes to the worst, they can rely on the expectation that certain minimum standards will prevail. But in the global market, people do not yet have that confidence. Until they do have it, the global economy will be fragile and vulnerable — vulnerable to backlash from all the 'isms' of our post-Cold-War world: protectionism, populism, nationalism, ethnic chauvinism, fanaticism and terrorism.

Embedding the global market within shared social values and institutional practices represents a task of historic magnitude. The reason is obvious: there is no government at the global level to act on behalf of the common good as there is at the national level, and international institutions are far too weak to fully compensate. Business has a critical role to play, Annan believes, because it has so much at stake — not only large multinational enterprises but also smaller national and local firms, many of which depend on, directly or indirectly, a stable and sustainable global economy. Moreover, business has capacities that other social actors lack: it has global reach, through transnational firms and supply chains; it directly affects communities in which it operates; and it can move at a speed that few governments or international agencies are able to match.

Accordingly, Annan proposed a 'global compact', enlisting corporate engagement in promoting nine principles drawn from the Universal Declaration of Human Rights,[2] the Declaration of Fundamental Principles and Rights at Work of the International Labour Organisation (ILO)[3] and the Rio Declaration on Environment and Development:[4]

- To support and respect the protection of internationally proclaimed human rights
- To ensure non-complicity in human rights abuses
- To ensure freedom of association and the effective recognition of the right to collective bargaining
- To eliminate of all forms of forced and compulsory labour

---

1 Kofi A. Annan, 'A Compact for the New Century', address to the World Economic Forum, Davos, Switzerland, 31 January 1999 (SG/SM/6881/Rev.1). Up-to-date information about the Global Compact and its activities may be found at www.unglobalcompact.org.

2 See www.un.org/Overview/rights.html; see also page 38.
3 See www.ilo.org/declaration; see also page 39.
4 See www.un.org/documents/ga/conf151/aconf15126-1annex1.htm; see also page 40.

- To ensure the effective abolition of child labour
- To eliminate discrimination in respect of employment and occupation
- To take a precautionary approach to environmental challenges
- To show greater environmental responsibility
- To encourage the development and diffusion of environmentally friendly technologies

These principles comprise the core elements of the UN normative agenda as it relates to business: human dignity, decent work and environmental sustainability, and, because they were adopted by the world's governments, they represent the aspirational goals of the entire international community. Companies are asked to help bridge the gap between aspiration and reality.

Annan's challenge was so well received that his proposal was soon turned into a programme. More than 1,000 companies worldwide now participate in it — nearly evenly balanced between developed and developing country firms — along with some 20 transnational non-governmental organisations (NGOs), international labour federations, representing 150 million workers, and five UN agencies. Governments provide financial support, and they participate fully at national and local levels in 50 or so country-based initiatives.

From the start, the Compact has differed from regulatory or quasi-regulatory approaches towards the corporate world; it was never intended to monitor and police the behaviour of firms. Instead, it constitutes a values-based platform for social capital formation: bringing the relevant social actors together to seek joint solutions to the imbalances and dislocations resulting from the gap between the global economy and national communities.

The Compact employs three instruments to achieve its aims:

- **Information sharing and learning.** Companies are asked to communicate their progress in internalising the principles through their annual reports or similar public vehicles. Also, a Learning Forum is intended to identify and disseminate good corporate practices. The UN system promotes these 'good practices', thereby providing a standard of comparison for — and public pressure on — industry laggards.
- **Policy dialogues.** Through such dialogues the Compact generates shared understandings about, for example, the socially responsible posture for companies when operating in countries afflicted by conflict. The zones-of-conflict dialogue has explored how companies can: conduct impact assessments and reduce the risk that their own behaviour may fuel conflicts; achieve greater transparency in their financial transactions with the host government or rebel groups; and devise revenue-sharing regimes that will benefit local populations.[5] The results from these dialogues inform not only companies but also the UN's own conflict-prevention and peacemaking activities, and they play a normative role in the broader public arena.
- **Partnership projects.** Through partnership projects in developing countries the Compact contributes to capacity-building where it is needed most. Examples include support for micro lending, investment promotion, HIV/AIDS awareness and treatment programmes for employees in sub-Saharan Africa, the devising of sustainable alternatives to child labour, and a host of initiatives in eco-efficiency and other dimensions of environmental management. One of the success stories at the Johannesburg World Summit on Sustainable Development was a Global Compact partnership effort to promote private-sector investment in the least-developed countries.[6]

Organisationally, the Global Compact consists entirely of a set of nested networks. The five participating UN entities themselves operate as a network. The Global Compact Office in New York is by far the smallest component; its main functions are to provide strategic direction, policy coherence

---

5   For summaries of these toolkits, consult www.unglobalcompact.org.

6   See 'Global Compact Launches Development Initiative at Summit', at www.unglobalcompact.org.

and quality control — what would be called 'brand management' in the corporate world. The other partners are the relevant UN agencies — the UN Office of the High Commissioner for Human Rights (UNOHCHR), the International Labour Organisation (ILO), the UN Environment Programme (UNEP), the UN Industrial Development Organisation (UNIDO) and the UN Development Programme (UNDP). They lend unparalleled sectoral and country-level expertise. The transnational NGOs — including Amnesty International, the World Conservation Union (IUCN) and Oxfam — also bring their expertise to bear, and they articulate more nearly universal human interests than are normally heard in intergovernmental forums. The same is true of labour, represented by the International Confederation of Free Trade Unions (ICFTU) and several of its constituent federations.

The operating network comprises the five UN agencies and the other partners: namely, companies, international labour, transnational NGOs and university-based research centres, which help analyse company case studies for the Learning Forum. Most of the 'heavy lifting' gets done in this larger circle. Gradually, other global efforts to promote corporate social responsibility, including the World Business Council on Sustainable Development (WBCSD), Business for Social Responsibility (BSR) and the Global Reporting Initiative (GRI), are entering into alliance-like relationships with the Global Compact, whereby they develop and operate additional tools and protocols for the implementation of the principles.

The Compact has also triggered numerous complementary regional, national and sectoral initiatives. Typically, these take a subset of interested Global Compact participants beyond the minimum commitments. For example, Norway's Statoil and the International Federation of Chemical, Energy, Mine and General Workers' Unions (ICEM) signed an agreement within the Global Compact framework whereby Statoil is extending the same labour rights and health-and-safety standards that it applies in Norway to all of its overseas operations — including in Vietnam, Venezuela, Angola and Azerbaijan.[7] The same labour federation also negotiated the first ever such agreement with a mining company, AngloGold.[8] A Nordic Global Compact Network has been established, as has a 'Friends of the Global Compact' network in Germany. Similar national efforts are under way in Brazil, China, Egypt, India, the Philippines, Thailand and several other developing countries and economies in transition.

A number of initiatives originally intended for entirely different purposes have associated themselves with the Global Compact — reflecting the expansive potential of its 'open systems architecture'. The most unusual is the multi-stakeholder Committee for Melbourne, which incorporated the Global Compact principles into the strategic plan it developed for that Australian city and which is encouraging all firms doing business there to adopt them.

The uptake of the Global Compact has exceeded the wildest expectations of any of its architects — suggesting that it does indeed respond to a critical need, at a critical time. It has attracted considerable acclaim in the world's press: in the USA, for example, it has been praised editorially by the venerable *Washington Post*, and the *Christian Science Monitor* lauded it as Annan's 'most creative reinvention' yet of the United Nations. But, most importantly, it has begun to make a difference where it really matters: in companies and communities. Compared with the profound challenges posed by globalisation, we have barely begun, but already we are on a truly extraordinary journey.

---

7 See 'Statoil Signs Agreement with ICEM', *Europe Energy*, 30 March 2001.
8 See 'Historic First for Mining in Africa: AngloGold Signs Global Labour Agreement', available online at www.icem.org/update/upd2002/upd02-36.html.

Part 1

CHAPTER ONE

THE UN GLOBAL COMPACT: A PRIMER ON THE PRINCIPLES

YOU MAY SKIP THIS CHAPTER IF YOU WISH — but only temporarily, because, if you dive into the next chapter, 'Getting Started', you will soon realise that you need to understand more about the basics of the Global Compact in order to address one or more of the following dilemmas:

- **An ethical dilemma.** At the deepest level, beyond your published declarations, where do your values, your business model or your activities clash with this set of universal principles?

- **A leadership dilemma.** Why should your company's vision and mission reflect the principles of the Global Compact? And, of all the expectations, which is the most important for your organisation? With limited resources, what should you change first?

- **A governance dilemma.** How legitimate is it to expect your employees and commercial partners to move beyond, or even against, local public policy?

- **A global–local dilemma.** What is the best way to ensure that the company applies the global principles of the Compact while also addressing local conditions, policies and perspectives?

- **A practical dilemma.** How will you adapt your daily routines to ensure that your company makes these principles operational and fulfils its commitments?

These dilemmas are related. Understanding the basics is necessary for making the most desirable choices and creating new approaches.

The Global Compact Principles are each based on concepts established in international agreements: the Universal Declaration of Human Rights,[1] the International Labour Organisation (ILO) Declaration of Fundamental Principles and Rights at Work[2] and the Rio Declaration on Environment and Development.[3] We have invited the relevant UN agencies to provide these introductions to the principles and are grateful to the UN High Commission on Human Rights, the International Labour Organisation and the UN Environment Programme for their contributions to this book.

The Global Compact Principles relating to human rights

International human rights standards have traditionally been the responsibility of governments, aimed at regulating relations between the state and individuals or groups. As the influence and reach of companies has grown, there is a developing consensus that human rights are also applicable to private bodies. Although the principle that human rights apply to business is far more widely accepted now than ten years ago, the *meaning* of the link between business and human rights remains

---

1 See footnote 2 on page 15.
2 See footnote 3 on page 15.
3 See www.un.org/documents/ga/conf151/aconf15126-1annex1.htm; see also page 40.

unclear for many. There remains substantial debate over which human rights can and should apply to business and in what way. There is also considerable debate on how business can support and respect human rights in conjunction with other actors.

Principle 1

Businesses should support and respect the protection of internationally proclaimed human rights within their sphere of influence.

Which internationally proclaimed human rights are covered by Principle 1?

The human rights encompassed in Principle 1 of the Global Compact arise out of the Universal Declaration of Human Rights (UDHR) adopted by the UN General Assembly in 1948. The Universal Declaration, defining itself as 'a common standard of achievement for all peoples and all nations', both proclaims a set of fundamental values shared by the international community and sets rules acknowledging rights and corresponding duties to protect those values. Many commentators recognise the Universal Declaration as an interpretation of the human rights values stated in the UN Charter and part of international customary law. The rights laid down in the Declaration have been further elaborated in a number of international treaties, with two of the most important being the International Covenant on Economic, Social and

Cultural Rights and the International Covenant on Civil and Political Rights.[4] The principles enshrined in these documents are, in many cases, brought into national laws when they are ratified by governments.

The Universal Declaration makes 'every individual and every organ of society' responsible for promoting and respecting the rights and freedoms it contains. This concept of 'every organ of society' has been broadly interpreted to cover private entities such as companies.

The Universal Declaration embraces three critical areas of human rights:

- **Rights protecting life and security of the person.** Among others, these include the right to:
  - Life, liberty and security
  - Freedom from slavery, servitude, torture and cruel, inhuman or degrading treatment or punishment
  - Equal protection of the law
  - Freedom from arbitrary arrest
  - Judicial remedy against human rights violations before a court

- **Economic, social and cultural rights.** These include the right to:
  - A standard of living adequate for health and well-being that includes food, clothing, housing, medical care and access to social services and social security
  - Education
  - Just and favourable remuneration ensuring workers and their families an existence worthy of human dignity
  - Form and join trade unions
  - Rest and leisure

  These rights are intended to be realised through national efforts and international cooperation in accordance with conditions in each state.

- **Personal and political rights and freedoms.** These include the right to:
  - Freedom of movement
  - Privacy in matters concerning family, home and correspondence
  - Own property and the prohibition of arbitrary deprivation of property
  - Freedom of expression, religion, peaceful assembly and association

In principle, all human rights apply to private corporations. However, their applicability will depend on a given situation. In summer 2003, the UN Sub-Commission on the Promotion and

---

4   Details of the International Covenant on Economic, Social and Cultural Rights may be found at www.unhchr.ch/html/menu3/b/a_cescr.htm; details of the International Covenant on Civil and Political Rights may be found at www.unhchr.ch/html/menu3/b/a_opt.htm.

Protection of Human Rights adopted a document containing a proposed set of 'norms'.[5] These seek to identify which human rights apply directly to companies. The Norms on the Responsibilities of Transnational Corporations and Other Business Enterprises with Regard to Human Rights include:

- The right to equal opportunity and non-discriminatory treatment
- The right to security of persons
- The rights of workers
- Economic, social and cultural rights

Much of the global debate about business and human rights has focused on preventing violations attributed to companies. Considerably less attention has been given to the opportunities companies have to contribute to the positive enjoyment of human rights. Principle 1 of the Global Compact encourages companies to consider how they can promote such progress, consistent with the role of business.

In fact, in many cases, companies may be acting to support and respect human rights without using the label of 'human rights'. To begin with, companies incorporate international human rights standards in their operations by adhering to national laws that have been adopted as a result of a state's international human rights obligations and

commitments. In other words, the kinds of human rights policies that businesses may be expected to implement as a result of a commitment to Principle 1 of the Global Compact include existing policy and practice linked to legal obligations or voluntary practice, such as provision of health insurance to workers, implementation of worker safety regulation, stakeholder dialogue, positive involvement in communities in which they operate and support for the rule of law and transparent and fair legal systems.

What is meant by 'support and respect'?

Respect for human rights means that corporations must refrain from any action or omission that would violate human rights or encourage or assist the commission of such violations. The notion of support for human rights means that, within their sphere of influence, corporations are expected to strive for full respect for human rights.

The Office of the UN High Commissioner for Human Rights has described the role of corporations — as 'organs of society' — under the Universal Declaration as follows:

> Corporations should strive for, and help uphold, democracy, the rule of law and full respect for human rights in the countries in which they operate. They should do nothing, directly or indirectly, to subvert these precepts. Corporations themselves should take particular care to ensure that their activities and practices do not contravene international human rights law . . . Corporations

should never be associated with, and should actively combat, racial, gender, social and other . . . forms of discrimination . . . They should play their part in implementing the right to work, to just and favourable conditions of work, the right of everyone to social security, including social insurance . . . the right of everyone to an adequate standard of living, the right to health, the right to education.

Further clarification of corporate responsibilities depends on the given situation in which a company is acting and on its relationship with other actors, all covered by the notion of 'sphere of influence'. Importantly, the human rights context of business varies across industries. Although all companies have the need to attend to labour rights (as all companies have employees), other issues — such as free expression, the use of security forces and access to certain goods considered public or quasi-public — are more prominent in some industries than they are in others.

What is the 'sphere of influence'?

Companies should assess their spheres of influence and design their human rights responsibilities accordingly.

At least three arguments have been said to underpin the importance of the idea of 'sphere of influence'. First, the people closest to a company, namely its employees, are those with whom it is most likely to have a direct relationship and for whom it has direct

---

5   For the Norms on the Responsibility of Transnational Corporations and Other Business Enterprises with Regard to Human Rights, see page 38.

responsibility. It follows that, whatever its general obligations to society, a company should take care not to harm its employees and should seek to ensure that they are treated properly. Second, within its sphere of influence, a company is most likely to know, or ought to know, the human rights consequences of its actions and omissions. If a company can predict or reasonably foresee that its actions or failures to act will result in human rights violations, then it is at least morally obliged to try to prevent them from occurring. Third, it is in relation to the people or institutions with whom it is closest that a company will have power, authority, influence, leverage or opportunity to protect victims or intervene with abusers.

A company's sphere of influence is an emerging concept in international human rights discourse. Various attempts in this regard focus on people and situations in political, contractual, economic or geographic proximity. One view of companies' spheres of influence — illustrated in Figure 1 — comes from a publication by Amnesty International and The Prince of Wales International Business Leaders Forum,[6] which provides the following framework, in order of priority:

1 **Core operations.** This includes human rights compliance under labour laws and in the direct use of security forces.

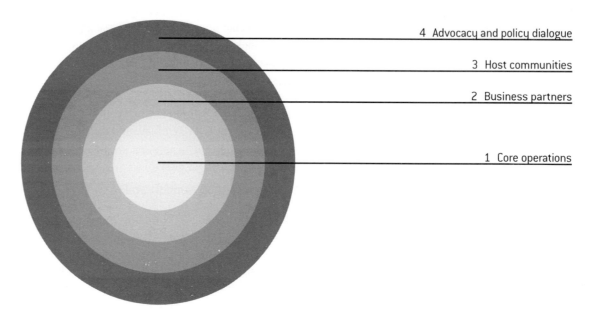

Figure 1 **A COMPANY'S SPHERES OF INFLUENCE**

4 Advocacy and policy dialogue

3 Host communities

2 Business partners

1 Core operations

---

6 Amnesty International and The Prince of Wales International Business Leaders Forum, *Human Rights: Is It Any of Your Business?* (London: Amnesty International, 2000).

2 **Business partners.** This includes ensuring that all contracts with partners and suppliers are in compliance with human rights and that compliance is subject to independent monitoring and verification.

3 **Host communities.** This includes stakeholder engagement and consultation, and partnership activities based on equity, transparency and mutual benefit.

4 **Advocacy and dialogue with government.** This applies to transnational corporations having considerable economic leverage with a government.

How can human rights be of help to companies?

Respect and support for human rights are conducive to business in general and to individual companies.

International human rights standards have been 'tried and tested' in corporate life, having proved their worth in policy and operational dimensions. Some companies implement these across functions and operations within the framework of policies addressing corporate social responsibility, health and safety, non-discrimination and the environment. Such principles have widespread legitimacy and are broadly accepted. Implementation can gain companies respectability and help to align their behaviour with the expectations of their stakeholders. The application

of internationally recognised standards also helps create a 'level playing field' on which business is competing on an even basis. In addition, respect and support for human rights are vital for upholding the rule of law, which is essential to sound business in that it contributes to a stable and predictable operational environment. Finally, actions based on human rights principles provide a moral dimension to companies' operations, which will help to address stakeholder concerns.

The international community is increasingly sensitive to human rights violations, and the image of a corporate actor is at serious risk if its human rights record raises doubts. Numerous campaigns against companies accused of violating human rights standards indicate the increased awareness of human rights within the general public. Companies operating in countries where serious human rights violations occur are under heightened scrutiny from local and international communities, non-governmental organisations (NGOs), consumer groups and the media. These companies will find that a human rights policy is an essential element of sound risk management and reputation assurance.

To which operations do human rights apply?

It is also useful to break down the aspects of a company's operations where human rights considerations might be applied. Indeed, this is another way to consider the spheres of influence a company has with respect to human rights. Although different products and projects may make

some of these areas more important than others for certain firms or sectors, Figure 2 provides a framework that can be used to consider in which operations human rights issues might arise.

Figure 2 **HUMAN RIGHTS IN A PROJECT LIFE CYCLE**
Source: Amnesty International/The Prince of Wales
International Business Leaders Forum

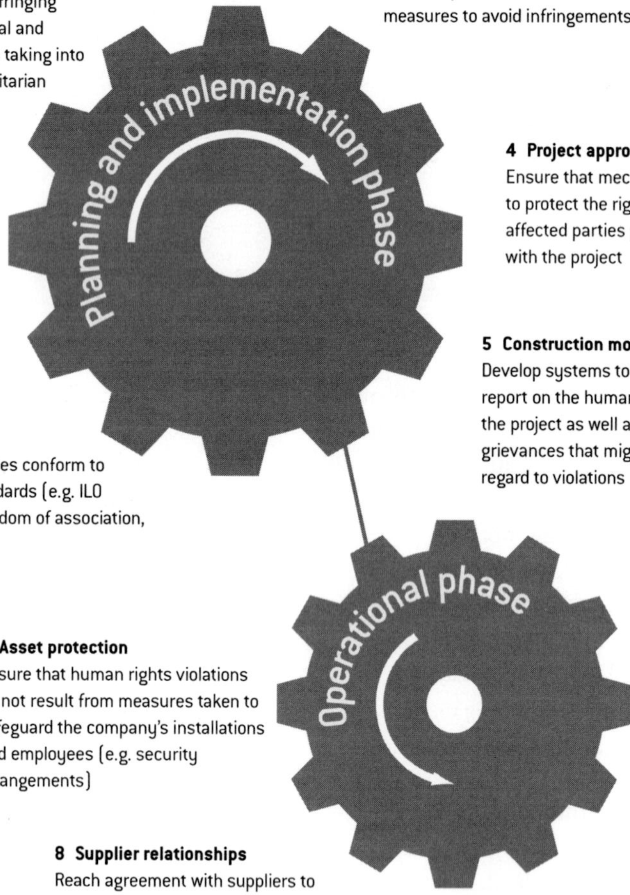

2 Pre-feasibility studies
Consider the risk of the project infringing
human rights in relation to political and
socioeconomic factors, as well as taking into
account legal, ethical and humanitarian
considerations

3 Feasibility studies
Include human rights implications in environmental and
social impact assessments and factor in the cost of
measures to avoid infringements

1 Project control
Consider the human rights context of
the project with regard to its location
and to internationally accepted
standards (e.g. UN and ILO
conventions)

Planning and implementation phase

4 Project approval
Ensure that mechanisms are in place
to protect the rights of interested and
affected parties prior to proceeding
with the project

5 Construction monitoring
Develop systems to monitor and
report on the human rights impact of
the project as well as to resolve any
grievances that might arise with
regard to violations

6 Employment practices
Ensure that employment practices conform to
international human rights standards (e.g. ILO
conventions) with regard to freedom of association,
non-discrimination, etc.

Operational phase

7 Asset protection
Ensure that human rights violations
do not result from measures taken to
safeguard the company's installations
and employees (e.g. security
arrangements)

10 Marketing and sales
Ensure that the human rights of
end users and others are
respected (e.g. avoid trading with
parties that might use the
company's products for
repressive purposes)

8 Supplier relationships
Reach agreement with suppliers to
ensure no forced labour, abusive forms of
child labour or ill treatment of workers
occur anywhere along the supply chain

9 Production processes
Provide a healthy and safe working environment, free of
harassment, intimidation and any form of degrading or
inhumane treatment of workers

Principle 2

**Businesses should ensure that their own
operations are not complicit in human rights
abuses.**

Much of the criticism of multinational corporations
has focused on companies that are perceived to be
associated with gross and systematic violations of
human rights in countries in which they operate.
Typically, the charge made is that a company
colludes, conspires or acquiesces in a pattern of
abuse committed by a government. In other words,
the companies are said to be 'complicit' in the
abuses committed by the authorities.

The direct violation of human rights is often clear,
but the question of complicity is not always as easy
to determine. Some have argued that merely
conducting business in countries where systematic
human rights violations are occurring constitutes
complicity. Many have also argued that a company's
failure to intervene publicly with a government
committing human rights violations in
circumstances where there is a link to the
company's own operations makes that company
complicit. Moreover, the relevance of this concept is
growing, as several multinational companies have
recently faced high-profile lawsuits for complicity in
human rights violations allegedly committed by
others.

In legal terms, the concept of 'complicity' means
facilitating someone else's violations of human
rights. To avoid such situations, both a determined
policy and a thorough understanding of the concept
of complicity are required.

In simple terms, complicity in human rights violations means that a firm is indirectly involved in violating the human rights of others. Direct involvement results from a firm's own employees acting as a function of company policy. Indirect involvement can take many forms but typically involves the violation of human rights by a firm's contractor, joint-venture partner, host government or other independent actor, acting on behalf of or with the active aid and encouragement of the firm in question. A company can be considered complicit in human rights violations if it authorises, tolerates or knowingly ignores the human rights violations of one of its business partners, committed in the furtherance of the two parties' common business goals. In addition, in some instances, the failure of the company to take action to prevent another party from committing violations may be interpreted as complicity, especially if the company is perceived to be a beneficiary of those violations.

A company may also be complicit in the human rights violations of the host government of a country where it operates. It is common for corporations to work with host governments on commercial projects in which both have an interest. In some instances, governments have committed human rights abuses in the process of these joint ventures. Companies that knowingly participate in a joint project with a host government that is committing human rights abuses in relation to that project may be considered complicit in such abuses.

If a company becomes aware of an indirect relationship to human rights violations related to any of its projects it should consider its role in that relationship carefully. Generally speaking, to be considered complicit in a human rights violation, the participation of the company need not actually cause the violation. Rather, the company's *assistance* or *encouragement* has to be to a degree that, without such participation, the violations *most probably* would not have occurred to the same extent or in the same way. A simple question for a company to ask itself is: if we or a company like ours were *not* doing business with the partner in question, what would be the effect on the violation of human rights? If the answer is that the human rights violations would occur to a lesser extent, or not at all, then that is a good indicator that the company may be complicit in the human rights violations.

Degrees of complicity

The final report of the South African Truth and Reconciliation Commission,[7] which examined the role of businesses under the apartheid regime, provides a useful illustration of how complicity can be applied to a specific situation.

The Commission concluded that business was central to the economy that sustained the apartheid state. Although it did not conclude that *all* businesses operating in South Africa supported or benefited equally from apartheid, it distinguished three levels of moral responsibility of businesses:

- Companies that actively helped to design and implement apartheid policies were found to have had 'first-order involvement'. The mining industry was especially guilty of working with the government to shape discriminatory policies, such as the migrant labour system, for its own advantage.

- Companies that knew the state would use their products or services for repression were accused of 'second-order involvement'. This is another form of complicity through active assistance, albeit of a more indirect form. The Commission cited banks, for example, that provided covert credit cards for repressive security operations, and the armaments industry, which knew the equipment it produced would be used to abuse human rights domestically and abroad.

- Finally, the Commission identified 'third-order involvement' — ordinary business activities that benefited indirectly by virtue of operating within the racially structured context of an apartheid society.

---

7 www.gov.za/reports/2003/trc

Figure 3 MAKING SENSE OF HUMAN RIGHTS INSTRUMENTS

Source: based on the figure produced by Amnesty International

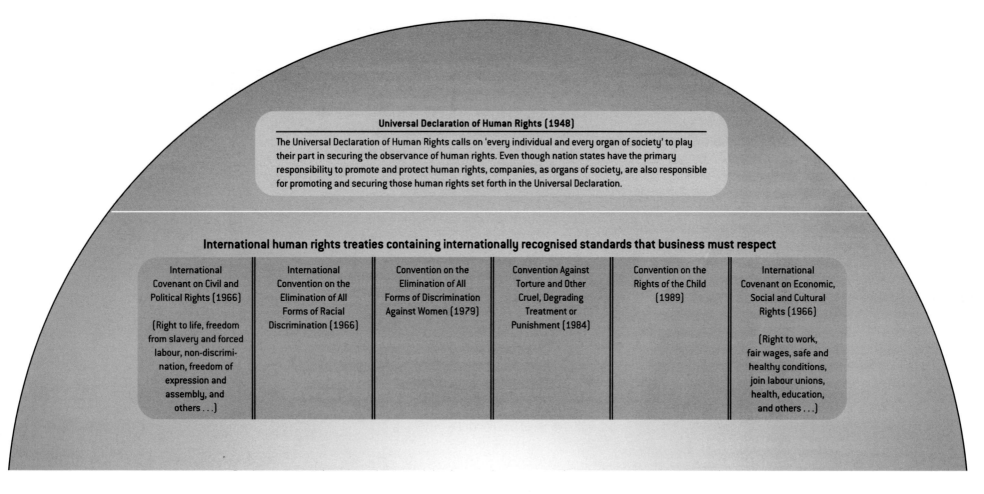

Universal Declaration of Human Rights (1948)

The Universal Declaration of Human Rights calls on 'every individual and every organ of society' to play their part in securing the observance of human rights. Even though nation states have the primary responsibility to promote and protect human rights, companies, as organs of society, are also responsible for promoting and securing those human rights set forth in the Universal Declaration.

International human rights treaties containing internationally recognised standards that business must respect

International Covenant on Civil and Political Rights (1966) (Right to life, freedom from slavery and forced labour, non-discrimination, freedom of expression and assembly, and others . . .)	International Convention on the Elimination of All Forms of Racial Discrimination (1966)	Convention on the Elimination of All Forms of Discrimination Against Women (1979)	Convention Against Torture and Other Cruel, Degrading Treatment or Punishment (1984)	Convention on the Rights of the Child (1989)	International Covenant on Economic, Social and Cultural Rights (1966) (Right to work, fair wages, safe and healthy conditions, join labour unions, health, education, and others . . .)

Regional human rights treaties containing internationally recognised standards relevant to business

European Convention for the Protection of Human Rights and Fundamental Freedoms (1950)	African Charter on Human and People's Rights (1981)	European Social Charter (1961)	American Convention on Human Rights (1969)	Arab Charter on Human Rights (1994)	Additional Protocol to the American Convention on Human Rights in the Area of Economic, Social and Cultural Rights (1988)

Specific international conventions, principles and codes relevant to business

UN Basic Principles on the Use of Force and Firearms by Law Enforcement Officials (1990); UN Code of Conduct for Law Enforcement Officials (1979); Convention on Combating Bribery of Foreign Public Officials in International Business Transactions of the OECD (2001); Rio Declaration on the Environment and Development (1992); World Summit on Sustainable Development Plan of Development (2002); International Code of Marketing of Breast-milk Substitutes (1981); ILO Convention No. 87 Concerning the Freedom of Association and Protection of the Right to Organise; ILO Declaration on Fundamental Principles and the Rights at Work (1998); ILO Convention No. 169 on Indigenous and Tribal Peoples (1989); and others . . .

Commitments specific to business containing human rights standards

UN Global Compact (2000); OECD Guidelines on Multinational Enterprises (2000); ILO Tripartite Declaration of Principles Concerning Multinational Enterprises and Social Policy (1977); and others . . .

Norms of Responsibilities of Transnational Corporations and Other Business Enterprises with Regard to Human Rights (2003)

The Norms were produced by an expert group of the UN Sub-Commission on the Promotion and Protection of Human Rights to be consistent with international, regional and multilateral agreements, conventions, principles and declarations. They relate these standards to specific human rights responsibilities of business.

The Global Compact principles relating to labour rights

The four labour principles of the Global Compact are taken from the ILO Declaration of Fundamental Principles and Rights at Work. Adopted in 1998 by the International Labour Conference, a yearly tripartite meeting that brings together governments, employers and workers from 177 countries, the Declaration calls on all ILO member states to apply the principles in line with the original intent of the core Conventions on which it is based. A universal consensus now exists that all countries, regardless of level of economic development, cultural values or ratification of the relevant ILO Conventions, have an obligation to respect, promote and realise these fundamental principles and rights. At the 2003 G8 meeting in Evian, France, the leaders of the industrialised world encouraged companies to work with other parties to implement the Declaration.

The principles and rights identified in the ILO Declaration comprise the labour portion of the Global Compact. They are:

- To promote and realise in good faith the right of workers and employers to freedom of association and the effective recognition of the right to collective bargaining
- To work towards the elimination of all forms of forced and compulsory labour
- The effective abolition of child labour
- The elimination of discrimination in respect of employment and occupation

The aim of the ILO is to harness the support of the business community for these principles through the Global Compact. The labour principles deal with fundamental rights in the workplace. The challenge for business is to take these universally accepted values and apply them at company level.

In the following we describe each of these labour principles. It should be noted that a thorough explanation of the principles, including the theory and legal aspects, is beyond the scope of this book but can be found on the ILO website, at www.ilo.org/business.

Principle 3

Businesses should uphold the freedom of association and the effective recognition of the right to collective bargaining.

Unfortunately, often the only time many people hear about the activities of unions and organised labour is when there is a disruption of services caused by walkouts or strikes. As a result, union roles and activities are often portrayed and perceived negatively. In reality, establishing a genuine dialogue with freely chosen workers' representatives enables workers and employers to understand each other's problems better and to find ways to resolve them. Security of representation is a foundation for building trust on both sides.

Freedom of association and the exercise of collective bargaining provide opportunities for constructive rather than confrontational dialogue, and this harnesses energy to focus on solutions that result in benefits to the enterprise, its stakeholders and society at large.

A number of studies — including a recent World Bank study[8] — indicate that the dynamic that results from freedom of association can set in motion a 'decent work-cycle' that increases productivity, income and profits for all concerned. The World Bank found that, at the macroeconomic level, high rates of unionisation led to lower inequality in earnings and can improve economic performance in the form of lower unemployment and inflation, higher productivity and speedier adjustment to economic 'shocks'.

The guarantee of representation through a 'voice at work' facilitates local responses to a global economy and serves as a basis for sustainable growth and secure investment returns. This can help bridge the widening representational gap in global work arrangements and facilitate the input of those people, regions and economic sectors — especially women and informal sector workers — who otherwise may be excluded from participating in processes that build decent work environments.

---

8 World Bank, *Unions and Collective Bargaining: Economic Effects in a Global Environment* (Washington, DC: World Bank, 2003).

Freedom of association

Freedom of association implies a respect for the right of employers and workers to join associations of their own choice. It does not mean that workforces must be organised or that companies must invite unions into the workplace. Rather, it implies that employers should not interfere in an employee's decision to associate or discriminate against the employee or a representative of the employee.

The freedom to associate involves employers, unions and workers' representatives freely discussing issues at work in order to reach agreements that are jointly acceptable. These freedoms also allow for industrial action to be taken by workers (and organisations) in defence of their economic and social interests.

Collective bargaining

Collective bargaining refers to the process or activity leading to the conclusion of a collective agreement. Collective bargaining is a voluntary process used to determine terms and conditions of work and the regulation of relations between employers, workers and their organisations. It is important to maintain harmonious industrial relations. This principle implies that the employers, employees and their organisations work together and make every effort to reach an agreement through genuine and constructive negotiations and that both parties avoid unjustified delays in negotiations. This does not imply a predefined level of bargaining or require compulsory bargaining on the part of employers or workers and their organisations.

Principle 4

Businesses should uphold the elimination of all forms of forced and compulsory labour.

Forced or compulsory labour is a concept that is often misunderstood. For example, the fact that wages or other compensation are paid to a worker does not guarantee that the labour is not forced or compulsory. In fact, forced or compulsory labour is any work or service that is extracted from any person under the menace of any penalty and for which that person has not offered himself or herself voluntarily. By right, work should be supplied without restraint, and employees should be free to leave in accordance with established rules.

Forced labour deprives societies of the opportunity to develop human resources for the modern labour market and to develop skills and educate children for the labour markets of tomorrow. The debilitating consequences of forced labour are felt by the individual, in particular by children, as well as by the economy itself as the degradation of human capital and social stability results in insecure investments.

By retarding the proper development of human resources, forced labour lowers the level of productivity and economic growth for society generally. The loss of income due to disruption of regular jobs or income-generating activities reduces the lifetime earnings of whole families and, with it, the loss of food, shelter and healthcare.

While companies operating legally do not normally employ such practices, forced labour can become associated with enterprises through their use of contractors and suppliers. As a result, all managers should be aware of the forms and causes of forced labour, as well as how it might occur in different industries. Forced and compulsory labour can take a number of forms:

- Slavery
- Bonded labour or debt bondage, an ancient practice still in use in some countries, in which adults and children are obliged to work in slave-like conditions to repay debts of their own, their parents or relatives
- Child labour in particularly abusive conditions where the child has no choice about whether to work
- Work or service of prisoners if they are hired to, or placed at the disposal of, private individuals, companies or associations involuntarily and without supervision by public authorities
- Labour for development purposes required by the authorities: for instance, to assist in construction, agriculture and other public works
- Work required in order to punish opinion or expression of views ideologically opposed to

the established political, social or economic system

- Exploitative practices such as forced overtime or the lodging of deposits (financial or personal documents) for employment

Principle 5

Businesses should uphold the effective abolition of child labour.

Child labour has occurred at some point in time in virtually all parts of the world as nations have undergone different stages of development. It remains a serious issue today in many developing countries — although it also exists (less visibly) in industrialised countries.

Child labour deprives children of their childhood and their dignity. Many children work long hours for low or no wages, often under conditions harmful to their health and to their physical and mental development. They are often denied the opportunity to a proper education and may be separated from their families. Children who do not complete their primary education are likely to remain illiterate and never acquire the skills needed to get a job and contribute to the development of a modern economy. Consequently, the use of child labour results in scores of underskilled, unqualified workers and jeopardises future improvement of skills in the workforce.

Child labour occurs because of the pressures of poverty and lack of development but also simply as a result of exploitation. It exists both in the formal and in the informal economy. However, it is in the informal economy where the majority of the worst forms of child labour are found.

Although children enjoy the same human rights as adults, their lack of knowledge, experience and power has resulted in the establishment of specific legal protections for them. These rights include protection from economic exploitation and work that may be dangerous to their health or morals and that may hinder their development. This does not mean that children should not be allowed to work, rather that there are standards that distinguish what constitutes acceptable or unacceptable work for children at different ages and stages of their development.

Employers should not use child labour in ways that are socially unacceptable and that lead to a child losing his or her educational opportunities. The complexity of the issue of child labour means that companies need to address the issue sensitively and not take action that may force working children into more exploitative forms of work. Nevertheless, as Principle 5 states, the goal of all companies should be the abolition of child labour within their sphere of influence.

The use of child labour can damage a company's reputation. This is especially true in the case of multinational companies with extensive supply and service chains, where the economic exploitation of children, even by a business partner, can damage a brand image and have strong repercussions on profit and stock value.

Definitions

ILO Conventions recommend a minimum age for admission to employment or work that must not be less than the age for completing compulsory schooling and, in any case, not less than 15 years. However, lower ages are permitted — generally, in countries where economic and educational facilities are less well developed, the minimum age is 14 years, and 13 years for 'light' work (see Table 1).

Type of work	Minimum age	
	Industrialised countries	Developing countries
Light	13 years	12 years
Regular	15 years	14 years
Hazardous	18 years	18 years

Table 1 GENERALLY APPLICABLE MINIMUM AGES FOR EMPLOYMENT

Priority is given to eliminating, for all persons under the age of 18 years, the worst forms of child labour, including hazardous types of work or employment. These are defined as:

- All forms of slavery, including the trafficking of children, debt bondage, forced and compulsory labour and the use of children in armed conflict

- The use, procuring or offering of a child for prostitution, for the production of pornography or for pornographic purposes
- The use, procuring or offering of a child for illicit activities, in particular the production and trafficking of drugs
- Work that is likely to harm the health, safety or morals of the child as a consequence of its nature or the circumstances under which it is carried out

Principle 6

Businesses should eliminate discrimination in respect of employment and occupation.

Discrimination can take many forms, both in terms of gaining access to employment and in the treatment of employees once they are in work. It may be direct, such as when laws, rules or practices explicitly cite a reason such as sex or race to deny equal opportunity. Most commonly, discrimination is indirect and subtle, arising where rules or practices have the appearance of neutrality but, in fact, lead to exclusion. This 'indirect' discrimination often exists informally in attitudes and practices which, if unchallenged, can perpetuate in organisations. Discrimination may also have cultural roots that demand more specific individual approaches.

The definition of discrimination in employment and occupation is 'any distinction, exclusion or preference which has the effect of nullifying or impairing equality of opportunity or treatment in employment or occupation', and is made on the basis of 'race, colour, sex, religion, political opinion, national extraction or social origin'. Obviously, distinctions based strictly on the inherent requirements of the job are not discrimination.

Discrimination can arise in a variety of work-related activities. These include access to employment and to particular occupations and to training and vocational guidance. Moreover, it can occur with respect to the terms and conditions of the employment, such as, for example, equal remuneration, hours of work and rest, paid holidays, maternity leave, security of tenure, advancement, social security and occupational safety and health. In some countries, additional issues for discrimination in the workplace, such as age and HIV status, are growing in importance. It is also important to realise that discrimination at work arises in a range of settings and can be a problem in all types of business.

Non-discrimination means simply that employees are selected on the basis of their ability to do the job and that there is no distinction, exclusion or preference made on other grounds. Employees who experience discrimination at work are denied opportunities and have their basic human rights infringed. This affects the individual concerned and negatively influences the greater contribution that they might make to society.

The Global Compact principles relating to the environment

Principle 7

Businesses should support a precautionary approach to environmental challenges.

What is 'a precautionary approach'?

Despite many years of scientific research, knowledge of environmental systems is still not sufficient to predict with certainty the effect of many human activities on the environment. The use of chlorofluorocarbons (CFCs) provides an example of how the hazardous nature of an activity can go unrecognised for many years. CFCs were introduced in the 1940s, but it was not until the 1970s that experts predicted that emissions of CFCs persisting in the atmosphere could lead to ozone depletion in the stratosphere. The first observation of ozone depletion over the Antarctic was reported in 1985, and the Montreal Protocol was signed in 1987.[9] This historic agreement brought about a phasing-out of the use of CFCs — nearly 50 years after their introduction.

If environmental protection is to be considered an integral part of the development process, how can the environmental risks associated with human

---

9 For the Montreal Protocol, see www.unep.org/ozone/index.asp.

activities be assessed and avoided? The Rio Declaration sets out an extremely important idea, now widely accepted by policy-makers, of a precautionary approach to environmental protection:

> In order to protect the environment, the precautionary approach shall be widely applied by states according to their capabilities. Where there are threats of serious or irreversible damage, lack of full scientific certainty shall not be used as a reason for postponing cost-effective measures to prevent environmental degradation.[10]

It is important here to point out the existence of two concepts — the 'precautionary approach' as embodied in Principle 15 of the Rio Declaration, and the 'precautionary principle'.

The precautionary *approach* is a softer formulation, as expressed in the Rio Declaration. The precautionary *principle* implies a systemic approach with more stringent requirements with respect to issues such as 'the burden of proof'. This concept of precaution has found its way into a number of multilateral environmental agreements (MEAs) in the 1990s. It has emerged from the German concept of *Vorsorgeprinzip*, which embraces notions of risk prevention, cost-effectiveness, ethical responsibilities towards the environment and a recognition of the uncertain nature of human knowledge and understanding. In its stronger formulation, precaution as principle has been reflected in national legislation in Sweden, Germany and other Nordic and German-speaking countries since the 1970s and also in EU legislation such as the Seveso Directive.[11] The 1992 Maastricht Treaty amendment elevated the precautionary principle to the level of constitutional goal in the EU Treaty (article 174).[12]

Precaution is founded on a number of key concepts, such as:

- **Preventative anticipation.** Action should be taken if necessary *before* scientific proof is available, on the grounds that a delay could cause damage to nature and society.

- **Safeguarding ecological 'space'.** In order to protect and widen the assimilative capacity of the natural environment, one should not impinge on ecological margins; that is, one should refrain from using resources unsustainably.

- **Proportionality of response.** A selected degree of restraint is not unduly costly; in other words, there is a need to show more concern for the possibly greater dangers to future generations arising from the undermining of important life-support systems.

- **Duty of care.** The onus of proof is on those undertaking an activity or carrying out change to demonstrate that they are causing no environmental harm.

- **Promoting intrinsic natural rights.** Natural processes should be allowed to function such that they maintain essential support for all life on Earth.

- **Paying for ecological 'debt'.** One should pay compensation for past errors of judgement as indicated by the notion of 'common but differentiated responsibility' enshrined in a number of multilateral environmental agreements.

A business approach to the concept of precaution

Precaution involves the systematic application of risk assessment (hazard identification, hazard characterisation, appraisal of exposure and risk characterisation), risk management and risk communication. The key element of a precautionary approach, from a business perspective, is the idea of prevention rather than cure. In other words, it is more cost-effective to take early action to ensure that irreversible environmental damage does not occur than to try to remedy it once it has happened. Companies should consider the following:

- Although it is true that prevention of environmental damage entails costs,

---

10 For details of the Rio Declaration see page 40.

11 For the Seveso Directive, see www.ess.co.at/HITERM/REGULATIONS/82-501-eec.html.

12 For the Maastricht Treaty and the EU Treaty, see www.europa.eu.int/abc/obj/treaties/en/entoc01.htm.

remediation can cost much more, both in terms of clean-up costs and damage to company image.

- Investment in unsustainable production methods has a lower long-term return than does investment in sustainable methods. In turn, improvements in environmental performance mean less financial risk, an important consideration for insurers.
- Research and development related to the creation of more environmentally friendly products can have significant long-term benefits.

Nevertheless, interpretation of the precautionary approach can present difficulties for companies. They will better assess any potential environmental harm if they have a thorough understanding of current environmental impacts as well as of the baseline environmental conditions within their sphere of influence. This requires the development of a life cycle approach to business activities that can manage uncertainty and ensure transparency.

With respect to assessing uncertainty and options for a precautionary approach, a number of useful tools are available to gather the necessary information, such as:

- **Environmental risk assessment.** This establishes the potential for unintended environmental damage alongside other risks.
- **Life cycle assessment (LCA).** This explores the opportunities for more environmentally

benign inputs and outputs in product and process development.

- **Environmental impact assessment (EIA).** This ensures that impacts of development projects are within acceptable levels.
- **Strategic environmental assessment (SEA).** This ensures that the impacts of policies and plans are taken into account and mitigated.

Principle 8

Businesses should undertake initiatives to promote greater environmental responsibility.

The 1992 Rio Earth Summit highlighted the true fragility of the planet. The message to companies was spelled out in Chapter 30 of Agenda 21, in which the role of business and industry in the sustainable development agenda is discussed. On the 'responsible and ethical management of products and processes' from the point of view of health, safety and environment, it states:

> Towards this end, business and industry should increase self-regulation, guided by appropriate codes, charters and initiatives integrated into all elements of business planning and decision-making, and fostering openness and dialogue with employees and the public.

In the ten years since the Rio Summit the imperative for business to conduct its activities in an environmentally responsible manner has not

lessened. In the Malmö Ministerial Declaration of May 2000, Environment Ministers stated:[13]

> A greater commitment by the private sector should be pursued to engender a new culture of environmental accountability through the application of the polluter-pays principle, environmental performance indicators and reporting, and the establishment of a precautionary approach in investment and technology decisions. This approach must be linked to the development of cleaner and more resource efficient technologies for a life cycle economy and efforts to facilitate the transfer of environmentally sound technologies.

The Malmö Declaration also welcomed the Global Compact as 'an excellent vehicle for the development of a constructive engagement with the private sector'. Two years later, government heads called for greater 'corporate environmental and social responsibility and accountability' in the Johannesburg Declaration and Plan of Implementation of the 2002 World Summit on Sustainable Development.[14]

It has become clear that, given the central role of the private sector in global governance issues, the public demands that corporations manage their operations in a manner that not only enhances

---

13 For the Malmö Ministerial Declaration, see www.unep.org/malmo/malmo2.pdf.
14 For details of the Johannesburg Declaration and the Johannesburg Plan of Implementation, see page 40.

economic prosperity and promotes social justice but also ensures environmental protection. Through Principle 8, the Global Compact provides a framework for business to take forward some of the key challenges made in Rio and, even earlier, at the first 'Earth Summit' in Stockholm 1972.

Towards environmentally responsible business practice

Business gains legitimacy by meeting the needs of society, and, increasingly, society is expressing a clear need for more environmentally sustainable practices. One way for business to demonstrate its commitment to greater environmental responsibility is by changing its *modus operandi* from the so-called 'traditional methods' to more responsible approaches to addressing environmental issues (see Table 2).

Such a change in business strategy brings with it a number of benefits. The United Nations Environment Programme (UNEP) has pinpointed the following reasons why a company should think about improving its environmental performance:

- Application of cleaner production and eco-efficiency leads to improved resource productivity.

- New economic instruments (taxes, charges, trade permits) are rewarding clean companies.

- Insurance companies and banks prefer to cover a cleaner, lower-risk company.

Traditional	Sustainable
Inefficient resource use	Resource productivity
End-of-pipe technology	Cleaner production
Public relations	Corporate governance
Reactive	Proactive
Use of management systems	Attention to life cycles and business design
One-way, passive communication	Multi-stakeholder, active dialogue

Table 2 **A COMPARISON OF TRADITIONAL AND SUSTAINABLE APPROACHES**

- Employees tend to prefer to work for an environmentally responsible company.

- Consumers want cleaner and healthier products and better information.

To take concrete environmentally responsible action the company can proactively chose to work on a consumption and production programme, define quantified improvement targets and report progress against those targets using the guidelines for sustainability reporting as developed under the Global Reporting Initiative (GRI).[15]

---

15 For more on the GRI, see www.globalreporting.org and pages 202-207.

Principle 9

Businesses should encourage the development and diffusion of environmentally friendly technologies.

What is meant by an 'environmentally friendly technology'?

Encouraging the development and diffusion of environmentally friendly technology is a longer-term challenge for a company that will draw both on the management and the research capabilities of the organisation. For the purposes of engaging with the Global Compact, environmentally friendly technologies are those described in Chapter 34 of Agenda 21 that:

protect the environment, are less polluting, use all resources in a more sustainable manner, recycle more of their wastes and products and handle residual wastes in a more acceptable manner than the technologies for which they were substitutes. [Environmentally sound technologies] are not just individual technologies, but total systems that include know-how, procedures, goods and services, and equipment as well as organisational and managerial processes.

Important here is an understanding that this broad definition not only includes end-of-pipe and monitoring techniques but also *explicitly encourages* more progressive preventative approaches, such as pollution prevention and cleaner production technologies. The aspiration of this principle is, therefore, towards clean technology, where the function is to provide a human benefit or service, rather than concentrating on products per se.

Reasons to develop and diffuse environmentally sound technologies

Environmentally proficient technologies allow us to reduce the use of finite resources and to use existing resources more efficiently. For example, improvements in the power–weight ratio of batteries has led to a significant reduction in the use of toxic heavy metals while bringing substantial benefits to the consumer.

Waste storage, treatment and disposal is costly both in financial and in environmental and social terms. As environmentally sound technologies (ESTs) generate less waste and residues, the continued use of inefficient technologies can represent increased operating costs for business. In addition, it results in a retrospective focus on control and remediation rather than on prevention. In contrast, the avoidance of environmental impacts through pollution prevention and ecological product design increases the efficiency and overall competitiveness of the company and may also lead to new business opportunities.

As ESTs reduce operating inefficiencies they also lead to lower occupational exposure levels and pollution emission, and contribute to reduced rates of accidents.

Methods to promote the use and diffusion of environmentally sound technologies

Engagement with Principle 9 will depend, to some extent, on the size and nature of the business. However, all companies will want to pursue the business benefits that come from a more efficient use of resources. As this principle captures 'hard' technologies and 'soft' systems the potential entry points are broad. At the level of the operating unit, technology improvement can be implemented through a combination of process change, raw material substitutions, product redesign and re-use on-site of the various materials resulting from the process. This implies a new approach to research and development and systemic thinking that encompasses the full life cycle of what is produced. It can also mean the building of new alliances between various cleaner technology providers and users.

And what about corruption?

Corruption is an overarching issue for the nine principles of the Global Compact. In its broadest definition, also taking into account private-to-private corruption, 'corruption is the misuse of entrusted power for private benefit'. In the case of the public sector, this involves behaviour on the part of officials, whether politicians or civil servants, in which they improperly and unlawfully enrich themselves or those close to them.[16]

In the area of labour, corruption is one of the major causes of the neglect of labour principles. Studies in export-processing zones have shown that bribery of public officials covered broken labour standards. In many countries, access to basic human rights such as education, food or transportation depends on corruption. The Organisation for Economic Cooperation and Development (OECD) has estimated that annual corruption payments amount to US$80 billion.[17] Examples from Russia, the Philippines and other countries show that many violations of human rights are committed to protect

---

16 This definition taken from the Transparency International *Sourcebook on Corruption* (www.transparency.org).

17 See www.oecd.org.

corrupt public officials.[18] Networks of corruption between authoritarian regimes and business elites lead government officials 'to turn a blind eye' not only to labour rights abuse but also to environmental non-compliance.

It has therefore been argued that the nine principles need to be strengthened by a strong stance against corruption, preferably in the form of a tenth principle. The signature in December 2003 of a UN Convention Against Corruption and the ensuing ratification process will provide the universal legitimacy that underpin the other principles.[19] The Global Compact is a formal commitment between a CEO representing the company and the UN represented by its Secretary-General. When it needs adaptation the process must be deliberate and transparent with advance notice and dialogue. Such a process began in the latter part of 2003 and was concluded recently. A tenth principle on corruption is expected to be introduced in the course of the second half of 2004. Put simply:

Businesses should work against corruption in all its forms, including extortion and bribery.

The fight against corruption has preoccupied business for decades now. Extortion of bribes increases business transaction costs and distorts competition and market efficiency. Corruption therefore weakens economic growth and social development, the consolidation of democracy and people's morality. Corruption is one of the main reasons for continuous poverty. Long-term economic, political and social development can be achieved only by good governance and by fighting corruption.

Corruption is not just a local or a national problem but also, to a large extent, a regional and global problem. Although almost all countries have criminalised domestic bribery, enforcement is patchy in many parts of the world. Therefore there is an increased interest in combating bribery and corruption from an international perspective.

The US Foreign Corrupt Practices Act of 1977[20] targets US companies involved in corruption abroad. It was the first piece of legislation that had an impact on international business. As a result, companies developed programmes to ensure that they could comply with its terms. However, the Act is powerless against companies that compete with US business on the basis of kickbacks and other facilitating payments. Also, in 1977, the International Chamber of Commerce (ICC) drafted the Rules of Conduct to Combat Extortion and Bribery[21] as a basis for corporate action, and a first attempt was made to negotiate a global framework of anti-corruption measures. This attempt failed, as developing and developed countries could not agree on the roots of corruption, and developing countries rejected being held solely responsible for this issue. The ICC, however, continued to encourage business initiatives. In its recent *Corporate Practices Manual: Fighting Corruption*[22] it recommends that companies should:

- Develop a clearly expressed manual or code of good corporate practice, with input from a range of company sources

- Give top management and the company's governing body responsibility for devising systems for implementing the manual or code

- Put into place an effective compliance programme containing measures aimed at education, training and appropriate disciplinary measures if the manual or code is violated

- Modify the manual or code if practices change or the original document proves to be inadequate

- Apply sanctions against code violators fairly, consistently and without bias

The ICC rules make it clear that, although governments have 'major responsibility' in controlling extortion and bribery, 'the international business community has the corresponding responsibility to strengthen its own efforts to combat extortion and bribery'.

18 E.P. Mendes, 'Corruption: The Cancer of the International Bill of Rights. Democracy and Freedom of Expression, The Main Treatments?', in E.P. Mendes and A. Lalonde-Roussy (eds.), *Bridging the Global Divide on Human Rights: A China–Canada Dialogue* (Aldershot, UK: Ashgate, 2003): 283-98.

19 On the UN Convention Against Corruption, see page 42.

20 Foreign Corrupt Practices Act (1977) 91 Stat. 1494, Dec 19, 1977 (Washington, DC: US Government Printing Office).

21 See www.iccwbo.org.

22 F. Vincke and F. Heimann (eds.), *Fighting Corruption: A Corporate Practices Manual* (Paris: International Chamber of Commerce, 2003).

It was not until November 1997 that international efforts succeeded with the adoption of the OECD Convention on Combating Bribery of Foreign Public Officials in International Business Transactions.[23] Since it came into force, the 35 signatory countries have enacted legislation. The Convention levels the playing field for companies situated in the signatory countries. This momentum grew with the development of further legal regimes by the Council of Europe (the Criminal Law Convention and the Civil Law Convention on Corruption),[24] and the UN Convention Against Corruption that will be open for signature by member states in December 2003.

Today, with the adoption of the UN Convention Against Corruption,[25] an ambitious global framework covering a wide range of actions on the demand and the supply sides of corruption has finally been introduced. The main areas covered by the Convention are embezzlement, misappropriation of influence, abuse of function, illicit enrichment and concealment. For the first time, confiscation and repatriation of illicit assets to the country of origin, as well as private-to-private corruption are covered by a convention. Although far-reaching in scope, the Convention does little for enforcing its provisions. This is left to the discretion of signatory states, which may choose to bring

unresolved disputes before the International Court of Justice. The actual implementation and the public monitoring of the provisions of the Convention will be crucial to provide a level playing field for all actors. However, as the UN Convention is the first truly global initiative it is considered to be a milestone in anti-corruption history.

Another aspect that has prompted companies to deal with anti-corruption measures is the rapid development of rules of corporate governance. These increasingly require companies to protect their reputation and shareholders through internal controls of integrity. An increasing number of ethical investment funds require companies in which they invest to undertake good business practice, including an explicit anti-corruption stance.

There has still been little enforcement of the new anti-corruption laws by national governments, other than by the USA. OECD monitoring of enforcement started more slowly than planned and, because of limited awareness in the business community, the adoption of corporate anti-bribery compliance programmes has also been limited. An OECD publication, *Business Approaches to Combating Corrupt Practices*[26] revealed that only 43 of the top 100 non-financial multinational enterprises include anti-corruption programmes on their websites. It was concluded that this low proportion might

reflect a lack of awareness of the issue, an unwillingness to discuss it publicly or the perception that corruption is not a major concern for companies. Transparency International's Bribe Payers Index,[27] published in October 2002, indicated that bribery by companies from 20 leading exporting states had not declined in the three years since the previous Bribe Payers Index was published.

Laws are stepping stones in the process of eliminating corruption; however, legal texts alone will not suffice, and the practical day-to-day work of fighting corruption must be done by enterprises before they become subject to sanctions imposed by the state. Voluntary initiatives and compliance by a large majority of companies is needed to establish the moral framework that makes law enforcement effective.

---

23 See www.oecd.org.
24 On the Criminal Law Convention and the Civil Law Convention on Corruption, see http://conventions.coe.int.
25 See www.odccp.org; see also page 42.
26 OECD (Organisation for Economic Cooperation and Development), *Business Approaches to Combating Corrupt Practices* (Paris: OECD, September 2003).
27 See www.transparency.org/surveys/index.html#bpi.

Global Compact Primer

Type of resource: resource package, available as CD-ROM or ring-bound

Author organisation: United Nations, interagency

Year of publication: 2003

The objective of this resource package is to serve as an introduction and awareness-raising tool for the Global Compact and its underlying principles. It can be used by anyone who seeks guidance on the background to and integration of the principles in their daily operations. It is available as a CD-ROM or as printed version in a ring-binder.

It comprises an introduction and comprehensive background to the Global Compact, separate presentations and subsequent case studies for each of the three main areas of the compact — human rights, labour and the environment — and a separate resource directory. The aim of the directory is to facilitate access to additional information on the Global Compact and the subject of corporate social responsibility. The resource directory is organised into three separate categories:

- Resources for companies
- Resources for training and management schools
- Resources for local networks

Introducing the Compact's principles in a systematic and simple manner, the presentations include explanations of where the principles came from, what they mean and how they can be implemented.

FURTHER INFORMATION
Website: www.unglobalcompact.org

Universal Declaration of Human Rights

Type of resource: declaration

Author organisation: United Nations

Year of publication: 1948

The Universal Declaration was adopted and proclaimed by UN General Assembly Resolution 217A(III) of 10 December 1948. The rights cover three areas:

- Life and security
- Economic, social and cultural rights
- Personal rights and freedoms

Everyone is entitled to all the rights and freedoms set forth in the Declaration, without distinction or discrimination of any kind. The Universal Declaration makes 'every individual and every organ of society' responsible for promoting and respecting the Declaration's rights and freedoms.

FURTHER INFORMATION
Website: www.unhchr.ch

Norms on the Responsibilities of Transnational Corporations and Other Business Enterprises with Regard to Human Rights

Type of resource: norms

Author organisation: UN Sub-Commission on the Promotion and Protection of Human Rights

Year of publication: 2003

In August 2003, the UN Sub-Commission on the Promotion and Protection of Human Rights, a body composed of 26 human rights experts, adopted the Norms and recommended that the UN Commission on Human Rights, which comprises 53 representatives of UN member states, review the document with a view to its formal adoption.

The document, which currently does not have any formal legal status, sets out the standards of international human rights law that transnational corporations and other business enterprises should respect, protect and fulfil within their sphere of influence. It covers:

- The right to equal opportunity and non-discriminatory treatment
- The right to security of persons
- The rights of workers
- Respect for national sovereignty
- Consumer and environmental protection

The Norms also set out general provisions for implementation, including periodic monitoring and adequate remedies for failure to comply.

FURTHER INFORMATION
Website: www.unhchr.ch
Document: www.unhchr.ch/pdf/55sub/38rev2_AV.pdf

ILO Tripartite Declaration of Principles Concerning Multinational Enterprises and Social Policy

Type of resource: declaration

Author organisation: International Labour Organisation

Year of publication: 2000

Adopted in 1977 by the ILO governing body and last revised in 2000 the principles laid down in this universal instrument offer guidelines to multinational enterprises, governments, employers' and workers' organisations in such areas as employment, training, conditions of work and life, and industrial relations. It constitutes the only corporate social responsibility instrument based on universal principles and agreed on a tripartite basis.

FURTHER INFORMATION
Website: www.ilo.org/multi

ILO Declaration of Fundamental Principles and Rights at Work

Type of resource: declaration/yearly report

Author organisation: International Labour Organisation

Year of first publication: 1998

Each year, the ILO publishes a report providing a 'global, dynamic picture' on one of the four categories of the ILO Fundamental Principles and Rights at Work. Discussion of the global report at the International Labour Conference sets the stage for the ILO governing body to draw conclusions about priorities for technical cooperation during the subsequent four-year period.

FURTHER INFORMATION
Website: www.ilo.org
Document: www.ilo.org/public/english/standards/decl/publ/reports/index.htm

ILO International Labour Standards

Type of resource: website

Author organisation: International Labour Organisation

The international labour standards website provides answers to basic questions about international labour standards — what they are, where they come from, how they are enforced and so on. In addition, the site has links to various ILO databases, such as ILOLEX, which covers international labour standards, and NATLEX, a database of national laws on labour, social security and related human rights.

FURTHER INFORMATION
Website:
www.ilo.org/public/english/standards/norm/index.htm
ILOLEX website: www.ilo.org/ilolex/english
NATLEX website: www.ilo.org/dyn/natlex/natlex_browse.home

ILO Codes of Practice in Safety and Health

Type of resource: codes of practice

Author organisation: International Labour Organisation

Year of publication: various

The ILO has developed a number of codes of practice, available from its website, that contain practical recommendations intended for all those with a responsibility for occupational safety and health both in the public sector and in the private sector. The most comprehensive is *Guidelines on Occupational Safety and Health Management Systems* (2001). Others concern ambient factors in the workplace, safety and health in forestry work, and technical and ethical guidelines for workers' health surveillance.

FURTHER INFORMATION

International Labour Organisation (ILO) website: www.ilo.org

Codes: www.ilo.org/public/english/protection/safework/cops/english/index.htm

ILO Code of Practice on HIV/AIDS

Type of resource: code of practice

Author organisation: International Labour Organisation

Year of publication: 2001

This code of practice was developed through a widespread process of consultation with governments and employer and worker constituents in all regions of the world. The code contains fundamental principles for policy development and practical guidelines from which concrete responses can be developed at enterprise, community and national levels in the following key areas:

- Prevention of HIV/AIDS
- Management and mitigation of the impact of HIV/AIDS on the world of work
- Care and support of workers infected and affected by HIV/AIDS
- Elimination of stigma and discrimination on the basis of real or perceived HIV status

The code is currently available in 17 different languages. Also available online is a comprehensive, modular training guide (in English only) to assist in the implementation of the code.

FURTHER INFORMATION

Website: www.ilo.org/public/english/protection/trav/aids/code/codemain.htm

The Stockholm, Rio and Johannesburg Declarations, Agenda 21 and the Johannesburg Plan of Implementation

Type of resource: publications

Author organisation: United Nations

Year of publication: various

The Rio Declaration and Johannesburg Declaration follow on from the Stockholm Declaration of 1972, when the first world environment conference was held under the auspices of the UN. Milestone conferences building on the Stockholm legacy were the UN Conference on Environment and Development of 1992 in Rio de Janeiro, and the 2002 World Summit on Sustainable Development in Johannesburg.

Along with agreements such as those concerning climate change and biodiversity, the 1992 Rio Summit produced Agenda 21, and the Rio Declaration, with its 27 principles. The 40 chapters in Agenda 21 include Chapter 30 on 'Strengthening the Role of Business and Industry'.

The two key documents from the 2002 Summit are the Johannesburg Plan of Implementation and the Johannesburg Declaration, with its 37 paragraphs. The Johannesburg Declaration recognises the 'need for private sector corporations to enforce corporate accountability, which should take place within a transparent and stable regulatory environment'.

FURTHER INFORMATION

United Nations, *Stockholm Declaration* (New York: UN, 1972)

United Nations, *Agenda 21* (New York: UN, 1992)

United Nations, *Rio Declaration* (New York: UN, 1992)

United Nations, *Johannesburg Declaration* (New York: UN, 2002)

United Nations, *Johannesburg Plan of Implementation* (New York: UN, 2003)

Website: www.un.org/esa/sustdev

ISO 14000 Series

Type of resource: standards

Author organisation: International Organisation for Standardisation

Year of publication: various

The ISO 14000 series was developed by the ISO environmental management committee, which was set up in 1993 following preparatory consultations held under the umbrella of the Strategic Advisory Group on Environment (SAGE). Today the ISO 14000 series consists of a set of standards that help companies to establish and maintain a structured and systemic effort to continually improve their environmental performance. ISO's technical committee works closely with the committee responsible for quality management and assurance to ensure compatibility between the ISO 14000 series and the ISO 9000 family of quality management standards.

The series is both organisation-oriented and product-oriented and includes the following:

- Environmental management systems and communication: ISO 14001, ISO 14004 and ISO 14063
- Environmental auditing: ISO 14010 series and ISO 19011
- Environmental performance: ISO 14030 series
- Environmental labels and environmental declarations: ISO 14020 series
- Life cycle assessment: ISO 14040 series
- Environmental aspects: ISO Guide 64 and ISO/TR 14062

These standards can be used both independently or in combination with one another.

FURTHER INFORMATION

Website: www.iso.org

OECD Guidelines for Multinational Enterprises

Type of resource: guidelines

Author organisation: Organisation for Economic Cooperation and Development

Year of publication: 2000

The OECD Guidelines for Multinational Enterprises contain voluntary principles and standards for responsible business conduct in such areas as human rights, disclosure of information, anti-corruption, taxation, labour relations, environment and consumer protection. They aim to promote the positive contributions multinational enterprises can make to economic, environmental and social progress.

Although observance of the guidelines is voluntary for companies, adhering governments formally commit to promoting them among multinational enterprises operating in or from their territories. The national contact point (NCP) — often a government office — is responsible for encouraging observance of the guidelines in its national context and for ensuring that the guidelines are well known and understood by the national business community and by other interested parties. The NCP promotes the guidelines, handles enquiries, assists in solving problems that may arise, gathers information on national experiences with the guidelines and reports annually to the OECD Committee on International Investment and Multinational Enterprises.

The Guideline procedures provide for something called 'specific instances', a facility that allows interested parties to call a company's alleged non-observance of the Guideline recommendations to the attention of an NCP. Over 60 such instances have been brought to the attention of NCPs since the revision of the guidelines in June 2000.

FURTHER INFORMATION

Website: www.oecd.org

OECD Principles of Corporate Governance

Type of resource: principles

Author organisation: Organisation for Economic Cooperation and Development

Year of publication: 1999

The OECD Principles of Corporate Governance, adopted in 1999, outline the core elements of good corporate governance and, in that sense, are useful to companies as well as governments, private associations, investors and other parties committed to improving corporate governance practices. Acknowledging that no one model of corporate governance can work for all countries and companies, the principles identify standards that can apply across a broad range of legal, political and economic environments. The principles have been endorsed by a number of organisations and have influenced corporate governance policy and practice at the regional, national and company level around the world. They are also designated as one of 12 key standards for international financial stability by the Financial Stability Forum, and the principles form the basis for the World Bank's Review of Standards and Codes (ROSC).

FURTHER INFORMATION

Website: www.oecd.org

United Nations Convention Against Corruption

Type of resource: convention

Author organisation: United Nations

Year of publication: 2003

The UN Convention Against Corruption was adopted on 31 October 2003 at the 58th session of the General Assembly of the United Nations and will be open for signature by member states from the end of 2003. The Convention includes prohibitions on transnational bribery and the tax-deductibility of bribes, as well as mandatory provisions on transparency in government procurement. It addresses mutual legal assistance, money laundering and asset recovery, where worldwide cooperation is essential. It is the first time that provisions are included that commit signatories to returning assets stolen and lodged overseas to their country of origin. Rules on the funding of political parties and on private-sector corruption are also included but are only optional.

The UN Convention proposes the implementation of effective anti-corruption policies and bodies. In the public sector, it envisages the elimination of vulnerability and opportunity for corruption, increased accountability and transparency and increased integrity in the judiciary. In the private sector, the UN Convention seeks increased cooperation between law enforcement agencies and private entities, appropriate internal accounting controls, the establishment of an adequate supervisory framework for financial institutions, the promotion of transparency among private entities, the prevention of misuse of public procedures regulating private entities and the imposition of restrictions on the professional activities of former public officials.

The UN Convention sets out a wide range of corruption offences. These include bribery of public officials, trading in influence, embezzlement, use of confidential information, the laundering of proceeds of corruption and the bribery of any person within the private sector. It also makes specific provision for money laundering as a corruption-related offence.

FURTHER INFORMATION

Website: www.unodc.org/unodc/en/crime_convention_corruption.html

CHAPTER TWO

GETTING STARTED: FIRST STEPS

THIS CHAPTER WILL SET OUT A SERIES OF simple steps to turn support for the UN Global Compact into a practical reality that motivates employees and provides early positive results. In tackling these steps, it is worth remembering that environmental and social responsibilities are not only for large companies — in fact, small operational units can be the best place to turn values and principles into success and opportunities.

We believe that this small-versus-big argument — only large organisations have the resources to undertake social and environmental initiatives — is mostly a fallacy. We have therefore written this book as a field guide for leaders of small operational units. What works for them will work for whole organisations.

Imagine, for a moment, that a few weeks ago your CEO attended a forum where several business and political leaders made a pressing call for supporting the Global Compact. The business leaders argued that business cannot ignore social and environmental problems; it must be part of the solution. The political leaders appealed to a sense of corporate citizenship and the need to show business

support for the universal principles that should apply to all nations. Inspired, your firm's CEO joined a number of other executives to send a letter of support to UN Secretary-General Kofi Annan. This included the following statement:

> The principles at the basis of the Global Compact are fully coherent with the values of our company and of our 1,200 women and men who make things happen around here. But we also realise that we have hardly started to work out the opportunities and the boundaries of this commitment. We must get started. We will endeavour to communicate our progress.

Whereas others may just leave it at that, this is not how things are done in your company — where a commitment is a commitment — where action must follow. But where do you start in practice to implement such a broad commitment?

Before we offer some practical guidelines, we should hear from one of the Global Compact role models. The pharmaceuticals giant Novartis was among the first group of companies formally to support the Compact.

Klaus Leisinger, president and executive director of the Novartis Foundation for Sustainable Development, comments on the progress and dilemmas Novartis has faced in the first few years of implementation.

On 14 July 2000, Daniel Vasella, the chair and CEO of Novartis, publicly announced that the company would support the Global Compact as a catalyst for concrete actions.

In retrospect, this early commitment at the highest level was the decisive factor that endowed the Global Compact at Novartis with the importance it enjoys today. Consistent signals from senior management are vital. Employees are alert to such signals. They transcend the internal pluralism of opinions, and help to channel and shorten discussions on the corporate strategy.

Since the basic question of whether or not to commit to the Compact was clearly answered at the outset by top management, the discussion moved quickly to 'How?'.

A few weeks after the initial commitment, a new version of the Novartis code of conduct was issued, with reference to the Compact. Items that had never before been covered were included — such as the Universal Declaration of Human Rights and application of the company's own quality standards to suppliers and business partners.

Implementation of the Global Compact was seen from the start as an open-ended *process*. The aim of this approach was to achieve a feedback-controlled management cycle, thus keeping the implementation process alive and continually renewing it by injecting new impetus. A comprehensive implementation programme must persuade and motivate employees at all levels. Then, what individuals know must be in harmony with what they do. Concrete action-specific objectives with performance indicators must be set and integrated into existing management systems and working practices. The results must be measured and obstacles analysed and overcome. Finally, since the social environment and its expectations are constantly changing, an ongoing process of learning and adjustment is needed.

A steering committee was set up to ensure a company-wide commitment to the Compact. This consists of senior personnel from various Novartis Group companies. The pluralism of interests and values keeps the discussion on complex process issues at the right strategic level. The committee provides general guidance on the process and fosters understanding within the company. It reports to top management on progress and dilemmas. Finally, it advises on the development of company rules. To strengthen the sense of ownership, one year on, the steering committee and the whole process were renamed the Novartis Corporate Citizenship Initiative.

Just as the need for experts on safety, computing or finance is taken for granted in companies so too does the Global Compact require experts on sustainable development and human rights. The Global Compact clearinghouse was therefore created to pool and develop the knowledge necessary for implementation.

Two kinds of knowledge are required to be a competent partner for Global Compact discussions with employees and external stakeholders:

- **Profound fact-based knowledge** remains the most important prerequisite for competent decision-making under complex conditions.

- **Value-based knowledge** is the ability to evaluate the ethical significance of different options for action, in order to identify those with an optimum balance of both social and business ethics.

The clearinghouse initiated a survey to identify potential deficits against the principles of the Global Compact in the company and with its business partners. The results showed that:

- Within the Novartis Group there were no direct or visible deficits.

- The performance of some business partners in a few countries raised questions.

- Creation of awareness and continual training are key to sustainable successful implementation.

Responsibility for follow-up was assigned to specific employees. Various Group companies also expressed the desire for a second, more detailed, survey.

A steering committee and clearinghouse may be a good thing, but, as with any other aspect of business, it was also necessary to ensure that all employees were sufficiently informed so they understood what the strategy and new corporate citizenship guidelines inspired by the Global Compact mean in practical terms. Operating in more than 140 countries among a variety of cultures always presents a communication challenge. Therefore, an interdepartmental communications team developed a 'roll-out kit' for all potential users of the guidelines.

Implementation would stall unless employees throughout the world and at all levels were well informed and trained. Tangible objectives had to be set because progress had to become part of the company-wide performance appraisal and bonus system. Without the allocation of appropriate time and money, a complex commitment of this kind would fail. Line management therefore had to budget adequate resources. Where conflicts of priorities occurred, a transparent process was introduced to resolve them.

Living up to the commitments requires substantial resources for both the conceptual work and the implementation programmes, through to compliance checks. Deficits that are legal but fail the Compact's principles must be cleared at a cost or at a loss of business that non-participating competitors continue to avoid. The public commitment to the Global Compact exposes companies to even more scrutiny by some pressure groups that seize the slightest chance to highlight hypocrisy. A company that supports the Compact also accepts a higher level of public accountability, of performance requirements and monitoring that go, at a cost, beyond compliance with laws and regulations.

FURTHER INFORMATION

Novartis Foundation for Sustainable Development website: www.novartisfoundation.com

An extensive description of the UN Global Compact implementation at Novartis is available at: www.parallaxonline.org/peglobalhuman5p.html

Source: K.M. Leisinger, 'Opportunities and Risks of the United Nations Global Compact', *Journal of Corporate Citizenship* 11 (Autumn 2003): 113-31

With 78,500 employees and US$24.9 billion of sales, Novartis is one of the world's largest corporations, with staff and consultants in a wide range of specialities and functions. How could a medium-sized company, let alone a small one, deploy and afford such an elaborate implementation programme? This is a fair question, and one that is asked frequently. Unfortunately, the usual response, that such initiatives are important but irrelevant for smaller organisations, leads to paralysis and inertia.

We take issue with this. The familiar argument of no time, no money and no staff does not, we believe, imply no brain, no ambition and no ethics. All companies, regardless of size, are simply groups of individuals. The smaller the company, the more it reflects the spirit of its owner and employees. Most large companies today began with a single dreamer or small team with no money but extraordinary personal energy and a passionate belief in a better world.

Small companies are key players in the economy (see Figure 4); they create new products and jobs like large ones. Thus, many large companies and most venture funds scout for small companies to rejuvenate their innovation portfolio through alliances or acquisitions.

The energy, creativity and sense of belonging of the small company are not lost in the management philosophy and disciplines of the larger company. Charles Handy, a long-time observer of the transformation of management realities, remarks: 'If today's corporations are going to work effectively

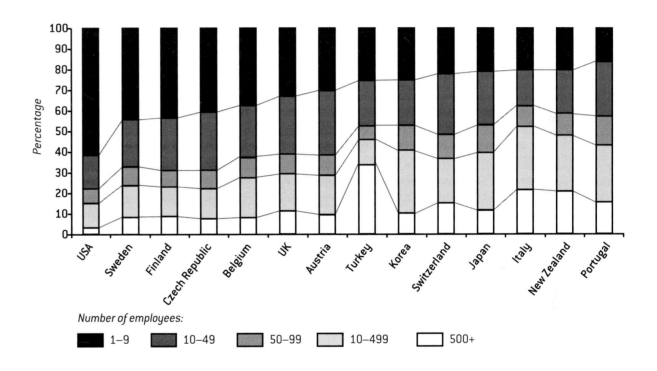

Figure 4 **DISTRIBUTION OF EMPLOYMENT IN MANUFACTURING, BY SIZE CLASS**
Source: OECD SME Database 2001

Number of employees:
■ 1–9   ■ 10–49   ■ 50–99   □ 10–499   □ 500+

they have to create operational units small enough for everyone to know everyone else by name'.[1] For a number of reasons, this has already happened.

For example, the big organisation with 100 or more units worldwide may indeed have a dozen large-scale production and administrative sites, but its branch office in Quito, Ecuador, or its formulating and packaging plant in Izmir, Turkey, are, like most of its other sites around the world, not much different from a small company. Even sites that employ thousands of people are organised into small units and teams with a small company-like autonomy within a larger networked organisation. The reason for this small-team focus is linked to performance and competitiveness. Small teams with a strong sense of ownership are more resilient, innovative and productive; they are more responsive to their customers and to the communities in which they operate. Another reason for this focus is the complexity of performance tracking. Real-time knowledge of how the company is doing relies on good input from the front line. No matter how efficient the computers that transfer and aggregate data from the company's worldwide system, someone needs to care for the inventory, scan the bar code or the credit card, move the material over the weighing scale and fill in the time-sheet. The quality and topicality of this data flow are directly related to the degree of accountability

and pride front-line teams have for the activity being measured.

Enabled by information technology, promoted by the total quality discipline and validated by business success, large companies are transforming themselves into what Handy calls 'federations of small enterprises'. They are simultaneously global and local, fostering a clear brand identity to bond their federation. When they seriously embrace a commitment such as the Global Compact they immediately start to ensure, as did Novartis, that it can be carried out in a local setting by employees at any site and at all levels. Designworks, a US subsidiary of German car-maker BMW, provides a telling example (see opposite).

In summary, we argue that the Global Compact and, more generally, all programmes of environmental and social responsibility are not the sole province of large organisations. On the contrary, such initiatives actually show more progress when driven through the small teams and companies.

However, there is a big difference between small teams or units operating under the umbrella of a 'great brand federation' and many small companies operating in isolation. Great brand federations can equip every member of every small team with a roll-out kit, marching orders, targets, budgets and a help-line. Along the way, the team is given checkpoints, steering, support, rewards and encouragement. With some regrettable exceptions, most big companies with great brands operate nearly perfect internal compliance systems. They

also have significant leverage on the socioeconomic context of their ramified network of operations and commercial partners. Thus, when UN Secretary-General Kofi Annan exhorted big companies to throw their weight behind the Global Compact, he was seeking rapid commitment and action.

But the Global Compact is for *all* companies of *all* sizes. It is just that a small or medium-sized enterprise (SME) needs to draw on its own energy and creativity to pull together an implementation agenda. But it also has access to a number of business networks, government agencies and clearinghouses.

The UN Industrial Development Organisation (UNIDO) and the International Labour Organisation (ILO) have developed practical guides to help SMEs to achieve continuous improvement in their social responsibility performance. In addition, CSR Europe, the European business campaign on corporate social responsibility, has an online support tool — the SME Key — specifically designed to strengthen the capacity of SMEs to deal successfully with such issues. In addition, UNEP is working with partners to expand its Efficient Entrepreneur environmental calendar for SMEs into a sustainability package (see pages 214-15).

---

1 C. Handy, *The Elephant and the Flea: Looking Backwards Into the Future* (London: Random House, 2001): 67.

THE LEVERAGE OF A SMALL DESIGNER GROUP: DESIGNWORKS

A $15 MILLION WHOLLY OWNED SUBSIDIARY of BMW Group, Designworks USA provides design and engineering services both to BMW Group and to external clients. Located just outside Los Angeles, CA, its 80 employees focus on designing vehicles and a wide array of consumer products.

Prompted by the BMW Group, Designworks USA began developing a sustainability management system (SMS) in 1999, recognising that designers are uniquely positioned to influence the environmental, social and economic impacts of products. Working with the BMW Group's corporate staff and with WSP Environmental, a London-based consultancy, Designworks USA developed an SMS framework that incorporates the 'triple bottom line' sustainability concept developed by UK consultant John Elkington. A sustainability policy was developed that includes commitments to continuous improvement of environmental, economic, social and ethical performance. It also dedicates the firm to encouraging its suppliers, contractors and clients to implement similar practices. Each department developed comprehensive lists of the environmental, social and economic aspects and impacts associated with its activities and then created action plans to address the high-priority issues. Action plans included objectives, targets and deadlines. The SMS is monitored through a system of periodic internal audits and external certifications.

Many features of the Designworks USA SMS support the principles of the Global Compact. By requiring each department to identify and prioritise its environmental aspects and impacts and to develop objectives and targets for prioritised aspects, this process represents the 'precautionary approach to environmental challenges' advocated by the Global Compact. In addition, the firm's efforts to minimise its on-site environmental impacts and to work with clients and suppliers to reduce their environmental impacts support the Compact's call to 'promote greater environmental responsibility'. The efforts of the purchasing and operations departments of Designworks USA to reduce the company's environmental impacts have led them to request contractors and suppliers to recommend environmentally superior technologies, which serves to 'encourage the development and diffusion of environmentally friendly technologies', a Global Compact principle.

Beyond these environmental issues, Designworks USA is addressing some of the Global Compact's human rights and labour principles. For example, it is reviewing its promotion, hiring and performance practices to facilitate gender and racial equity, which serves to 'eliminate discrimination in respect of employment and occupation'. In addition, it has initiated efforts to better understand its suppliers' practices in relation to child and forced labour. In analysing its potential social aspects, the purchasing department considered its suppliers' possible use of child and forced labour to be a significant aspect. As such, the department developed a questionnaire to screen existing and potential suppliers. This questionnaire included issues on child and forced labour as well as other social and environmental criteria. The firm's top 100 suppliers have already been sent and responded to the questionnaire, and all other existing and new suppliers are in the process of responding.

FURTHER INFORMATION

Designworks USA website: www.designworksusa.com

See also:

M.W. Toffel, N. Hill and K.A. McElhaney, 'Developing a Management Systems Approach to Sustainability at BMW Group', *Corporate Environmental Strategy: International Journal of Corporate Sustainability* 10.2 (2003): 29-39

M.W. Toffel, N. Hill and K.A. McElhaney, 'BMW Group's Sustainability Management System: Preliminary Results, Ongoing Challenges and the UN Global Compact', *Corporate Environmental Strategy: International Journal of Corporate Sustainability* 10.3 (2003): 51-61

THE SME KEY

CSR Europe

A GOOD STARTING POINT FOR SMALL AND

medium-sized enterprises (SMEs) unfamiliar with corporate social responsibility (CSR) and the UN Global Compact, the SME Key is a self-analysis for companies that asks them to communicate their social, economic and environmental performance and, by doing so, forces them to think about the impact they are making. The aim of CSR Europe's SME Key is to communicate the business case for CSR and to explain why it is important for SMEs to engage with CSR. Having communicated the business case, the key provides a means of supporting SMEs to better evaluate and take forward their responsible business practices.

The key is easy to use and can be downloaded from the website (www.smekey.org) in a handful of languages (Dutch, English, French, Finnish, Italian and Spanish) and is set out in a visually familiar way. It is divided into three sections: economic, environmental and social. Each section expands into a set of questions and measures that should help users to assess their responsible business practices and shape future strategy. The tool is sufficiently flexible to allow users to skip sections that are not directly relevant to their current situation. This enables users to take an incremental approach, making the task less intimidating and emphasising that responsible business is an evolving process.

Depending on the size of the company, either one person can work on the key, or the sections can be divided among colleagues. CSR Europe found that SMEs needed no more than eight hours to complete the guide.

According to M. Patrick Vandamme of Triselec, a 250 employee French SME specialising in waste sorting and management:

> The SME key enabled us to establish and record the state of play. We already had ISO 9000 certification, but the key allowed us to go deeper into the subject matter, to address areas where we had been active but where we had not formally recorded our activities. It also helped us identify gaps in our strategy — for instance with our suppliers — and plan what remains to be done to further develop responsible business practices. By writing a report using the key, we gave ourselves the opportunity to take time to reflect and rethink the parameters of our strategy. The tool is designed to support progress and is also a useful management tool. The report can be revisited every one to three years to measure progress made. It is also a useful tool for external communications. In our business, we need to publicise the achievements of the company to recruit new people.

M. Vandamme concludes:

> The key achieves a good balance between environmental and social responsibility. Both aspects are very important to us.

FURTHER INFORMATION:

SME key website: www.smekey.org

Website of CSR Europe, European Business Campaign on CSR, Brussels: www.csreurope.org

Ten steps

Based on the experience of many, as well as on plain common sense, we offer a simple and systematic way to make the Global Compact principles come alive in ten steps (see Table 3). They will structure your progress. For each step, different chapters of this book provide more in-depth guidance and examples.

Although it makes sense to take the steps in order, from 1 to 10, there is no compelling reason why the reader cannot approach the book differently. The ten steps follow the presentation of the quality model familiar to most companies dedicated to continuous improvement. They are an integrated store of tools and resources that you can access when needed. Like a tourist, you will not stop at every sight and every museum, nor will you visit every restaurant or hotel. You will visit those that fit your itinerary, your needs at the time, your financial resources and your interests.

Steps 1–3 represent nothing more than the 'Yes' or 'No' phase that Klaus Leisinger highlights in relation to the beginning of the Novartis journey (see pages 43-44). Although this is not time-intensive, it does draw on good business and ethical judgement. It is heavy on consequences, because the internal 'go' signal to the organisation must be loud and clear to provide time, openness and motivation for Step 4. For many, that will seem like the real start.

Table 3 TEN STEPS TO GET STARTED, AND SOME PROBING QUESTIONS ON THE WAY

STEP	ACTION AND QUESTIONS	MORE IN CHAPTER . . .
0. Decide to commit to the UN Global Compact	The CEO support letter is posted.	2 Getting started
1. Share the commitment	Is everyone aware of this commitment? Who have we missed?	5 Forming a vision 7 Empowerment for implementation
2. Seek value	Philanthropy is good but business reasons are stronger: How can the principles in the Global Compact deliver business value? How will the company make the Global Compact relevant and build support?	Performance and value creation
3. Make time	What signals are needed for everyone to make this an appropriate priority? What expertise do we have? What is needed? Where could we get free know-how?	6 Leadership decisions 7 Empowerment for implementation
	The organisation hears the 'go' signal	
4. Understand the basics	What is the scope of this commitment? What do the Global Compact principles mean for us?	1 A primer on principles
	The core of the quality process starts here	
5. Where are we?	As we get familiar with the basics, where do we find issues for our organisation? What are our strengths and weaknesses? How would others answer that question?	10 Processes and innovation 4 On stakeholder engagement and partnerships
6. What's first?	If we could resolve only one or two issues in the near term, which would they be? What should we do about them, and what will it take?	6 Leadership decisions 8 Policies and strategies
7 How will we organise resources?	How will we get and deploy the resources? What is the most effective and efficient way?	9 Allocating resources
8. How will we do it?	What do we need to change? How do we do this with side benefits for other aspects of our business?	10 Processes and innovation
9. How will we chart our progress?	How will we know that we are progressing? As time passes, are we getting there? What remains to be done? Who else should know about this?	11 Impact on employees 12 Impact on value chain 13 Impact on society 14 Communication of progress and results
	The end of the beginning	
10. Learn from the project	What have we learned? How do we feel about progress?	6 Leadership decisions 7 Empowerment for implementation
Expand and go back to Step 5	What have we left out? What is important now?	4 On stakeholder engagement and partnerships 11 Impact on employees 12 Impact on value chain 13 Impact on society

Why the Global Compact?

Before leaving the starting block there are a cluster of questions that are likely to bother you or some colleagues:

Why another programme?
We are strongly committed to quality, safety, eco-efficiency and people success. We were slowly catching up with sustainable development when we heard the real thing is corporate social responsibility or maybe corporate citizenship . . . And now the Global Compact? Where is the STOP button?'

This is a valid reaction. A growing number of concepts and campaigns claim the attention of business people. But these concepts and campaigns *do* hang together. Before we move on, here is a bare-bone review of the main concepts to show their connections.

There is no shortage of definitions of sustainable development, but effectively they can be summed up as the transformation of our economy into one that would ensure a fair chance and an appropriate quality of life to everyone on this planet, in the near term and for future generations. This transformation should not occur at the expense of the natural resources and living systems that support our economy. Sustainable development has a social side as it aims to promote equity and quality of life, and it has an efficiency dimension for it must balance our development needs with the capacity of our planet to sustain those needs. It is a complex and vital undertaking. Sustainable development is the overarching objective of all other programmes and campaigns.

Who is responsible for making this happen? The answer is everyone, of course, but business has been singled out as a powerful and influential actor. Any foresighted business person understands that corporations cannot succeed in a society that fails. It is around this basic function of providing solutions rather than creating more problems that the idea of corporate social responsibility revolves. Some call it corporate citizenship because they stress the sense of duty towards the community or the idea that business should act with the same rights and responsibilities as an individual.

CSR or corporate citizenship is the behaviour that gets business to contribute to society's transformation towards sustainable development. Others, too, have roles and responsibilities. Business cannot do it alone. Therefore corporate citizenship also implies a social dialogue and partnership with other stakeholders.

And where does the Global Compact come in? The idea of CSR matured in the mid-1990s. The debate still goes on about its boundaries as well as its multiple incarnations, depending on activity sector, culture and political environment. The CSR approach should remain adaptive but the Global Compact anchors it with a set of fundamental principles that should be the starting point and form the core of any forward-looking business agenda.

In summary, we suggest the Global Compact principles should be the non-negotiable basis of your corporate citizenship agenda to make your contribution to sustainable development (while also achieving your business goals!).

Corporate Social Responsibility: Implications for Small and Medium Enterprises in Developing Countries

Type of resource: publication

Author organisation: United Nations Industrial Development Organisation

Year of publication: 2002

This study from the United Nations Industrial Development Organisation (UNIDO) reviews the relevance and implications for small and medium-sized enterprises (SMEs) in developing countries of the increasing adoption of corporate social responsibility (CSR) by transnational corporations (TNCs) and examines the motivations, potential benefits and obstacles of CSR practised in SMEs. It could be of interest to practitioners actively engaged in CSR-related activities in the field and to executives in TNCs seeking to enhance the firm's CSR performance within its entire value chain.

FURTHER INFORMATION

Website: www.unido.org

Publication: www.unido.org/userfiles/BethkeK/csr.pdf

Global Compact Self-assessment Tool

Type of resource: tool

Author organisation: Business for Social Responsibility

Launch date: 2004

This tool is being developed by Business for Social Responsibility (BSR) to help companies understand and assess their work specifically applicable to the principles of the Global Compact in their operational policies and practices. The objectives are to enable companies of all sizes, and individual business units within companies, to review their performance, address any gaps in their performance in relation to the Global Compact principles and then to make improvements to achieve and demonstrate implementation of the principles. The tool is designed to be used in a simple manner. It involves a set of questions, and compilation of documents, that reflects concepts and functions familiar to most businesses.

FURTHER INFORMATION

Website: www.bsr.org

The Employers' Guide to the Global Compact

Type of resource: guide

Author organisation: International Organisation of Employers

Year of publication: 2001

This short guide from the International Organisation of Employers offers an employers' perspective of the Global Compact. It answers a number of questions that employers have raised about the Global Compact but at the same time stresses the freedom of action inherent in the Compact. It includes a Foreword by Secretary-General Kofi Annan.

FURTHER INFORMATION

Website: www.ioe-emp.org

Publication: www.ioe-emp.org/ioe_emp/pdf/ Employers%20Guide%20-%20Global%20Compact.pdf

Seven-Step Model for Turning CSR into Corporate Social Opportunity

Type of resource: book

Authors: David Grayson and Adrian Hodges

Year of publication: 2004

This seven-step business process model enables businesses to align their stance on social, ethical and environmental issues with their purpose, values and strategic objectives — to the benefit of the business and the wider community. The seven steps were first described in *Everybody's Business*, published by Dorling Kindersley and the *Financial Times* in 2001 and is updated, expanded and road-tested in *Corporate Social Opportunity*, published in July 2004. The model follows a logical flow yet allows for the uncertainties and interdependence of events in real life. Business is subject to heightened expectations from a range of increasingly vocal and organised stakeholders. They act as the trigger for companies to shift and change behaviour. The seven steps are as follows:

- Step 1: Recognising the trigger
- Step 2: Scoping
- Step 3: Articulating the business case
- Step 4: Committing to action
- Step 5: Integrating strategies
- Step 6: Engaging stakeholders
- Step 7: Measuring and reporting

FURTHER INFORMATION

D. Grayson and A. Hodges, 'Seven-step Model for Turning CSR into Corporate Social Opportunity', in *Everybody's Business: Managing Risks and Opportunities in Today's Global Society* (London: Dorling Kindersley and Financial Times, 2001)

Source: D. Grayson and A. Hodges, *Corporate Social Opportunity: Seven Steps to Make Corporate Social Responsibility Work for your Business* (Sheffield, UK: Greenleaf Publishing, 2004; www.greenleaf-publishing.com/catalogue/cso.htm)

CHAPTER THREE

THE GLOBAL COMPACT PERFORMANCE MODEL

THIS CHAPTER EXPLAINS THE ORIGIN OF THE UN Global Compact performance model and its strong links with the management of quality and excellence. This model provides a way of achieving continuous improvement and for sharing experience. Its application will help you gain a better understanding of the relations between principles, codes and standards and how you can integrate them into your daily business activities with the help of a new group of management tools.

In 2002, a number of business practitioners met for a series of workshops related to the Global Compact. They all had more than two years' experience of working to implement the Global Compact in their companies, building on considerable previous experience in the area of corporate social responsibility. The purpose of the workshops was to gain an improved understanding of the conditions and dynamics of implementation and to identify the approaches that work best so that they can be used to help others starting, or strengthening, their own Global Compact programme.

The workshops were part of the Global Compact series of Policy Dialogues. These are a good illustration of the shared learning that is fostered between leading-edge companies, even those that compete with each other for markets and capital. Such companies have realised that the complex challenges of sustainable development need an active balance of cooperation and competition. In this sense, the Global Compact operates as a catalyst for shared learning.

There is also another important reason for identifying and sharing good implementation practices: none of those actively committed wants to see the Global Compact, as it extends its reach, turn into a 'two-speed' initiative with only a small number committed while others drag their feet and act as free-riders. It is therefore in the interests of the integrity of the Global Compact to achieve a real change in attitude throughout the business community — even more so in light of the pressure from a growing number of non-governmental organisations (NGOs) who are demanding demonstrable and tangible progress from the initiative.

As participants in the 2002 workshops recounted their early successes and failures, and outlined their current programmes, it became apparent that most programmes were adopting a similar approach, with the following success factors:

- Clear signals and expectations from the leadership
- High employee commitment and awareness
- Clearly established priorities
- Ambitious objectives to stimulate new ideas and business innovation
- Measurable targets to assess and communicate progress
- Learning from successes and failures to ensure the ability to act and adapt
- Discussions of social objectives with the concerned stakeholders

It was quickly recognised that aligning Global Compact implementation with the management of quality excellence would offer a familiar framework to thousands of well-managed companies around the world and that the Global Compact would add another dimension to good management.

The workshop discussions therefore turned to the formulation of a Global Compact performance model with an adaptable structure similar to the prevalent quality excellence model. Of course, this is not the only way to progress. There are many schools of thought and models of how to manage organisations. Although not denying the value of more complex approaches and recent thinking in the theory of management, we deliberately chose 'the vanilla flavour' approach — a simpler taste that facilitates access and alignment to the Global Compact but which, as a comprehensive management framework, links principles, business processes and results. For hundreds of companies that have stated their commitment to the Global Compact the performance model can be the key to efficient implementation.

What do you get from a performance model? By 'performance' we mean the maximisation of outputs with the minimisation of inputs. Targets are more likely to be met or exceeded using less time, effort and financial resources. The execution will also provide a clearer understanding about why a particular approach works, and how it may be improved. Individual skills will be enhanced, as will the capacity of the organisation.

In the context of the Global Compact principles, performance is mostly related to the elimination of failures. Accidents, pollution, breaches of human rights or labour standards, corruption, discrimination, hunger, public health crises and

even poverty can all be defined as failures at various levels and among various sectors of society. Whether they are symptoms of human failures or, more generally, system or institutional failures, the goal is to strive for ever lower rates of failure — or continual improvement.

To achieve this continual improvement, the performance model provides a system of practices, means and rules. Business schools and consultants thrive on spreading models. Management guru Henry Mintzberg[1] recently reviewed about 2,000

---

1 H. Mintzberg, B. Ahlstrand and J. Lampel, *Strategy Safari* (London: Financial Times/Prentice Hall, 1998).

papers on management strategy produced since the 1960s and classified them into no less than ten major schools of thought or models about how an enterprise should conduct its affairs. Similarly, Joan Magretta[2] wrote that business models are, 'at heart . . . stories that explain how enterprises work'. Business models express company culture, brand personality and the people behind the brand. Considering the richness of the business world and its people, the multiplicity of models should not be so surprising.

---

2 J. Magretta, *What Management Is: How It Works, And Why It's Everyone's Business* (Glenview, IL: The Free Press, 2002).

Figure 5 **THE EFQM EXCELLENCE MODEL**

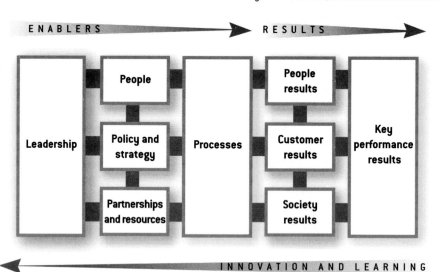

EUROPEAN FOUNDATION FOR QUALITY MANAGEMENT (EFQM) MODEL AND GUIDELINES

W. EDWARDS DEMING AND JOSEPH JURAN — THE fathers of total quality management — were not successful in convincing US business that their quality management approaches were the most effective. In contrast, Japan, which had to rebuild its economy after the Second World War, listened more carefully. As early as 1951, it created the Deming Prize, the first-ever quality management award, to promote total quality management (TQM). It was not until the 1980s that awareness of total quality as a management method burgeoned in the USA, leading to the Malcolm Baldrige Award in 1987. In 1988, 14 leading European companies, encouraged by the European Commission, decided to create the European Foundation of Quality Management (EFQM) excellence model and launched the European Quality Award.

The EFQM model helps enterprises and public-sector organisations achieve quality excellence. It was set up to take into account expectations from different stakeholders such as shareholders, customers, employees and society. The model is used by 15 of Europe's largest companies (in terms of revenue) and by over 20,000 organisations across Europe, including many small and medium-sized enterprises.

The EFQM model is a non-prescriptive management framework with nine criteria split into five 'enabler' criteria and four 'results' criteria. The enabler criteria relate to what an organisation does and the results criteria cover what it achieves. Results are influenced, improved and caused by what is done within the enablers which are, in turn, improved by using feedback from results. The model recognises that there are many approaches to achieving sustainable quality excellence in all aspects of performance. It is based on the premise that excellent results with respect to performance, customers, people and society are achieved through leadership driving policy and a strategy that is delivered through people, partnerships with resources and processes.

The model's nine boxes (see Figure 5 on page 54) represent the criteria against which to assess an organisation's progress towards excellence. Each of the criteria has a high-level definition, supported by a number of explanatory elements. Criteria elements pose a number of questions that should be considered in the course of a progress assessment, and each element is supported by suggested guidance points to further explain its meaning.

Example of EFQM model criteria and elements

Criterion 1, 'Leadership', is divided into five sub-criteria:

- Leaders develop the organisation's mission, vision, value and ethics and are role models for a culture of excellence.
- Leaders are personally involved.
- Leaders interact with customers.
- Leaders reinforce a culture of excellence.
- Leaders identify and champion organisational change.

According to research carried out in 2000 by Dr Vinod Singhal of the Georgia Institute of Technology and Dr Kevin Hendricks of the University of Western Ontario,[3]

'organisations that use a holistic framework such as the EFQM excellence model perform considerably better than others on a wide range of measures do'.

With the appearance of concepts such as corporate social responsibility (CSR) and sustainable development, many EFQM members have seen the need to integrate new behaviour and new stakeholders (e.g. the planet, future generations or vulnerable ethnic minority groups) into their management strategy.

EFQM has built a 'community of practice' comprising interested member organisations, including Siemens, Unilever, TNT, Deutsche Telekom, British Telecommunications plc, EDF and Lloyds TSB, to develop an EFQM framework for CSR as a way of using the EFQM model to manage CSR and so meet external expectations. This development started with an international research project on existing CSR standards, models and guidelines, identifying the main focus and application of each approach.

Through this work, EFQM has been able to integrate UN Global Compact principles into the CSR framework to: 'help enterprises become more responsible, have a good stakeholder balance and, therefore, to be more sustainable'.

FURTHER INFORMATION

European Foundation of Quality Management website:
www.efqm.org

---

3 'The Impact of TQM on Financial Performance: Evidence from Quality Award Winners', www.efqm.org.

CASE STUDY

DEXIA GOES 'SIX SIGMA' WITH THE GLOBAL COMPACT

Putting the European Foundation for Quality Management model and guidelines into practice

DEXIA GROUP, A FRENCH AND BELGIAN BANK

with 24,000 employees, is a Global Compact signatory. One of its French subsidiaries, Dexia-Sofaxis, a local authority insurance broker, has integrated the requirements of the Global Compact into its management system, thanks to the European Foundation for Quality Management (EFQM) excellence model. The practical experience acquired by the company shows the power of the model to implement the Global Compact principles in a coherent way and to move the company towards 'excellence' based on 'Radar': results–approaches–deployment, assessment–review.

Each year, Dexia-Sofaxis synthesises stakeholder needs and expectations at its annual strategy review and sets targets for the following year. The requirements of the Global Compact are integrated through five key stakeholder groups:

- **Customers.** Increasingly, and particularly during the tendering process, customers are asking Dexia-Sofaxis if it respects the Global Compact requirements.
- **Staff.** Through employee satisfaction surveys and their representatives, staff express their views with regard to ethics, justice, and health and safety at work.
- **Partners, suppliers, subcontractors.** These stakeholders want to enhance their reputations by cooperating with companies that comply with the Global Compact requirements.
- **Society.** Legislators and non-governmental organisations demand more stringent social and environmental performance from companies.
- **Shareholders.** As a wholly owned subsidiary, Dexia-Sofaxis is required to respect the values of its parent, the Dexia Group, which is a Global Compact signatory.

The approaches that Dexia-Sofaxis has deployed to 'walk the talk' comprise certification to ISO 14001, OHSAS 18001 and SA8000, combined with a system of permanent risk assessment for environmental, social, ethical, compliance and safety risks.

The deployment of the objectives and approaches covers all processes, especially those relating to Global Compact implementation:

- The legal, ethical and partnership process
- The security and safety process
- The environment process
- The human resource management process

For sound assessment, these four processes have performance indicators, perceived quality indicators and capability indicators (Six Sigma).[4] The consolidated results are published on the Global Reporting Initiative website (www.globalreporting.org).

The annual review of these processes makes it possible for Dexia-Sofaxis to improve its capacity year by year to take into account the requirements of the Global Compact in its internal processes.

Moreover, the Global Compact requirements are also taken into account by the innovation and product development process. Thanks to innovations in the field of prevention, hygiene and safety at work among its customers, Dexia-Sofaxis has became an active promoter of the Global Compact among French local authorities.

FURTHER INFORMATION

Website: www.sofaxis.com

---

4 For an explanation of the concept of 'Six Sigma' (6s), see Chapter 10, page 131.

The starting point

There are two main reasons for applying one performance model. First, discussions at the 2002 Global Compact workshops revealed a common pattern among those most advanced in integrating the Global Compact and, more generally, CSR into their businesses. Second, it is important to agree a starting point or baseline from which knowledge can be shared in a systematic way. Ten baselines would be too many. Even among the ten schools of thought identified by Mintzberg and others, there are several 'market leaders' that are better adapted to operational units and supported by an extended network of resources. The performance model outlined here draws from these market leaders. It is a starting point and an occasion for learning; it is a possibility for each business to develop its 'own story' or model for working towards even higher performance.

The quality excellence model has already enabled thousands of organisations to boost their performance. The model's 'booster engine' is the never-ending cycle of improvement, the Deming cycle (see Figure 6), named after Dr W. Edwards Deming who made it a core of the quality management discipline. It propels the organisation on a course of continuously more demanding benchmarks. Every cycle brings the organisation to a new level of mastery and control that is focused on the needs of the 'customer'. The 'customer' can also include the community and the environment, or whoever and whatever the organisation decides to include in its sphere of influence and responsibility.

The Deming cycle or the 'plan–do–check–act' cycle can be applied at Step 5 of the ten-step 'Getting Started' roadmap set out in Chapter 2 (page 48; see also Table 3, page 49). Step 5 is a diagnostic of issues that present themselves to you as you review the demands of the Global Compact principles outlined in the primer (Chapter 1). Although far from being a trivial task for a large and complex organisation, this early phase does not require perfection; a sound rule of thumb is the 80/20 rule that prioritises the easiest options for improvement. In the case of a small independent organisation, this diagnostic is significantly easier. It completes Step 6 of the 'Getting Started' roadmap and, with a short list of issues to solve, leads to the 'act' phase of the Deming circle (see Table 4).

The Deming cycle requires managerial capability. The model that we describe deconstructs managerial capability into a specific set of elements — the European Foundation for Quality Management (EFQM) model defines them as *enablers* and *results* (see page 55). Together they are sufficient to ensure that the organisation achieves excellence in every objective it chooses to pursue.

The *enablers* are those elements that define how the organisation operates, and the *results* group are those elements that define what the organisation achieves and contributes. Figure 7 depicts the close integration of those elements into the performance model. Each element will be covered in detail in subsequent chapters.

Figure 6 THE DEMING CYCLE

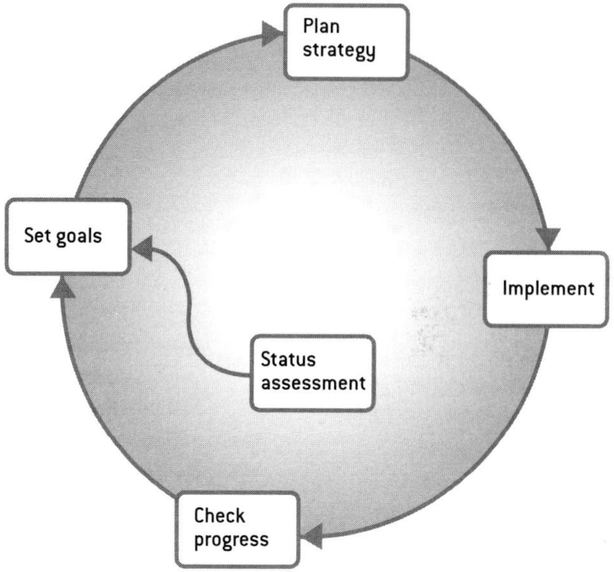

The performance model is applicable to all organisations regardless of sector, size or geography. It can work for a small furniture producer in Indonesia, a global producer of fertilisers, a sporting goods marketer with a global network of suppliers, an oil producer with extraction platforms, refineries and gas service stations or a local food catering business. Nevertheless, each of these organisations will apply specialised tools that represent its specific circumstances and know-how. The recipes of the food caterer are different from the formulations of the fertiliser producer. The

Figure 7 THE UN GLOBAL COMPACT PERFORMANCE MODEL AND THE DEMING CYCLE

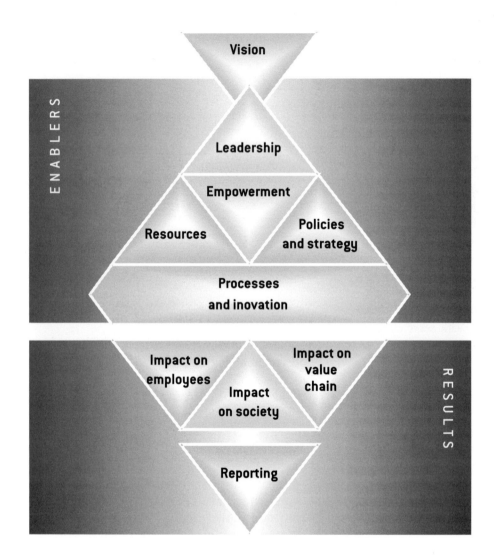

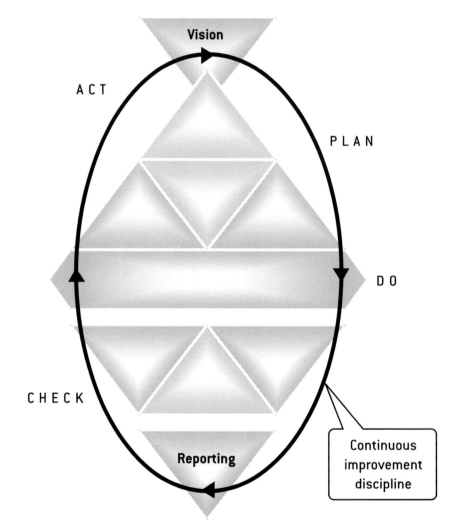

STEP	ACTION AND QUESTIONS
	The core of the quality process starts here
5. Where are we?	Status assessment
6. What's first?	**Act** on the top opportunities by setting specific performance targets
7 How will we organise resources?	**Plan** the resources that you will need to reach the targets
8. How will we do it?	**Do** what is planned to reach the objectives
9. How will we chart our progress?	**Check** the results achieved against targets
	The end of the beginning
10. Learn from the project	**Act** to correct deviations and integrate learning from doing Consider issues you left out before or which have emerged

Table 4 **INTEGRATING THE DEMING CYCLE INTO THE 'GETTING STARTED' ROADMAP**

design and testing of swimwear is of little help in the manufacture of garden furniture from sustainable certified tropical wood. This appreciation of difference is also required when it comes to the Global Compact and corporate citizenship, which need specific tools to deal with issues of human and labour rights, corruption and environmental protection.

In this context, the word 'tool' does not describe a physical instrument such as a drill. Instead, it refers to a conceptual instrument. Presented here, for the first time, are tools that will help you to engage effectively with the Global Compact. They have the following essential functions:

- They provide a methodology to collect information about the behaviour of an organisation or a system or about those related to it.

- They organise the information in ways to improve knowledge and understanding of the dynamics of the system, the drivers of behaviour and the reasons for failure.

- They either give a description of generally accepted adequate performance or prompt the setting of performance targets.

- They propose proven ways to modify behaviour to reach or exceed satisfactory performance.

- They monitor progress.

Management tools are part of the school of thought that sees organisations as information and knowledge systems. This leads to the development of rational and scientific approaches to business strategy. The literature and training modules of total quality management (TQM) are largely based on tools that combine surveys, checklists, root-cause analysis, decision trees and flowcharts, critical variable statistics and reports. This is not the only way to manage a company, however. Some managers intuitively 'see' the challenge and the correct solution without the conscious help of tools, which they may reject as being too cumbersome. However, when it comes to sharing knowledge and learning new skills, particularly at a distance and through published material, tools work best.

A growing toolbox

The business toolbox is still growing. Tool-making is part of business life, but specific tools for implementation of the Global Compact are few. Rather, existing tools are there to be adapted. This has always been the case. For example, in the early 1970s when the world was faced with significant oil shortages, some business people were quick to adapt the accountant's tool of cost analysis. Energy streams were converted into a single currency — the calorie, joule or British thermal unit (BTU) — and production systems were surveyed to count every input, output and loss in this common currency. This approach revealed tremendous opportunities for stemming losses, for energy cascades and recycling loops and for fuel substitutions. Energy accounting was born to enable the systematic management of energy efficiency.

A decade later, in the 1980s, when the issues of waste and product disposal came to the forefront, some remembered energy accounting and adapted it to other material streams. Life cycle assessment (LCA) became a new field of tool development that continues to produce ramifications in the area of sustainable consumption and product design. Tools are therefore presented not only to be used but also to be adapted and combined with others to reach new levels of performance.

The toolbox associated with the Global Compact performance model will continue to grow as companies share and standardise their approaches to implementation. An overview of all the tools, cases, and information and resources available in this book is presented, according to focus (human rights, labour, environment and corruption), on pages 10-13.

Linking tools, principles, codes and standards

Any discussion of tools should also consider some related concepts, notably the position and status of principles, codes and standards. These can be linked in a way that makes sense to operational managers.

Imagine a bookcase with four shelves. Principles occupy the top shelf (see Figure 8). They are formulations of fundamental values and beliefs. In broad terms they define civilised values and they change slowly. In the political context, they are universally adopted by all governments through the UN process. The content of this shelf inspires meaning and personal or organisational 'vision'.

Codes, national and regional regulations and directives are located on the second shelf down. They define the right way of operating, not just what should be done but also what should *not* be done. They are rules formulated in accordance with the principles. They define social expectations and culture. They can also define the culture of a single organisation — 'this is the way we do things; this is our business model'. You use the content of this shelf to line up your priorities and your policies.

The third shelf from the top is for practice standards. These describe the ideal processes through which to achieve a certain status (e.g. accountability), to be listed as a socially responsible purchaser or to implement an adequate environmental management system. The content of this shelf is for business planning and licence to operate.

Finally, at the bottom, comes the deep shelf of content standards. These define parameters that determine whether a service, a product or a public statement meets a minimum expectation. The content of this shelf defines your minimum output requirements and compliance limits.

Standards emerge from initiatives of common interest groups. They can be purely business-driven or develop as a result of multi-stakeholder discussions with governments, NGOs or trade unions. They can be endorsed and legislated by specific governments or may achieve international status under the auspices of the International Organisation for Standardisation (ISO). Many are of a voluntary nature, without legal penalties for non-compliance. Others, however, have been elevated to universal principles through endorsement by all governments, which is true of the four labour standards of the Global Compact. They work like standards but have moved up a shelf on the bookcase to become principles.

Management tools, generally, are of use and available for every shelf, yet a majority deal with the standards shelves. This is a result of the continuous search for efficiency. Most managers try to avoid 'reinventing the wheel' and look for knowledge and practices already packaged to help them deal with similar situations. They also use various existing standards and approaches in new combinations for new challenges. The Global Compact relies particularly on this dynamic of creative voluntary initiatives. The issues at hand are often so complex that upfront rules and regulations are impossible to set. In many regions of the world there is a lack of functioning institutions to enforce the universal principles as a basis for respected legislation. Corporate leadership and voluntary alliances are then the best way forward.

Voluntary initiatives should not be seen as a soft option. Public commitments such as support for the Global Compact create public expectations for results. Companies who make such declarations without follow-up and tangible performance

Figure 8 FROM UNIVERSAL PRINCIPLES TO STANDARDS: A HIERARCHY OF CONNECTIONS TO THE PERFORMANCE MODEL

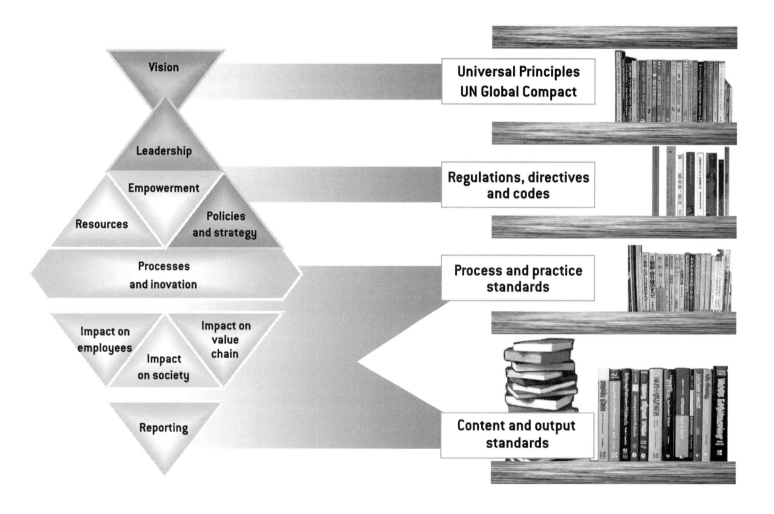

improvements can damage the morale of their employees and of partners, who believed them to be serious. They can also hurt the standing and the brand of their organisation — and of the Compact itself. As the field develops, there is likely to be a trend for standardisation within business sectors and based on specific strands of the Compact. After a phase of experimentation and multiple approaches will come a phase of convergence towards the best solutions. Suppliers will want to streamline the variety of audits imposed by major clients, and listed companies will need to find solutions to cope with the flood of questionnaires from financial ratings experts.

The subject continues to move quickly, but the Global Compact performance model, which evolved from the experience of the 'first movers', can help managers to make sense of this changing territory and to borrow and adapt knowledge that can enhance their performance on the way to responsible excellence.

Voluntary initiatives: reasons for success

In an effort to improve performance on sustainability and social issues, voluntary initiatives involving industry and governments have increased in number since the early 1990s. In the environmental sphere, they cover a variety of commitments by individual companies to achieve environmental targets that go beyond existing regulations. Generally, they take the form of codes of conduct adopted at the national or international level by industrial sector associations, or agreements on performance targets between a government, public authority or civil society organisation and a company, a group of companies or an industry sector.

Although voluntary, such an initiative may nevertheless be:

- Legally binding in the case of a signed, contractual agreement, and thus enforceable if broken
- Mandatory if it becomes a condition for membership of an industry association
- Compulsory, if it becomes a de facto marketing requirement (e.g. ISO 14001) or when, as in countries with an established consensus-based approach, it has the same weight as traditional regulations
- Used to encourage compliance with existing laws

At the international level, various industry associations have been involved in the creation of international voluntary codes and guidelines in the environmental field.[5] Experience with these initiatives has shown the following aspects are needed to make them effective:

- **Commitment.** There is a need to establish a clear sense of purpose, reasons to implement the code and the involvement of internal and external stakeholders.
- **Content.** There is a need to take a triple-bottom-line approach and to include key management elements.
- **Collaboration.** Associations can help with general dissemination, providing guidelines on management and use of tools, peer support and networking.
- **Checking.** This is used to review awareness and to monitor implementation and results.
- **Communication.** There is a need to listen to the public and to communicate implementation and results.

These aspects have been defined by the United Nations Environment Programme (UNEP),[6] and the Canadian government has identified the following eight-step model for developing effective voluntary initiatives:[7]

- Step i: Gather information

---

5 For an assessment of the impact of national-level voluntary agreements, see OECD (Organisation for Economic Cooperation and Development), *Voluntary Approaches for Environmental Policy: Effectiveness, Efficiency and Usage in Policy Mixes* (Paris: OECD, 2003).

6 DTIE (Division of Technology, Industry and Economics), *Voluntary Industry Codes of Conduct for the Environment* (Technical Report 40; Paris: DTIE, United Nations Environment Programme [UNEP], 1998).

7 Government of Canada, *Voluntary Codes: A Guide for Their Development and Use* (Ottawa: Industry Canada and the Treasury Board, 1998).

- Step ii: Undertake preliminary discussions with major stakeholders
- Step iii: Create a working group
- Step iv: Prepare a preliminary draft of the code
- Step v: Consult on the preliminary draft
- Step vi: Publish and disseminate the code
- Step vii: Implement the code
- Step viii: Review the code

Examples of sectoral voluntary initiatives

Since the early 1990s a number of international voluntary initiatives for different industry sectors have been created between UNEP and industry. The participating companies pool resources in developing and advancing environmentally sound practices.

In each initiative, participants commit themselves to a set of principles under the umbrella of sustainable development. These provide sectoral avenues for Global Compact participants to explore the meaning of its principles in greater detail at the sectoral level.[8]

Examples of these, and other, initiatives are listed in Table 5.

Other international voluntary initiatives on social issues and sustainable development include the Voluntary Principles on Security and Human Rights.

INITIATIVE	WEBSITE
Initiatives from the United Nations Environment Programme	
Finance initiative	www.unepfi.net
Tour operators initiative for sustainable tourism development	www.toinitiative.org
Global e-sustainability initiative	www.gesi.org
Automotive forum	www.uneptie.org/outreach/vi/initiatives.htm#automotives
Advertising and communication forum	www.uneptie.org/pc/sustain/advertising/advertising.htm
Sustainable building and construction forum	www.unep.or.jp/ietc/sbc
Other initiatives	
Fair Labor Association	www.fairlabor.org
Ethical Trading Initiative	www.ethicaltrade.org
International Cocoa Initiative	www.chocolateandcocoa.org
Kimberley Process on conflict diamonds	www.kimberleyprocess.com
Voluntary Principles on Security and Human Rights	www.state.gov/www/global/human_rights/001220_fsdrl_principles.html

Table 5 INITIATIVES

Voluntary codes of conduct with labour-related provisions exist in nearly all the 22 sectors of activity of the International Labour Organisation (ILO). An overview of 258 codes from the ILO has shown that sectoral participation in them varies widely. Only 12% provided for external monitoring.[9]

---

8 See www.globalreporting.org.

9 M. Urminsky (ed.), *Self-regulation in the Workplace: Codes of Conduct, Social Labelling and Socially Responsible Investment* (Management and Corporate Citizenship [MCC] Working Paper 1; Geneva: International Labour Office, 2001; www.ilo.org/dyn/empent/docs/F1936481553/1_mcc_wp.pdf).

CHAPTER FOUR

ON STAKEHOLDER ENGAGEMENT AND PARTNERSHIPS

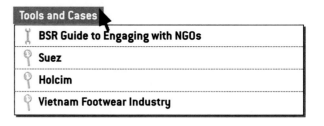

Tools and Cases

- BSR Guide to Engaging with NGOs
- Suez
- Holcim
- Vietnam Footwear Industry

IN THE PAST GENERATION WE HAVE MOVED from a world where even the most basic dialogue between companies and external stakeholders was rare, to the situation today where many companies and civil society organisations recognise the basic truth that without dialogue and partnership lasting social progress is unlikely.

Often, the term 'stakeholders' is used to refer to groups external to the company, and it is this group that is the focus of this chapter. However, many researchers, including Archie Carroll,[1] have provided a definition of stakeholders as 'individuals and groups who may affect or be affected by the actions, decision, policies practices or goals of an enterprise'. In this context, one can differentiate between internal or 'primary' stakeholders and external stakeholders. Although each company's stakeholders will vary, many distinguish between internal, or 'primary', stakeholders, who are often defined as employees and their representatives (trade unions), investors, customers and business partners, and external stakeholders, who often are defined to include non-governmental organisations (NGOs), communities, public officials and others whose partnership with business has become a defining feature of company efforts to implement the UN Global Compact's principles.

Many experts in corporate social responsibility (CSR) have pointed out the importance of dialogue with external stakeholders. This too will vary according to the issues being addressed. For example in the case of the labour principles of the Global Compact, partnership and dialogue will typically start inside the workplace with employees and their representatives. Dialogue with internal stakeholders will help ensure that those most directly affected by decisions are consulted, and also that companies benefit from their employees' extensive knowledge of the issues most pertinent to the company and their experience in the local community in which the company operates. In other cases, such as with environmental issues, the principle proposed in 2004 on bribery and corruption, there may be other stakeholders, often external, who will have an important contribution to make.

Historically, the relationship between companies and community groups has been at 'arm's length' — usually limited to corporate philanthropy initiatives. But that world has changed. In *A Guide to Working with Multilaterals*,[2] a publication co-authored by Tara Rangarajan of Business for Social Responsibility (BSR) and Simon Zadek, chief executive of AccountAbility, the emerging objectives of partnerships undertaken in the stakeholder world were identified as:

- **Learning and knowledge.** As companies have come to embrace a wider set of issues related to their operations, they have found that

---

1 A.B. Carroll, *Business and Society: Ethics and Stakeholder Management* (Cincinnati, OH: South Western College Publishing, 1996): 74.

2 For more details, see page 71.

NGOs have been an essential source of information. Many are familiar with NGO campaigns on various social and environmental matters. These public debates — and many more private discussions — have mutually reinforced understanding of critical issues.

- **Voluntary standards.** Companies and NGOs have joined together to establish voluntary guidelines on issues that previously had not been addressed. There are numerous examples of efforts to create standards for managing labour practices in global supply chains. One such effort, the Voluntary Principles on Security and Human Rights,[3] an initiative convened by the US, UK, Dutch and Norwegian governments, brings companies, NGOs and trade unions together to create a set of principles on an issue of critical importance to all stakeholders.

- **Operational delivery.** In even more cases, companies and NGOs have found that their ability to solve essential social and environmental questions is dependent on partnership. The marriage of companies' operational knowledge with NGOs' understanding of social needs and delivery of social services is of paramount importance, especially in environments where government

resources are lacking. This helps to create the social infrastructure that allows the Global Compact principles to be applied more effectively.

- **Policy dialogue.** The notion that the work of companies and NGOs to develop voluntary standards is a replacement for official policy-making is incorrect. In fact, formal policy dialogue on matters of importance to the private and independent sectors can help to create a constituency for policy initiatives, with one recent example being support for the UN Convention Against Corruption.[4]

- **Mobilising funds.** Civil society and business can help to mobilise funds. Partnerships that take a collaborative approach to problem-solving have been supported by bilateral and multilateral funds as there is confidence that such coalitions leverage the skills and constituencies needed to make lasting change happen.

Triggers for stakeholder engagement

The decision to establish an engagement between companies and civil society groups takes careful consideration on all sides. Even when agreement is reached on what an engagement or partnership might accomplish, there must be a continuing

effort to ensure that the collaboration proceeds on a mutually satisfactory basis.

Individual companies will want to assess the direct benefits to their business, whether they have the necessary resources available and what their obligations are as 'corporate citizens'. Companies should also be aware that they will have less control over a joint project, and that NGOs often have different agendas and ways of working.

For an NGO, careful consideration should be given to ensuring that a corporate partner is sympathetic to the NGO's operating principles and values. NGOs have their own 'brand' to protect, in particular their reputation for independence and their vision and values. They will not want to risk this unduly. Finally, many NGOs are resource-constrained, so they will need to consider carefully whether investment in the partnership is worthwhile.

How do stakeholder partnerships relate to the performance model?

Companies may not look to engage with stakeholders on every aspect of their business, and stakeholders may neither expect nor desire this. In the performance model, there are five areas in particular in which companies can usefully benefit from the perspective of wider stakeholder groups — vision, leadership, policies and strategies, impact on society and reporting (see Figure 9):

---

3 For more information on the Voluntary Principles on Security and Human Rights see page 119.

4 On the UN Convention Against Corruption, see page 42.

- **Vision.** Stakeholder engagement and partnerships can have an impact on the vision of a company. For example, a number of oil companies are now describing themselves as 'energy companies', partly as a result of stakeholder engagement and the ongoing debate about renewable energy. Some companies have invited stakeholders to help them look 'beyond business-as-usual' and are moving into what might be a non-traditional direction.

- **Leadership.** Stakeholder engagement and partnerships can develop leadership skills at all levels of the company, especially at the top, as they often involve setting priorities on social and environmental goals, risk-taking, new forms of working and the crossing of traditional boundaries within and between companies and other organisations.

- **Policies and strategies.** Especially when companies begin to address new issues, working with stakeholders to define the issues and understand desired outcomes can be essential to the successful creation of policies and strategies. The relative newness of the issues addressed by the Global Compact has meant that many signatory companies have consulted widely with NGOs on, for example, the meaning of human rights for business. Questions arising from new technology, such as concerns regarding the use of genetically modified organisms in the production of food

Figure 9 **THE FOUR BEST ELEMENTS FOR MEANINGFUL STAKEHOLDER ENGAGEMENT**

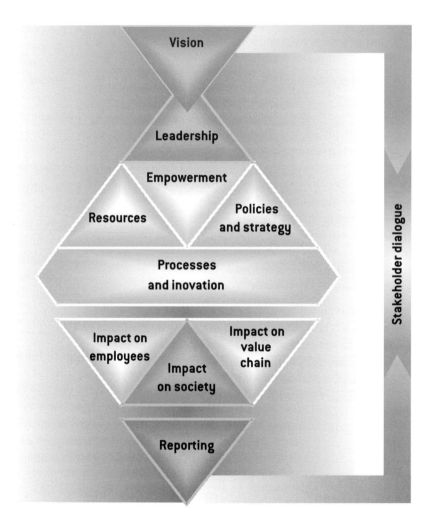

or regarding electromagnetic fields in the use of mobile phones, also require stakeholder dialogue when understanding 'risk' in the application of precaution.

- **Impact on society.** Stakeholders can offer guidance on the likely impact on society that company actions will have, given that for many groups assessment of social conditions is at the core of their activities.

- **Reporting.** Related to the above item, the views of stakeholders, and an analysis of how a company has taken those views on board, can increase trust in the performance data and outcomes featured in a public report or communication of progress. More and more companies consult with selected stakeholders to strengthen and add credibility to their public reporting.

We have come to realise that progress towards sustainable development is a very complex systemic issue. The Global Compact performance model is a way to deal with change and progress. But change is not just a technical fix; it needs a social approach, more so for complex systems where no one is quite in charge. Stakeholders and partnerships are not new 'buzzwords' in the field of business. They are signs of a new paradigm that sees success in managing complex change through the association of interdependent actors with a shared purpose, real accountability in parts of the system and a real stake in the success or failure of the endeavour.

GUIDE TO ENGAGING WITH NON-GOVERNMENTAL ORGANISATIONS

Business for Social Responsibility

AS COMPANIES WITH GLOBAL OPERATIONS seek to enhance their corporate social responsibility efforts, many are finding value in dialogue and other engagements with non-governmental organisations (NGOs). Business for Social Responsibility (BSR) has worked with its member companies and other stakeholders to create a framework for understanding the growth and evolution of these partnerships. The *Guide to Engaging with Non-governmental Organisations* presents a process for proactive relations and engagement.

Part 1 of the guidebook traces the emergence of such partnerships, explores the benefits and risks to companies, provides insights into the motivations for NGOs to partner and describes lessons learned from ongoing engagements. Part 2 of the guidebook outlines practical steps and key considerations to help companies identify relevant NGOs, assess and select among potential NGO partners and implement an effective project involving NGOs.

The functionality of the guidebook is enhanced further through the presentation of benefits and risks and of basic steps that can be taken to ensure that maximum benefits to business and society are achieved. The guidebook also seeks to provide NGO perspectives in a manner that enhances business's understanding of the potential concerns and interests that NGOs will have during the course of engagement.

The tool itself is relatively simple to use; any complexities arise more from the nature of partnerships themselves than from the tool.

FURTHER INFORMATION

Business for Social Responsibility (BSR) website: www.bsr.org

Publication: www.bsr.org/BSRStore/ShowProducts.cfm?DID= 15&Action=Detail&objectgroup_id=9&Product_ID=88

CASE STUDY

SUEZ: HOW PUBLIC–PRIVATE PARTNERSHIPS CONTRIBUTE TO SOCIAL INCLUSION

POOR AREAS TYPICALLY HAVE LIMITED ACCESS to basic services such as water, waste or energy. Public–private partnerships have been central to improving local environmental conditions and promoting community organisation and participation as well as to the operational and economic sustainability of the services themselves, with the communities playing a role in maintaining service infrastructure and paying affordable fees for the services provided.

Suez is a Paris-based major energy, water and waste services company with 241,000 employees and global sales of €46 billion.

As a specific contribution to the Global Compact in Buenos Aires, Suez and its subsidiaries such as Aguas Argentinas, Cliba and Safège, along with several public, private and community stakeholders, undertook a project to improve understanding of the preconditions for successful small, local partnerships, with a view to replicating the findings in other contexts. Ten indicators of sustainability agreed by all the stakeholders showed that environmental education, local capacity-building and a high level of contractualisation enhance partnership effectiveness. Ongoing interaction between public, private and community stakeholders generates a climate of trust and enhances the credibility needed for the sustainable delivery of services or products. The payment of affordable fees generates rights and responsibilities, raises awareness of citizenship among marginalised people and promotes their social inclusion.

In its water service public–private partnership activities, Suez runs training programmes contributing to the development of the communities it serves. Its Chilean subsidiary, Aguas Andinas, has trained 21,000 women from low-income households to carry out basic plumbing repairs. Over 1,000 workshops have been held to date, and the model has been transferred to La Paz and El Alto, Bolivia, and Manaus, Brazil.

In the field of refuse collection and sorting, Suez has also had opportunities to innovate in the field of social inclusion. In São Paulo, Brazil, another subsidiary, Vega, trained 90 unemployed people to become environmental educators within a partnership involving the municipality and non-governmental organisations (NGOs). Moreover, Vega built a cooperative sorting and recycling centre employing 200 'rag-and-bone men' who had previously worked, with their families, at unauthorised dumps. Besides reducing the volume of waste dumped, the income made has raised parents' ability to sending their children to school instead of making them work at the dump. In Buenos Aires, Cliba raises the awareness of health risks among low-income communities and trains people to collect waste before employing them.

These actions mobilise and motivate employees as well as engendering loyalty to the company and raising enthusiasm and ideas for new productive partnerships. They also show how private–public partnerships can empower community and business development when partners assume their responsibilities both in line with their contracts and in line with the UN Global Compact principles.

FURTHER INFORMATION

Suez website: www.suez.com

FROM TENSION TO COOPERATIVE DIALOGUE: HOLCIM'S COMMUNITY ADVISORY PANEL APPROACH

HOLCIM IS ONE OF THE WORLD'S LARGEST

suppliers of cement, as well as aggregates (gravel and sand), concrete and construction-related services. The Holcim Group, which includes Union Cement of the Philippines, has majority and minority interests in more than 70 countries on all continents. The company has a long history of constructive engagement, particularly with local communities in many countries. A productive way of addressing specific issues that emerge from stakeholders in areas close to its operations is represented by the community advisory panels (CAPs).

With a broad cross-section of representative voices, CAPs can directly generate substantive input from the community as well as from experts in specific technical fields.

Before Holcim invested in Union in 1988, Union's relationship with external stakeholders was based on limited or selective engagement, in some cases characterised by an adversarial relationship with local communities. However, it was recognised that this did not present a supportive environment in which to maintain its licence to operate.

In one instance, a flood that devastated the area close to Union's Lugait plant in 1999 became a turning point in community relations for the company. Prior to this, people in the local community knew of the company, but they did not know its people. In response to the flood, Union employees volunteered assistance, with provision of food and medicine, infrastructure repair and emotional support for victims, and in so doing opened the door to improved relations.

A CAP was then created, involving company management, unions, local community representatives, non-governmental organisations (NGOs), government agencies and local government units. Membership of this committee, is both by invitation from the company and by nomination from local officials or an NGO.

The mandate of this committee is to assess and validate the plants' proposals for community activities, which are identified through local stakeholder engagement processes. Projects are then carried out in collaboration with partner organisations.

For example, the Women's Livelihood Programme trains women in sewing and in the production of various handicrafts. The objective is to augment the family income and help provide for family needs. To date, membership of the Women's Livelihood Programme has increased from less than 50 participants to more than 200, and a livelihood centre has been constructed for production and display. This programme was established in partnership with the local government, the women's association and the Department of Social Welfare and Services.

Since the formation of the CAP committee at the Lugait plant, the relationship with the community has blossomed. The company now regularly opens its doors to the community every Friday and Saturday so that local officials, NGOs, students and community residents can visit the plant. Similar community groups are also being organised at the other plants of Union.

CAPs are also good for business. Zita Diez, Union's CSR coordinator and Communications Manager highlights that:

> At the Lugait plant, security concerns are high due to the presence of rebel groups in the area. But if you are responsible and open to discussion then your community can actually become your first line of defence. In fact our security guard numbers have not increased but on the contrary they have reduced to about 20% over the last three years — primarily because we have improved our relationship with the community and we know that they will help 'protect' us.

In addition to helping develop community projects, strong community relations have also helped the company introduce the use of alternative fuels and raw materials (AFR). Union has held specific consultations on the topic of AFR to inform local communities and key people. As a result, the company has received overwhelming support. And this is not because the community understands specifically how the AFR works but because — as surveys have shown — they know and trust the company. As a result, AFR permits were received quickly.

The shift in community relations for Union Cement has not only positively impacted the community but also the company's employees who now feel and understand that they are part of a bigger community. Engagement with different stakeholder groups has led to increased awareness about environmental responsibility and the overall role the company and its employees can play in the community.

FURTHER INFORMATION

Holcim website: www.holcim.com

CASE STUDY

FOOTSTEPS TO WORKER HEALTH AND SAFETY: THE VIETNAM FOOTWEAR INDUSTRY BUSINESS LINKS INITIATIVE

THE FOOTWEAR INDUSTRY IN VIETNAM IS expanding rapidly and is one of the key industries leading Vietnam's economic development. It is important, therefore, that the industry can participate fully in the international market, for which it will need to meet exacting workplace standards.

With three-year support funding from the UK Department for International Development, and an alliance of three major international sportswear companies, The Prince of Wales International Business Leaders Forum (IBLF) and the Vietnam Chamber of Commerce, the industry jointly established the Vietnam Footwear Industry Business Links Initiative (VBLI) in December 1999. The objective of the programme is to improve working conditions in the footwear industry, including private, state-owned and foreign-invested factories. It focuses on occupational health and safety issues, especially on the choice, storage, handling, use and disposal of chemicals used in the manufacturing process. It is also concerned with improving housekeeping and with reducing noise, fumes and dust, thereby providing a healthier and safer environment for workers in the industry.

VBLI is a tri-sectoral partnership between 23 Vietnamese and international companies. It is a Vietnamese programme managed and run by local professionals, and is licensed by the Vietnamese Ministry of Planning and Investment. In its third full year of operation, the achievements of VBLI achievement are

well recognised by all participants and external bodies, seeing the VBLI as an effective agent in bringing real improvements to working conditions in the footwear industry.

Its key achievements include:

- Establishment of a formal management structure (i.e. a steering committee, management committee and advisory groups) which allows all participating organisations and companies to be actively involved in various aspects of the programme

- Involvement of over 60% of local footwear businesses in the programme activities

- Presentation of 12 'train the trainer' courses in Hanoi, Ho Chi Minh City and Haiphong on occupational health and safety management, chemical safety management, equipment safety and maintenance and management support systems. These were attended by over 400 local factory managers and supervisors

- Development of a management support system manual comprising 19 chapters, distributed to over 130 local factories

- Research on topics such as worker consultation, female labour and gender issues, allowable levels of hazardous factors (e.g. dust, chemicals, fumes, noise and heat), monitoring and inspection systems and the sourcing from Vietnam by international footwear companies

- Promotion of a single governmental inspection and monitoring agency in order to streamline current non-cohesive and inefficient practice

In addition to continuing its existing activities, the anticipated key tasks for the VBLI are:

- To expand gradually into the garment and textile industry, which faces similar occupational health and safety issues and is sourced by similar sportswear companies

- To involve Taiwanese and Korean businesses, which are major foreign investors both in the footwear industry and in the garment industry

- To conduct training both for factory inspectors and for government inspectors and to advise local academic institutes in formulating occupational health and safety curricula

- To develop checklists for self-monitoring and inspection by local factories

- To identify and secure funding from local entities (e.g. government, industrial associations and factories) to ensure its long-term sustainability

FURTHER INFORMATION

Vietnam Footwear Industry Business Links Initiative website: www.vcci.com.vn/vbli

International Business Leaders Forum website: www.iblf.org

Partnership Guide

Type of resource: publication

Author organisation: United Nations Industrial Development Organisation

Year of publication: 2002

The purpose of this guide from the United Nations Industrial Development Organisation (UNIDO) is to serve as a framework for actors in the public and private sector who may become involved in a UNIDO business partnership for industrial development.

In order to facilitate the process approach, the guide is structured in a way that allows easy and practical highlighting of actions to be taken:

- Partners: Their Basic Roles, Objectives and Contributions
- The Basics of UNIDO Business Partnerships
- Types of Partnerships
- Partnership as a Process

FURTHER INFORMATION

United Nations Industrial Development Organisation (UNIDO) website: www.unido.org

Publication: www.unido.org/userfiles/ Bethkek/BPGuide.pdf

A Guide to Working with Multilaterals

Type of resource: publication

Author organisation: Business for Social Responsibility with AccountAbility

Year of publication: 2001

This publication from Business for Social Responsibility (BSR) outlines for businesses the rationale for entering into partnerships with multilateral organisations, reviews the risks and benefits of such arrangements and explains the different and mutual objectives businesses and multilateral agencies have for working with one another, with the ultimate goal of demonstrating the value of these partnerships and therefore catalysing the creation of more partnerships.

FURTHER INFORMATION

Business for Social Responsibility (BSR) website: www.bsr.org

Stakeholder Dialogues: The WBCSD's Approach to Engagement

Type of resource: publication

Author organisation: World Business Council for Sustainable Development

Year of publication: 2002

This report from the World Business Council for Sustainable Development (WBCSD) provides the reader with a better understanding of the WBCSD's dialogue experience, offers ten keys to success and explains why business should engage in dialogue.

FURTHER INFORMATION

World Business Council for Sustainable Development (WBCSD) website: www.wbcsd.org

Publication: www.wbcsd.org/DocRoot/ fHkJNncZmiLvRSeHxFQo/stakeholder.pdf

Putting Partnerships to Work: Strategic Alliances for Development between Government, the Private Sector and Civil Society

Type of resource: book

Editors: Michael Warner and Rory Sullivan

Year of publication: 2004

This book, edited by Michael Warner and Rory Sullivan, provides evidence not only of the viability of partnerships through a number of detailed case studies but also that partnership approaches can provide substantially better outcomes for all parties than can more traditional approaches to development or corporate social responsibility.

FURTHER INFORMATION

Publication:
M. Warner and R. Sullivan (eds.), *Putting Partnerships to Work: Strategic Alliances for Development between Government, the Private Sector and Civil Society* (Sheffield, UK: Greenleaf Publishing, 2004; www.greenleaf-publishing.com/catalogue/partners.htm)

Part 2

CHAPTER FIVE

FORMING A VISION

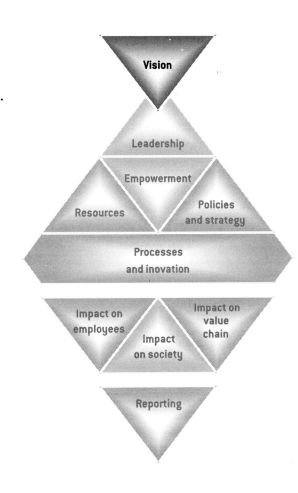

IN 1969, ALAN RICHARDSON, AN AUSTRALIAN

psychologist, reported on a fascinating experiment.[1] Choosing three groups of students at random, on day 1 he took each group to a basketball court and recorded their respective scores in shooting the ball through the basket. Group A continued to practise making free throws every day. Group B did not touch a ball again. Group C did not touch a ball either, but spent 20 minutes every day visualising themselves shooting the ball and going through the routine of aiming, scoring or missing. When they missed they visualised their effort to correct the movement and aim again, successfully. On day 20 the groups reconvened in front of the basket. Group A reaped the benefit of daily practice and scored 24% better than on day 1. Group B did as on day 1. But, surprisingly, Group C did 23% better than on day 1. The power of vision is revealed in this simple test — a significant improvement in 20 days through six hours of positive thought.[2]

Vision is also essential for business and organisations. Although it is true that many organisations embrace change only after a crisis, the real driver of progress, innovation and value is a vision of what the organisation wants to become. Bill Gates writes in *The Road Ahead*[3] how he dropped out of Harvard in the spring of 1975 to start his software business with Paul Allen, who had left his job at Honeywell:

> People often ask me to explain Microsoft's success . . . Of course, there is no simple answer, and luck played a role, but I think that the most important role was our original vision . . . We believed there would be computers everywhere because of cheap computing power and great new software that would take advantage of it. We set up shop betting on the former and producing the latter when no one else was. Our initial insight made everything else a bit easier.

Lack of vision only leaves a business drifting with the trends while the odds for competitive attacks and crises rise.

Vision is a shared ambition of a highly desirable end-state.

This is how Jean Philippe Deschamps, professor at the Lausanne Institute of Management Development, defines 'vision' — the core driver of entrepreneurship — in his course on innovation. This definition implies a powerful question: 'Whose highly desirable end-state?' The narrow answer is: the company's — higher margins,

---

1 A. Richardson, *Mental Imagery* (New York: Springer, 1969).

2 For more on scoring, see Chapter 10, page 131.

3 W. Gates, *The Road Ahead* (Harmondsworth, UK: Penguin Books, 1995): 18.

a bigger market, a new head office and the CEO praised in the *Financial Times*. The ambition to reach this desirable end-state is surely shared by the CEO, the shareholders and, maybe, a number of employees. Fine and true, but this is not what you are looking for in this book.

The ideal answer to the question 'Whose highly desirable end-state?' is: society at large. Or is this, rather, the *idealistic* answer? How large a boundary can you afford to stretch to take responsibility for society's future? This is at the heart of the corporate citizenship debate — the redefining of the boundaries of the company. It is not a new question. For years, leading-edge companies have been adopting product stewardship programmes and managing their environmental impacts beyond their site perimeters, including those of their suppliers. They have also developed community relations initiatives or nature conservation programmes or have followed other philanthropic interests. These companies see their responsibility somewhat wider than their limited liability status. But the question nowadays calls for sharper, strategic answers. In 1962, Milton Friedman could forcefully state his oft-quoted attack on social responsibility:[4]

> Few trends could so thoroughly undermine the very foundations of our free society as the acceptance by corporate officials of a social responsibility other than to make as much money for their stockholders as possible.

---

4 M. Friedman, *Capitalism and Freedom* (Chicago: University of Chicago Press, 1962).

Despite its apparent narrowness, Friedman's position held an underlying assumption: that wealth created by a few would somehow trickle down through society and that the metaphor of the tide raising all boats together could describe the market economy. That assumption was popular among the economists and politicians of the postwar boom.

Some 40 years later, the world is indeed three times richer, as measured by gross domestic product (GDP), but the trickle-down effect dried up very early: too many boats have capsized in the wake of the larger power boats. In counterpoint to Friedman, Henry Mintzberg and two other eminent business professors, Robert Simons and Kunal Basu, exposed the stark truth in June 2002:[5]

> In the past decade, we have been experiencing a glorification of self-interest perhaps unequalled since the 1930s. It is as if, denying much of the social progress made since then, we were thrown back to an earlier and darker age.

They depict the model that is destroying engagement:

> A tight little model — we call it a syndrome of selfish-ness — has taken hold of our corporations and our societies, as well as our minds. It builds on a set of half-truths — shown in Figure 10 as 'wedges' — from a narrow view of ourselves, as economic man; to a distorted view of our values, reduced to shareholder value; to a partic-ular view of leadership, as heroic and dramatic; to a nasty view of our organisations, as lean and increasingly mean; to an illusory view of society, as a rising tide to

---

5 H. Mintzberg, R. Simons and K. Basu, 'Memo to CEOs', *Fast Company Magazine*, June 2002.

prosperity. All of this looks rather neat, as does a house of cards. Before it collapses outright, we would do well to balance it with a rather different set of beliefs.

A vision needs to engage a wider agenda than just narrow value creation. Achieving the vision requires an understanding of the boundaries and limits of your business and the contribution it can make to the 'common good' on the strength of universal principles and your own capabilities and values. The common good is not a blank page. The past 40 years have produced an ever-growing list of universal declarations and international conventions that describe a consensus around a 'highly desirable end-state'. These reflect a noisy and diverse consensus around complex issues with large margins of uncertainty, but they do offer a map for where we would like to be as human beings.

The Information and Resources section at the end of this chapter (pages 84-85) provides access to the major signposts to this end-state. On the one hand are a number of principles and codes pointing towards a more balanced economy where technology and finance are in harmony with people and the environment. On the other hand are a number of desired development outcomes, among them the Millennium Development Goals for 2015 (see page 76) or the call for a Factor 10 improvement in eco-efficiency (see page 78). Also critical are the multilateral declarations and conventions behind the UN Global Compact principles. In the face of continuous population growth and people's aspirations for a better quality of life, many of these goals are daunting. A bold vision is needed in order to reconcile development and sustainability.

Half-truths

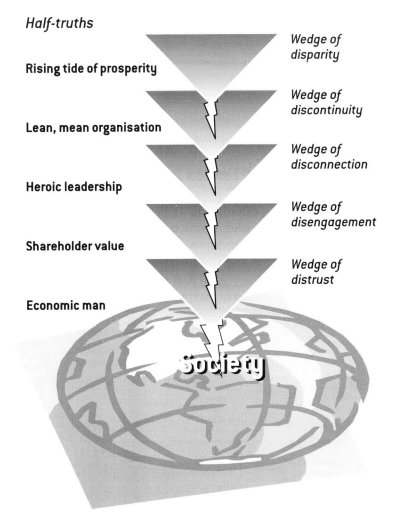

Rising tide of prosperity — Wedge of disparity

Lean, mean organisation — Wedge of discontinuity

Heroic leadership — Wedge of disconnection

Shareholder value — Wedge of disengagement

Economic man — Wedge of distrust

Society

Figure 10 **A SYNDROME OF SELFISHNESS**

Source: H. Mintzberg, R. Simons and K. Basu, 'Memo to CEOs', *Fast Company Magazine*, June 2002

Failure to make progress will undermine peace, markets, democracies and our health. However, success brings with it countless business opportunities.

A vision that embraces values and a purpose that is wider than profitability alone can also bring benefits to the bottom line. For those who still need convincing, take a look at the data from Dow Jones Sustainability Index presented in Chapter 15 of this book (page 221), which indicates that companies aligned with Global Compact principles marginally outperform those that are not.

Deschamps's belief that 'vision is a shared ambition of a highly desirable end-state' takes on a new dimension when we agree that the end-state should be one of a company with redefined boundaries, operating beyond its strict legal limits and with a will to engage with others to create a better world. It is not only sharing with employees and business associates — who are all essential to achieve the vision (as described in Chapters 11 and 12) — but it is also sharing with other stakeholders (as described in Chapter 4). It is not only sharing the vision after it is formulated but during the formulation itself. The charismatic CEO whose epiphany provides a compelling vision formed after solitary reflection is a silly stereotype, but would it not make things easier?

Many among the leaders who support the World Business Council for Sustainable Development (WBCSD) think not:

In terms of leading an organisation, it is crucial to have both a vision of where you want to be and a clear idea of what can practically be achieved at any time. One is on the way to the other. But if you try to jump straight to the vision, it will either not work, or your vision is not very visionary.[6]

On page 80 the case study from Northumbrian Water takes the visioning process through its principal steps. It illustrates several important success factors:

- Take time out of daily activities: set aside at least a couple of days.
- Get external input to focus on the big picture: 10–20 years on.
- Involve employees.
- Use a framework to identify the meaningful and practical elements of the vision.
- Look for simple formulations: they must express people's energy and shared ambition; the vision must be alive in a year's time (and beyond).

Vision is a process, not a sudden inspiration. As we heard at the start of this chapter, Richardson's students worked on their vision of perfect free throws every day.

6 Quoted in C.O. Holliday, Jr, S. Schmidheiny and P. Watts, *Walking the Talk: The Business Case for Sustainable Development* (Sheffield, UK: Greenleaf Publishing, 2002): 136.

THE MILLENNIUM DEVELOPMENT GOALS

THE MILLENNIUM DEVELOPMENT GOALS ARE an ambitious agenda for reducing poverty and improving lives that world leaders agreed on at the Millennium Summit in September 2000. For each goal one or more targets have been set, mostly for 2015, using 1990 as a benchmark:

Goal 1: Eradicate extreme poverty and hunger

- *Target for 2015:* halve the proportion of people living on less than US$1 a day and those who suffer from hunger.
- *Comment:* more than a billion people still live on less than US$1 a day. Sub-Saharan Africa, Latin America and the Caribbean, as well as parts of Europe and Central Asia, are falling short of the poverty target.

Goal 2: Achieve universal primary education

- *Target for 2015:* Ensure that all boys and girls complete primary school.
- *Comment:* as many as 113 million children do not attend school, but the target is within reach.

Goal 3: Promote gender equality, and empower women

- *Target for 2005 (preferred target year):* eliminate gender disparities in primary and secondary education.
- *Target for 2015:* eliminate gender disparities at all levels.
- *Comment:* two-thirds of illiterate people are women, and the rate of employment among women is only two-thirds that of men.

Goal 4: Reduce child mortality

- *Target for 2015:* reduce by two-thirds the mortality rate among children under five years old.

- *Comment:* every year nearly 11 million young children die before their fifth birthday, mainly from preventable illnesses, although that number is down from 15 million in 1980.

Goal 5: Improve maternal health

- *Target for 2015:* reduce by three-quarters the rate of women dying in childbirth.
- *Comment:* in the developing world, the risk of dying in childbirth is 1 in 48, but virtually all countries now have safe motherhood programmes.

Goal 6: Combat HIV/AIDS, malaria and other diseases

- *Target for 2015:* halt and begin to reverse the spread of HIV/AIDS and the incidence of malaria and other major diseases.
- *Comment:* 40 million people are living with HIV, including 5 million newly infected in 2001. Countries such as Brazil, Senegal, Thailand and Uganda have shown that the spread of HIV can be stemmed.

Goal 7: Ensure environmental sustainability

- *Targets:* integrate the principles of sustainable development into country policies and programmes and reverse the loss of environmental resources.
- *Target for 2015:* reduce by half the proportion of people without access to safe drinking water.
- *Target for 2020:* achieve significant improvement in the lives of at least 100 million slum dwellers.
- *Comment:* more than one billion people lack access to safe drinking water and more than two billion lack sanitation. During the 1990s, however, nearly one billion people gained access to safe water and the same number to sanitation.

Goal 8: Develop a global partnership for development

- *Targets:* develop further an open trading and financial system that includes a commitment to good governance, development and poverty reduction — nationally and internationally.

  Address the least developed countries' special needs, and the special needs of land-locked and small island developing states.

  Deal comprehensively with developing countries' debt problems.

  Develop decent and productive work for youth.

  In cooperation with pharmaceutical companies, provide access to affordable essential drugs in developing countries.

  In cooperation with the private sector, make available the benefits of new technologies — especially information and communications technologies.
- *Comment:* many developing countries spend more on servicing debts than on social services. New aid commitments made in the first half of 2002 could mean an additional US$12 billion per year by 2006..

FURTHER INFORMATION

Website: www.developmentgoals.org

For more on progress towards achievement of the MDGs, please refer to the Global Governance Initiative (opposite)

Source: www.undp.org/mdg

Fact Sheet: World Economic Forum Global Governance Initiative: From Aspiration to Action

Type of resource: report

Author organisation: World Economic Forum

Year of publication: 2004

The Geneva-based World Economic Forum, in partnership with the Brookings Institution (Washington, DC), formed the Global Governance Initiative (GGI) in 2003 to measure progress towards achievement of the Millennium Development Goals (MDGs). The GGI's expert working teams reviewed progress achieved through the combined efforts of the public sector, private sector and civil society organisations, including trade unions, NGOs and others. The first report of the GGI, issued at the WEF's Davos meeting in January 2004, assigned scores of between one and ten, with ten representing the highest achievement, for each of the MDG categories. In this initial assessment, scores ranged between three and four, reflecting the broad view by the working parties that considerable additional work is required to achieve the targets outlined in the MDGs.

FURTHER INFORMATION

Global Governance Initiative document:
www.weforum.org/pdf/Initiatives/GGI_Factsheet.pdf?SEARCH.X=13\&SEARCH.Y=14

Business and the Millennium Development Goals

Type of resource: publication

Author organisation: United Nations Development Programme and The Prince of Wales International Business Leaders Forum

Year of publication: 2003

This briefing provides a framework for action on how companies and business coalitions can work with the UN System, governments and civil society organisations to help achieve the Millennium Development Goals. It answers three key questions:

1. What are the Millennium Development Goals?
2. Why are they important to business?
3. How can business contribute to their achievement?

The framework proposes a set of options to contribute to each of the eight development goals in the core business activities, as social investment or philanthropy, and in the realm of policy and advocacy.

It is completed with examples from, among others, major Global Compact signatories.

FURTHER INFORMATION

Website: www.iblf.org/csr/csrwebassist.nsf/content/f1d2b3aad4.html

See also:
www.undp.org/business
www.iblf.org

FACTOR 4 / FACTOR 10 AND ECO-EFFICIENCY

THERE IS GROWING AGREEMENT AMONG

policy-makers, academics, businesses and non-governmental organisations (NGOs) that total resource productivity needs to be increased significantly in order to move towards a sustainable world economy. A number of studies estimate that efficiency should improve by a factor of 4 within the next decade[7] and by a factor of 10 in industrialised countries within one generation.[8] Factors 4 and 10 refer to total material flow reductions (including material flows for energy production) within the economy and express a visionary goal of sustainable resource efficiency. Such reductions have been set as long-term targets by some countries; for instance:

- The Ecocycle Commission set up by the Swedish Government is driving for a Factor 10 within the next 25–50 years.[9]

- The Netherlands' Ministry of Housing, Spatial Planning and the Environment formulated a Factor 4 goal in its National Environmental Policy Plan in 1996.[10]

In *Sustainable Development in Germany*, its draft programme for priority areas in environmental policy, the German Federal Ministry for the Environment, Nature Conservation and Nuclear Safety suggested a 2.5-fold increase in raw material productivity by 2020 compared with 1993 and a 2-fold increase in energy productivity by 2020 compared with 1990.[11]

To achieve such targets, resource use must be optimised at every level of society, from the national level to regional levels, from total sectors of activity to the individual company and household levels.

This does not mean that the resource productivity of every single process or every phase of a product life cycle can be drastically increased. Each industrial sector contributes to the Factor 10 goal according to its potential to reduce resource consumption. Overall, it may turn out to be ecologically preferable to 'invest' more resources in a particular sector (e.g. into new energy sources) or at specific stages in the life of a product (e.g. to develop new engines for vehicles) in order to increase overall resource productivity (of transportation and mobility). What counts is the rapid composite progress towards Factor 10.

The Nordic Council of Ministers conducted four case studies in Denmark (transport sector), Finland (forestry sector), Norway (real estate and building sector) and Sweden (food chain). Each case study included a description of the sector before and after implementing Factor 4 and Factor 10 targets. Furthermore, the case studies considered the role of government in implementation and the responsibilities and opportunities for business, academic institutions and NGOs.

Each of the studies concluded that it is possible to reach a Factor 4 improvement by 2030 or a Factor 10 improvement by 2050 only with considerable changes to individual and societal values as well as to regulatory regimes. Changes in consumer behaviour are a critical requirement. Governments have a number of powerful policy options available that may help to stimulate these changes. Core elements in the approach are:

- The internalisation of environmental costs
- Legal and economic instruments
- Elimination or reform of subsidies detrimental to sustainable development
- Improved education and awareness
- Indicators to measure eco-efficiency and energy productivity
- Time-specific national targets

It is also important to introduce measures that encourage a 'bottom-up' change, including processes involving development of new forms of technology, life organisation, learning and innovation and subsequent changes to values.

7 E.U. von Weizsäcker, A.B. Lovins and L. Hunter Lovins, *Factor Four: Doubling Wealth, Halving Resource Use* (London: Earthscan Publications, 1997).

8 The Factor Ten Club, *The Carnoules Declaration: Statement to Government and Business Leaders* (Wuppertal, Germany: Wuppertal Institute for Climate, Environment and Energy, 1997).

9 Ecocycle Commission (1997) *Hallbrat Sa Klart: en Kretsloppstrategi* (Kretsloppsdelegationens report 1997/13; Stockholm: Ecocycle Commission).

10 VROM (Ministerie van Volkshuisvesting, Ruimtelijke Ordening en Milieubeheer [Ministry of Housing, Spatial Planning and Environment]), *National Environmental Policy Plan* (The Hague, The Netherlands: VROM, 1996).

11 BMU (Bundesumweltministerium für Umwelt, Naturschutz und Reaktorsicherheit [German Federal Ministry for the Environment, Nature Conservation and Nuclear Safety]), *Perspektiven für Deutschland: Unsere Strategie für eine nachhaltige Entwicklung* (*Perspectives for Germany: Our Strategy for Sustainable Development*) (Berlin: BMU, 2002).

FURTHER INFORMATION

Wuppertal Institute website: www.wupperinst.org

THE SIGMA MANAGEMENT FRAMEWORK

British Standards Institution, Forum for the Future, and AccountAbility

'SUSTAINABILITY: INTEGRATED GUIDELINES

for Management' (SIGMA) was launched in 1999 as a partnership between the British Standards Institution, Forum for the Future, and AccountAbility. SIGMA seeks to provide clear practical advice to organisations that enables them to make a meaningful contribution to sustainable development, by improving their social, economic and environmental performance.

The SIGMA Management Framework describes a four-phase cycle to manage and embed sustainability issues within core organisational processes and decision-making. These four systematic phases (leadership and vision; planning; delivery; and monitor, review and report) are broken down into detailed sub-phases to allow an organisation to develop, plan, deliver, monitor and report on its sustainable development strategy and performance. The management framework explains clearly and concisely necessary activities, the anticipated outcomes and lists further resources. It also helps an organisation understand how to build on what it already has in place.

The aim of the SIGMA Management Framework is to manage and enhance five types of capital that most organisations apply to the development and delivery of their products and services: namely, natural capital, human capital, social capital, manufactured capital and financial capital — yet remaining accountable to their stakeholders.

Organisations are part of our increasingly complex and global system, drawing on and impacting on that system. Sustainable development poses a challenge to the traditional mind-set of organisations. Increasingly, their performance is judged not just by the services, products and profits they make but also by the impacts they have on human and social well-being and on the natural environment on which we all depend for life. Expectations are changing, bringing risks and opportunities.

The SIGMA Management Framework helps organisations to structure their thinking, vision and strategic direction. It allows organisations to incorporate all aspects of sustainable development into their day-to-day operations and to appreciate and maintain their licence to operate, grow and use natural resources in a responsible way — taking account of the needs, views and expectations of stakeholders. As such, the SIGMA Management Framework offers much to organisations seeking to align themselves with the principles of the UN Global Compact.

The SIGMA Management Framework is intended to be used by all types and sizes of organisation and has been 'road-tested' with a range of organisations from the private and public sector, including small and medium-sized enterprises (SMEs), multinational companies and government departments.

FURTHER INFORMATION

The SIGMA Project website: www.projectsigma.com

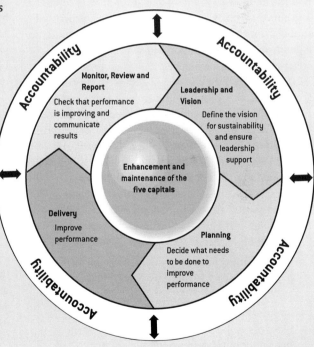

Figure 11 **THE SIGMA MANAGEMENT FRAMEWORK**

CASE STUDY

THINK 2020 AT NORTHUMBRIAN WATER

THIS CASE STUDY FOCUSES ON HOW

Northumbrian Water Ltd (NWL) used The SIGMA Project pilot programme and its guidelines to develop a vision that enabled it to create a route map towards a more sustainable future. The process enabled NWL to bring together senior managers from across the business to focus on the development of a vision for the company. The outputs from the visioning process also formalised thoughts on the new sustainable development policy, so enabling NWL to communicate its vision more coherently to its stakeholders.

NWL is among the 250 largest UK listed companies. It serves 4.3 million people with drinking water and 2.6 million with sewerage services and operates in the north (where the brand name Northumbrian Water is used) and in the south (where the brand name Essex and Suffolk Water is used). The company manages holiday accommodation and conference and recreational facilities. It also provides services to home-owners relating to water connections, contaminated land, flooding and planning applications.

Creation of the vision was done in two stages:

- Brainstorming in small groups, focused on the big picture of what a sustainable NWL could look like in 2020
- Application of these 'big-picture ideas' to the five types of capital of the SIGMA guiding principles — financial capital, human capital, manufactured capital, natural capital and social capital

The day began with external input, in this case a presentation from Jonathan Porritt, programme director at Forum for the Future. The presentation ensured that everyone was at the same level in their understanding of sustainable development and also challenged NWL to identify the key issues that it would need to address to be more sustainable. The presentation was followed by a brainstorming exercise, which allowed people to 'think 2020', and formed the creative basis for the rest of the workshop. It resulted in a combination of innovative, big-picture ideas and some more specific changes that were captured by the facilitators.

By mapping these elements against the five types of capital the participants developed the vision by incorporating more specific objectives. Workshop participants were asked to identify what the management and optimisation of the five stocks of capital would ideally look like in NWL. These outputs were ultimately developed into five vision statements — one for each type of capital — and an overarching, integrating statement. These statements were then consolidated into a draft vision.

The final part of the workshop identified the actions that would be necessary to achieve the vision, again using the five capitals model as a framework. The workshop formed the first step in developing a vision for a sustainable NWL. This is now being refined, shared with stakeholders and communicated more widely. In parallel with establishing the vision, NWL is developing

a sustainable development policy and strategy by using the SIGMA Management Framework .

Lessons learned, potential for improvements and pitfalls to avoid are as follows:

- The ability of a group of people to think beyond their current priorities is critical for the success of the visioning approach.
- The effectiveness of visioning workshops is generally enhanced by external facilitation and by being away from the place of work.
- The initial input was important in creating a good understanding across the group of the five capitals and SIGMA guiding principles.
- The five capitals element of the SIGMA guiding principles provided a useful framework for visioning and provided some structure. The provision of information in advance meant that less time was spent explaining these principles and more time was spent on the vision for NWL.
- Workshops are a first step in creating a vision; the next steps are more challenging.

FURTHER INFORMATION
Northumbrian Water website: www.nwl.co.uk

RETHINKING BUSINESS: FROM BUILDING MATERIALS TO RESOURCE MANAGEMENT — RMC GROUP

THE RMC GROUP PLC IS A LEADING PRODUCER and supplier of aggregates and cement and is the largest manufacturer of ready-mixed concrete in the world. The Group has over 31,500 employees, operating in 27 countries. Through organic growth and acquisition it has become the world's fourth largest building material group, by annual turnover.

RMC UK Ltd (RMC) piloted the SIGMA Guidelines on behalf of RMC Group. RMC first produced a corporate environmental report in 1998 and a sustainable development report in 2001, which was updated the following year on the Internet.

The objective of RMC's SIGMA pilot project was to understand where and how enhancements could be made to a number of existing management systems and approaches by using the SIGMA Management Framework. The company has a very strong health and safety, quality and environmental management system culture, with various systems applied across the group in line with local conditions and priorities.

During The SIGMA Project pilot programme the focus for RMC was on the first two stages of the SIGMA Management Framework: the leadership and vision and planning phases. In particular, RMC used the SIGMA Management Framework to draw together its numerous strategic and tactical initiatives with sustainability considerations and to understand how they contributed to the overall business strategy. Strengths, weaknesses and the relationships between existing initiatives became clearer and helped to focus business planning activity.

To facilitate the pilot project internally, RMC developed a matrix to assess just how aligned companies within the Group were with sustainable development policy (on the business case matrix, see pages 87-88). This matrix was then used to compare:

- Sustainable development initiatives with business priorities, policies and RMC projects
- Stakeholder dialogue activities with RMC projects
- Sustainable development opportunities and risks

This enabled communication of how the sustainable development initiatives fit in with other initiatives.

As a result of the pilot project, RMC found the Management Framework helpful in providing a new clear and simple structure for the Group's strategic sustainability work. At the operational level, where RMC before had used many different approaches, SIGMA offered RMC the chance of aligning this diversity. This avoided the need to reinvent the wheel, saving time and money and aiding the integration with existing RMC sustainability structures.

RMC sees this as just a beginning; SIGMA has provided RMC with direction for the long-term, as Tim Pinder, their UK Environment Manager, explains:

> SIGMA has helped us to innovate; to look 20 years ahead and understand how our business can develop and become increasingly sustainable and accountable. In the future we hope to be viewed not only as a sustainable building materials producer but also as a resource management

business. This approach will present us with new commercial opportunities, and we are already developing new activities based on this long-term view.

RMC's top tips on using the SIGMA Management Framework are as follows:

- Alignment with existing management systems is essential.
- Time spent on a vision, on mapping and on future proofing is well repaid.
- Don't throw away existing management systems and approaches.
- Don't try to implement all parts at once; consider prioritising.
- Avoid jargon at all costs.
- Stakeholder engagement processes require careful planning.
- Choose carefully the company 'evangelists' who are to provide leadership (whether senior managers or individuals working at the operation level). These initiatives must have a high-level 'owner' overall to provide the leadership.
- Ensure effective internal communication and hold workshops to achieve 'buy-in' at all levels of the company.

FURTHER INFORMATION

RMC Group plc website: www.rmc-group.com

THE COMPASS

Wuppertal Institute

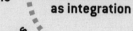

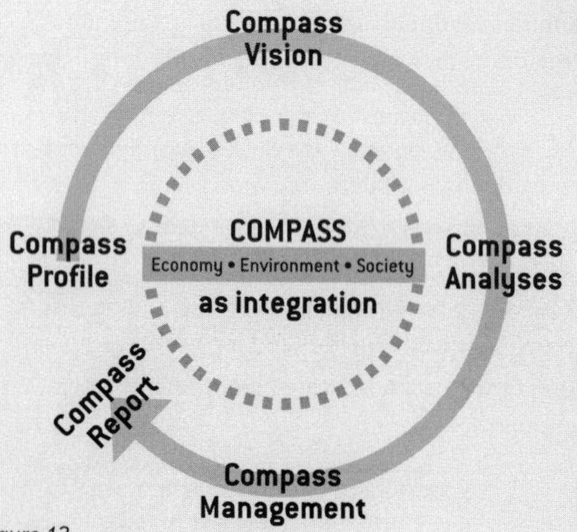

Figure 12

Source: M. Kuhndt and C. Liedtke, Wuppertal Institute

IN 1998 THE WUPPERTAL INSTITUTE'S

Eco-efficiency and Sustainable Enterprise Team defined a methodology named Compass (Companies' and Sectors' Path to Sustainability).

Compass aims to select — according to the 'plan–do–check–act' management cycle (the Deming cycle; see Chapter 3, page 57) — a set of indicators that drive and measure economic, social and environmental performance. Compass works for single companies and whole sectors. It supports a step-by-step understanding of the life cycle-wide impacts and stakeholder demands for different performance issues. The methodology provides information to enable decision-makers to optimise products and services towards a sustainable satisfaction of demand. Compass combines five elements:

- Compass aims to describe the state of knowledge about economic, social and environmental performance issues within the company or sector and the expectations of different stakeholders.

- Compass helps to develop a sustainability vision for the company or sector and to define goals and targets.

- Compass assists in the selection of a set of relevant indicators and explores performance measurement and benchmarking.

- Compass ensures the translation of the target set and indicators selected into decision-making processes by providing suitable management instruments.

- Compass prepares a communication plan that helps to report according to international standards and guidelines, such as those provided by the International Organisation for Standardisation (ISO, www.iso.org) and the Global Reporting Initiative (GRI, www.globalreporting.org), to internal or external stakeholders, on performance improvements and achievements.

In order to communicate aggregated results for internal decision-making processes, Compass, which provides a graphical illustration, can be used.

The Compass methodology can be adapted to the specific needs or sizes of corporations: for example, it can be applied in multinational organisations as well as in small and medium-sized enterprises (SMEs). It can be utilised at different strategic levels, such as strategic planning, product design or production.

According to the level of resources (financial, human, time) available to the company, the level of ambition in using the tool can be determined beforehand. In the case of limited resources, input from stakeholders can be collected from secondary resources, and collection of primary data via stakeholder surveys and workshops would provide more solid data for indicator development. Hence, Compass is a flexible, process-oriented tool.

Compass can also be used at levels beyond a single company. Collective action at the sectoral level can offer a better understanding of external demands and common problem areas, can develop cost-effective solutions and, eventually, can lead to innovation opportunities. However, the start-up of sector-level efforts can be a real challenge because of the difficulty of identifying priority areas, the difficulty of tracking performance in these areas and, most importantly, the difficulty of creating trust among the corporations.

FURTHER INFORMATION

Wuppertal Institute website: www.wupperinst.org

A STAKEHOLDER RADAR FOR THE EUROPEAN ALUMINIUM INDUSTRY

FOR THE EUROPEAN ALUMINIUM INDUSTRY,
Compass has been helpful in detecting and facilitating sector-wide sustainability improvements. Starting with the industry's ambition to improve the overall sustainability performance of the sector, the Wuppertal Institute has been carrying out a project — Towards a Sustainable Aluminium Industry — on behalf of the German Gesamtverband der Aluminiumindustrie (GDA) and the European Aluminium Association (EAA).

As a preliminary to a vision, Compass was used to compare the views of external stakeholders with those of a number of industry insiders. The graphical representation as a radar (see Figure 13) enabled the visualisation of 'hot issues' and perception gaps between internal and external stakeholders before moving to the formulation of a vision for change towards sustainable development.

FURTHER INFORMATION

Aluminium Industry Project website:
www.oekoeffizienz.de/english/content/agzu/index.html

Figure 13 COMPASS STAKEHOLDER RADAR FOR THE EUROPEAN ALUMINIUM INDUSTRY

ENVIRONMENTAL ISSUES

SOCIAL ISSUES

ECONOMIC ISSUES

Index: 0 = not relevant
3 = highly important

Stakeholder views: Internal
External

Route Map

Type of resource: publication

Author organisation: WWF-UK

Year of publication: 2001

This publication from WWF-UK is an example of a partnership project between a conservation non-governmental organisation (NGO), WWF-UK, and a global Internet and data services company, Cable & Wireless. They researched and produced a guide for creating the business case for sustainable development. One chapter in particular is pertinent to the start of a vision as well as to a number of elements of the performance model. The Route Map guides senior managers to ways that can create and conserve value while avoiding responses that limit or destroy value. It identifies six steps:

- Step I: identify significant impacts.
- Step II: identify key issues.
- Step III: establish sources of potential threat and opportunity.
- Step IV: identify and prioritise proposed actions.
- Step V: highlight actions with strategic implications.
- Step VI: determine preferred actions for inclusion in a business case.

The first three steps correlate well with the vision element. The final three steps correlate well with leadership decisions.

FURTHER INFORMATION

Publication: WWF-UK, 'Route Map', in *To Whose Profit?* (Godalming, Surrey, UK: WWF-UK, 2001)

Publication online: www.wwf-uk.org/filelibrary/pdf/towhoseprofit.pdf

Self-regulation in the Workplace

Type of resource: publication

Author organisation: International Labour Organisation

Year of publication: 2001

This is an International Labour Organisation (ILO) paper on codes of conduct, social labelling and socially responsible investment. The purpose of the paper is to provide information on recent trends in the area of voluntary initiatives. It first examines the general context within which voluntary private initiatives are developing, the actors involved and the institutional context. The paper then focuses on the three major issues:

- Codes of conduct
- Social labelling
- Investment initiatives

The section on codes of conduct is based on a review of 258 codes collected from multinational enterprises, employers' organisations and trade unions, governments, non-governmental organisations (NGOs) and academic institutions. It looks at the labour issues covered by the codes, considers questions of implementation and monitoring, tries to extrapolate important sectoral trends and considers the relationship between codes and national standards. Next, social labelling programmes are examined, concentrating on their origins, characteristics, content, structure and effectiveness. The paper then examines the area of investment and discusses socially responsible investment initiatives such as shareholder initiatives and investment screens. The final section concerns the ILO position on voluntary private initiatives.

FURTHER INFORMATION

International Labour Organisation (ILO) website: www.ilo.org

Publication: www.ilo.org/dyn/empent/docs/F1936481553/1_mcc_wp.pdf

Values in Action: Formalising Your Company's Values

Type of resource: publication

Author organisation: Business for Social Responsibility

Year of publication: 2001

Many forward-thinking businesses are defining and implementing company values in formal business principles. Business principles can take the form of corporate policies, mission and value statements, or codes of conduct and can help guide day-to-day operations, decision-making and strategic planning. This document from Business for Social Responsibility (BSR) briefly outlines trends, highlights emerging best practice and suggests concrete steps to consider if you are one of those working to incorporate values into every aspect of your business.

FURTHER INFORMATION

Business for Social Responsibility (BSR) website: www.bsr.org

Sustainable Development Opportunity and Risk Guide

Type of resource: publication

Author organisation: The SIGMA Project

Year of publication: 2003

The SIGMA Sustainable Development Opportunity and Risk Guide provides a flexible process to allow organisations to identify, assess and manage opportunities and risks relating to sustainable development. It helps organisations to identify where there are strong links between some aspects of risk and opportunity assessment and many other management needs, such as procurement processes, health and safety assessments and sustainable marketing processes.

As many organisations already have risk management processes in place, the guide seeks to enhance and integrate these processes rather than trying to create a new layer of risk and opportunity management.

The guide is not intended to be a comprehensive risk and opportunity management approach — more an introduction to the topic that provides useful and practical guidance to a range of non-specialists within an organisation.

FURTHER INFORMATION

The SIGMA Project website: www.projectsigma.com

SIGMA Sustainability Scorecard

Type of resource: publication

Author organisation: The SIGMA Project

Year of publication: 2003

The SIGMA Sustainability Scorecard draws from the traditional balanced scorecard by using a driver model that links the different aspects of organisational performance. It therefore strengthens an organisation's understanding of its own operations and supports decision-making. However, the SIGMA Scorecard makes two key revisions to the traditional model. It adopts a sustainability perspective (triple bottom line) rather than a financial perspective (single bottom line) and a stakeholder rather than a customer perspective.

The SIGMA scorecard measures the company from four perspectives of management performance:

- Sustainability perspective
- External stakeholder perspective
- Internal perspective
- Knowledge and skills perspective

FURTHER INFORMATION

The SIGMA Project website: www.projectsigma.com

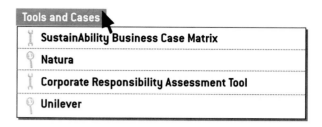
CHAPTER SIX

LEADERSHIP DECISIONS

I don't spend a lot of time talking about vision; I focus on leadership reality. To me, leadership reality is vision, grounded. Sustainability is such a grand and noble vision that people can subscribe to it and then go about business as usual, never making it a reality. At DuPont we've grounded the vision of sustainability in the reality of real activity and performance measures that tell us whether or not we are moving in that direction.

The biggest challenge any leader faces is what will be the first step — what action will you take?

So advises DuPont's chair and CEO Chad Holliday.[1] There is little to add.

Leadership is to know what is important, what comes first. To ground a vision, a company needs leadership at all levels. Leadership is not a function of a unique person. It is everyone's responsibility, at various times, to take the lead, inspire others and create positive change towards the vision.

It is both important and appears disarmingly simple: you have this shared ambition of a highly desirable future — your vision — and you have

current reality. Your most important decision is to select the first, second and other steps to bring you from current reality to the vision. This is your call and the call of your colleagues.

Mads Øvlisen, chair of Novo Nordisk's board, comments:[2]

Leadership is so personal. In most cases, there are no books to open, no databases to check; you simply have to use your judgment, your basic values in determining what is the right thing to do.

In line with this view we have chosen to avoid the tools that address the art and skills of leadership. There may well be too many books — a major online bookstore offered more than 50,000 titles with the words *leadership* and/or *leaders* in the title! But we think that we can help leaders to decide on their priorities. We therefore suggest a number of tools and examples that can assist in the context of the Global Compact, by assessing the current situation and so enabling decisions about urgent steps and opportunities. The tools that follow have

---

1 C.O. Holliday, Jr, S. Schmidheiny and P. Watts, *Walking the Talk: The Business Case for Sustainable Development* (Sheffield, UK: Greenleaf Publishing, 2002): 129.

2 M. Øvlisen, 'The Importance of Being Mad', *Perspective: The International Magazine for Novo Nordisk Stakeholders*, November 2003 (Corporate Communications, Novo Nordisk A/S, Novo Allé 2880 Bagsværd, Denmark): 4.

been developed in recent years. Many are derived from other integrated assessment tools that help in priority-setting, such as the 'balanced scorecard' or the older SWOT (strengths–weaknesses– opportunities–threats) analysis.

Leaders also need to be clear about the importance of doing things the *right* way, and of being in tune with the accepted codes and culture of their social environment. The major codes relevant to human rights, labour and environmental issues are collected in the Information and Resources section at the end of Chapter 1 (pages 38-42) to provide an explicit background of the universally accepted principles bundled into the Global Compact.

Although we promote the view that in excellent organisations a large number of employees live up to the quality of leadership and create change to move the organisation closer to the vision, we do not underestimate the critical role of top management. If top management does not campaign relentlessly for the vision, set clear signals of priorities and behave as a role model, change will slow down and the organisation will return to business as usual.

THE BUSINESS CASE MATRIX

SustainAbility, the United Nations Environment Programme, the International Finance Corporation and Instituto Ethos

IN A SERIES OF PUBLICATIONS,

SustainAbility, the United Nations Environment Programme (UNEP), the International Finance Corporation (IFC) and Instituto Ethos have developed a basic 'business case framework' to help companies uncover hidden value.[3] The framework is intended to highlight how separate 'sustainability factors' can improve business success. It distinguishes seven sustainability factors:

- **Governance and management:** concerning the management systems that underpin a company's sustainability performance as well as its governance structures
- **Stakeholder engagement:** involving consulting with business and non-business stakeholders on key sustainability issues facing the company
- **Environmental products and services:** involving reducing the environmental impacts associated with the use (rather than the production) of products and services (also called 'product stewardship' or 'design for environment')
- **Environmental process improvement:** involving producing the same level of output with fewer resources and less waste (also called 'eco-efficiency')
- **Local economic growth:** focusing on processes for ensuring that companies share the benefits from their investment activity with local businesses and provide tools for economic growth in local communities
- **Community development:** going beyond economic growth, involving supporting the development of health, education, water provision, sanitation, human rights and other positive impacts in the community
- **Human resource management:** concerning the conditions under which employees work, the benefits they receive and their opportunities for development

These impact on the six most important 'business success factors':

- Revenue growth and market access
- Cost savings and productivity

continued over ➜

---

3 SustainAbility and United Nations Environment Programme, *Buried Treasure: Uncovering the Business Case for Corporate Sustainability* (London: SustainAbility, 2001); SustainAbility, International Finance Corporation (IFC) and Instituto Ethos, *Developing Value: The Business Case for Sustainability in Emerging Markets* (London: SustainAbility; Washington, DC: IFC, 2002).

THE BUSINESS CASE MATRIX

TOOL

Figure 14 THE BUSINESS CASE MATRIX: WHERE SUSTAINABILITY FACTORS ENHANCE BUSINESS SUCCESS

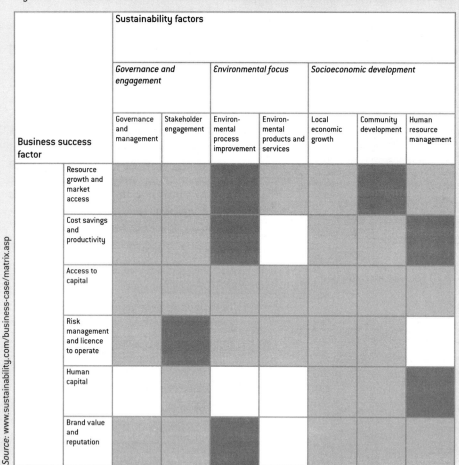

Source: www.sustainability.com/business-case/matrix.asp

Key. Level of evidence of a positive impact of each sustainability factor on each business success factor:

■ = strong   ▨ = limited   □ = none

- Access to capital
- Risk management and licence to operate
- Human capital
- Brand value and reputation

The full business case matrix is based on an analysis of 240 cases from 176 companies. It shows where there is strong (dark grey), limited (light grey) or no (white) evidence of a positive impact of each sustainability factor on each business success factor (see Figure 14).

Whether companies are interested in 'doing the right thing' or just improving their chances of business success, the business case matrix is intended to illustrate how good social and environmental performance connects to strong financial performance and reveal where the strongest 'win–win' opportunities are likely to be.

For companies just starting out in this area, the matrix can be used to identify which sustainability actions are most likely to deliver value in line with internal business priorities and programmes. Companies investing in new infrastructure, for example, will find that stakeholder engagement is likely to be a critical issue in their overall approach to risk management and protecting the company's licence to operate. For others, where the priority is building brand value and reputation, the matrix points strongly towards investing in environmental process improvements.

For many of the cells in the business case matrix, there is still only limited information available. Nonetheless, what information there is suggests a significant financial value in improving various aspects of social and environmental performance.

FURTHER INFORMATION

SustainAbility website: www.sustainability.com

Matrix: www.sustainability.com/business-case/matrix.asp

DEVELOPING A BUSINESS CASE AT NATURA, BRAZIL

FOUNDED IN 1969, NATURA SELLS COSMETICS, personal hygiene products, perfumes and nutritional supplements throughout Latin America. Sales in 2001 were 1.66 billion reals (US$630 million), an increase of 14% over the previous year. At the beginning of 2002 Natura employed 3,100 people directly and had 286,000 sales consultants in Brazil.

Natura believes that investing in the quality of all its relationships is fundamental to creating a united enterprise, attracting and maintaining professional talent, establishing constructive dialogue with communities and achieving consistent economic results.

Launched in 2000, the Natura Ekos line of hygiene and beauty products is based on natural Brazilian flora extracted in a sustainable manner by local people. Natura uses in its products many raw materials found in nature, such as flowers, fruits, seeds and vegetable oils. It works in partnership with the non-governmental organisation (NGO) ImaFlora to ensure that the extraction of these materials is performed in an environmentally sustainable and socially fair way, in accordance with Forest Stewardship Council (www.fscoax.org) principles for sustainable management of forests.

Another environmental initiative is support for environmental restoration projects in the 650 hectare Fazenda Bulcão and of the Pomar project, which promotes restoration of polluted areas on the banks of the Pinheiros River.

Natura is also heavily involved in social projects, with an amount equal to 10% of shareholders' dividends invested in social programmes each year.

For example, since 2000, product labels are printed at Laramara, an institution that cares for visually impaired people. Natura has also developed a programme with the Abrinq Foundation — an NGO that promotes the rights of the child — called Seeing is Believing. The proceeds from a line of special products support the development of educational projects involving 3,600 schools and 768,000 children in Brazil. A total of 9 million reals (US$3.4 million) has been invested since the start of the programme in 1995.

Natura believes it has benefited from:

- Increased skills and motivation (human capital)
- Improved ability to attract and keep employees
- Increased brand value and reputation, demonstrated by a high ranking in assessments by Ethos and the Good Citizenship Guide, prepared by *Exame* and *Carta Capital* magazines
- Consumer loyalty and willingness to pay a price premium (an annual study of Natura consumers has found that the company's social responsibility is regarded as its most important attribute)
- Better evaluation from financial institutions

FURTHER INFORMATION

Natura website: www.natura.net/relatorio [in Portuguese and Spanish]

SustainAbility website: www.sustainability.com

CORPORATE RESPONSIBILITY ASSESSMENT TOOL

The Conference Board of Canada and the Canadian Centre for Philanthropy

THE CORPORATE RESPONSIBILITY ASSESSMENT

(CRA) tool is a comprehensive web-enabled management system for corporate responsibility, designed to help companies manage, measure, improve and report on their corporate responsibility practices and performance.

The Conference Board of Canada and the Canadian Centre for Philanthropy worked with a number of companies and practitioners on the CRA tool. By using the tool, companies can benchmark and report their performance against a set of practices derived from sources such as the UN Global Compact, the Guidelines for Multinational Enterprises of the Organisation for Economic Cooperation and Development (OECD), the Dow Jones Sustainability Index, the Global Reporting Initiative and the Tripartite Declaration of Principles Concerning Multinational Enterprises and Social Policy of the International Labour Organisation (ILO).[4]

The survey data are organised into five 'pillars':

- Governance and management practices
- Human resources management
- Community investment and involvement
- Environment, health and safety
- Human rights

Through the CRA tool, a company can focus on enhancing its relationship with stakeholders, measuring and tracking performance data and internalising performance information for continuous learning and improvement. The information collected through this internal assessment process provides management with a clearer understanding of how the company's practices compare with public expectations for responsible behaviour. In addition, companies can automatically produce detailed or summary reports for individual sections or for the entire assessment.

The tool includes a comprehensive, online knowledge centre and e-learning capability to provide companies with the latest information on corporate responsibility and voluntary codes.

The CRA tool is a packaged product. When purchased, users receive customer and technical support, a training workshop and a number of licences. The cost is based on company size and position within the Fortune 500 or equivalent index. Purchase prices range from US$8,000 to US$16,000 (prices correct at time of publication).

The CRA tool is fully customisable and can be altered to include company-specific or industry-specific codes of conduct. In its current format it is more applicable to large companies.

FURTHER INFORMATION

Website: www.crtool.com

---

4   For more details on the OECD Guidelines and the ILO Tripartite Declaration, see pages 41 and 39. For more details of the Dow Jones Sustainability Index and the Global Reporting Initiative, see Chapter 15.

LEADERS INTO ACTION: UNILEVER

UNILEVER IS A BRANDED CONSUMER PRODUCTS company operating in around 100 countries. Setting itself ambitious targets for business success, the company pursues its goals guided by clear values and a commitment to social responsibility that are set out in its Code of Business Principles. Central to meeting and sustaining these targets is a recognition that its people need a passion for winning and a culture that encourages and rewards enterprise.

Developing leadership competence that supports and develops this culture, across all levels of the business, is core to such empowerment in Unilever. This is a shared responsibility between leaders and their teams and is now fully integrated into company communications, training and reward schemes.

Unilever's intranet, company magazine and corporate publications provide continuous information about leadership competence initiatives and opportunities. They demonstrate commitment and engagement among senior management while providing information and access to personal development programmes for people at all levels in the company.

Leadership development training includes a focus on learning by experience. Activities in some programmes range from smaller practical tasks to stretch each individual's skill base, to setting up large-scale community service projects. It recognises that the leaders of tomorrow will need to be very different from the leaders of the past — that business success requires leaders doing things for others including the communities in which the company operates. It also requires a sense of community and the need to bring out the best in different people.

Leader and team performance calls for a high level of motivation. In this regard, opportunities to align business and personal values are actively pursued, providing scope to develop enterprise skills and explore new avenues for personal achievement.

For example, through Unilever's engagement in the global Living Lakes Network, marketers in Unilever Canada have worked in partnership with conservationists in British Columbia to develop a brand strategy for the East Kootenay Environment Society (EKES), which works to protect the Columbia River Wetland — North America's longest pristine wetland. Developing the marketing strategy for this environmental movement provided a rare opportunity for Unilever people to create a brand from scratch. At the same time, EKES have gained insight into how to communicate their work effectively at the national and international levels. The experience has raised motivation among the Unilever team and its associates and has opened the eyes of team members on to how to realise their full team potential.

Through an annual Leadership Growth Journey, Unilever's chairpeople engage with high-potential managers on a journey of personal discovery. In preparation for the journey, participants, including the chairpeople, spend two days 'getting into the skin' of someone else — living a life totally different from their own — often working with severely disadvantaged people. This is followed by a week of physical challenge in a remote location where they have time to reflect on their lives and personal goals and discuss these with the chairpeople.

At operating company level, the local chairpeople and their boards are fully empowered to develop and implement diverse initiatives contributing to society and environment. Examples are: a packaging recycling scheme in Brazil, the Lifebuoy Friendship Hospital in Bangladesh, the Unilever Foundation for Education in Ghana, reduced transport emissions in the United Kingdom, the Netherlands and Italy, and the protection of wildlife and the promotion of biodiversity in tea plantations in India.

Through these empowerment initiatives, Unilever hopes to nurture leadership competences that recognise the importance of societal engagement to future business success.

FURTHER INFORMATION

Website: www.unilever.com/environmentsociety

Tomorrow's Markets: Global Trends and their Implications for Business

Type of resource: publication

Author organisations: World Resources Institute, World Business Council for Sustainable Development, and United Nations Environment Programme

Year of publication: 2002

Although the future is always uncertain, probable market scenarios are bounded by global trends. *Tomorrow's Markets*, a joint publication from the World Resources Institute (WRI), the World Business Council for Sustainable Development (WBCSD) and the United Nations Environment Programme (UNEP), identifies the trends that are shaping a new 'market-scape' — the landscape through which business must navigate to succeed. The features of the market-scape continue to be dominated by business fundamentals such as competitive advantage, price, product channels, cost of capital and operating costs, but the pathways to market success are increasingly signposted by indicators of environmental and social performance. Each topic is presented in a succinct, lively format that can be easily adapted for business use.

FURTHER INFORMATION

World Resources Institute website: www.wri.org

United Nations Environment Programme website: www.uneptie.org

World Business Council for Sustainable Development website: www.wbcsd.org

Document: www.wbcsd.org/DocRoot/NomqBWD9ZafICkslurQQ/ tomorrows-markets.pdf

CHAPTER SEVEN

EMPOWERMENT FOR IMPLEMENTATION

FACED WITH THE CHALLENGE OF CHANGE, some organisations stand out and perform better than others. It is people who make that difference. Every organisation is, first of all, a community of people who cooperate towards common objectives. Performance therefore depends on how the organisation releases the full potential of its people and enhances their cooperation and alignment with the vision and the priorities defined by the leadership.

Many performance models call this element 'people management'. We prefer to use the term 'empowerment'. This term may sound faddish; but it implies a notion that in responding to the challenges of sustainable development and corporate citizenship no one has all the answers. In order to make progress, the creativity of each individual must be stimulated and nurtured.

In studying new organisational designs, Russell Ackoff, professor emeritus at the Wharton School, University of Pennsylvania, observed:

> Because, today, most employees in corporations do their jobs better than their bosses can, the

traditional notion of management as supervision of subordinates must be abandoned. Instead, managers have a responsibility for creating working conditions under which their subordinates can function as well as they know how. This requires that their subordinates have a great deal more freedom to work as they want than they have had up to now.[1]

This freedom is what empowerment is about. Professor Jamshid Gharajedaghi,[2] a close associate of Ackoff's at Wharton, proposes that power should be viewed in the same way as knowledge — it can be delegated without being lost. Front-line employees are empowered to innovate and make sound decisions in complex business situations as long as they share the same decision criteria. Although it is impossible to plan in advance the specific solutions to every possible real-life business

---

1 R.L. Ackoff, *Re-creating the Corporation: A Design of Organisations for the 21st Century* (New York: Oxford University Press, 1999): 287.
2 J. Gharajedaghi, *Systems Thinking: Managing Chaos and Complexity, A Platform for Designing Business Architecture* (Boston, MA: Butterworth Heinemann, 1999).

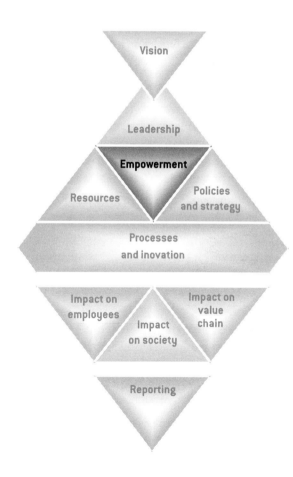

situation, it is important for performance that everyone understands why the company has set its priorities and how it generally wants them accomplished. This is why, as we will see in the next chapter, it is critical to be explicit about policies and strategies.

Empowerment is based on a set of critical success factors:

- **Training and learning.** Employees are involved in training or learning sessions that help them understand and discuss the vision and leadership priorities.

- **Dialogue and listening.** Employees are invited to provide input on specific strategies and policies. A learning process is a two-way road. It stimulates the individual and creates collective initiative.

- **Personal and team objectives.** Employees translate the leadership priorities into specific objectives for their team and themselves.

- **Rewards for performance.** Performance and breakthroughs are rapidly rewarded and communicated, with a preference for team rewards. Mistakes are also accepted as opportunities for trying and learning. Career progression recognises skills for leadership and teamwork.

- **Recruitment profile.** Recruitment looks for employees who, in addition to having the required professional skills, provide evidence of values and experience aligned with the purpose of the organisation.

- **A spirit of partnership.** A top-down hierarchical structure is replaced by a purpose-centred organisation that lives up to its principles, vision and priorities in ways that are adapted to the diverse cultures and environments of its employees.

The UN Global Compact principles and the pursuit of sustainable development introduce a massive set of concepts that are not yet part of most professional education programmes. The Global Compact resource package, the Global Compact Primer, offers ideas on how to include this information into existing management courses.[3] Here, we present a number of training modules that aid empowerment 'on the job' — some directly, through the wider application of labour and human rights, and some indirectly, through the empowerment of employees to implement the broader corporate social responsibility agenda throughout their companies.

---

3 For more information on the Global Compact Primer, see page 38.

CHRONOS E-LEARNING TUTORIAL

World Business Council for Sustainable Development and
University of Cambridge Programme for Industry

COMPANY VISIONS, PRINCIPLES AND POLICIES

play an important role in sustainable development, but more is needed to move sustainable development into the heart of the organisation — its employees. To respond to this need the World Business Council for Sustainable Development (WBCSD) developed CHRONOS, a concise, motivational, e-learning tutorial on the business case for sustainable development.

CHRONOS is designed to make sustainable development relevant and meaningful to the everyday practice of employees, equipping them with the knowledge they need to deliver on corporate priorities. Its success will be judged by the degree of reflection it causes among employees, the number of conversations it inspires and the amount of enthusiasm it creates for exploration and action on sustainable development.

The product is an easy-to-navigate, self-guided tool that is:

- **Learner-focused.** Personal initiative is valued above expert 'answers', and experience is valued above memorisation.
- **Challenging.** Positive opportunities for individuals and companies to contribute to society and to create business value are highlighted.

- **Inclusive.** Inspiration comes from a wide range of voices, both business and non-business.
- **Flexible.** Available on the Internet, and soon to be joined by versions for CD-ROM and corporate intranets, it can be deployed by itself or as an accompaniment to other learning methods, reinforcing existing programmes and deepening the impact on employees.
- **Appealing.** A range of training methods are drawn on to appeal to individual learning styles.

CHRONOS provides a foundation on which further layers of learning can be built. It is not a total learning solution: for it to be successful, it needs to be integrated into the learning strategy of a company, and individual learners need to be supported and guided and their expectations managed.

Although currently available in English only, a Spanish version is under development and future translations are planned.

The tool takes approximately three hours to complete, although it has eight hours of embedded learning for those who wish to return at a later stage. If used as recommended, in a blended learning environment, completion will take longer.

CHRONOS provides an introduction to the business case for sustainable development — it is not for the sustainability expert. In reality, every employee — not just the company's leaders and specialists — needs to make the link between sustainable development and business value. The target audience for CHRONOS will depend on the company's position and strategy on sustainable development.

CHRONOS can be customised to suit the specific needs of individual companies. Shell, together with CPI and the WBCSD, tailored the contents to include: in-house case studies, the adoption of 'Shell language', and the incorporation of links to Shell resources. Prices range from US$80 for a single user, to increasingly lower unit costs in variable-quantity packs, ranging from five to 100,000 packs. WBCSD members and not-for-profit groups receive a 50% discount.

FURTHER INFORMATION

Website: www.sdchronos.org

TOOL

GLOBAL COMPACT TRAINING MATERIAL ON THE FOUR LABOUR PRINCIPLES

International Labour Organisation, Multinational Enterprises Programme

THE TRAINING MATERIALS ON THE LABOUR

principles of the UN Global Compact were completed in 2003 by the International Labour Organisation (ILO) in response to an increased demand for educational materials regarding the Global Compact principles. The objectives of the training materials are twofold: to convey to managers that it is in their own interest to undertake activities that support the labour principles of the Global Compact and to ensure that they fully understand and can therefore implement the principles within their companies.

The Global Compact training programme on the four principles is:

- **Action-oriented.** The contents of the manual are based on the day-to-day experiences of companies dealing with the principles. The business principles and methods imparted in this programme benefit from problems and solutions found to work within companies.

- **Direct and participatory.** It promotes hands-on learning and encourages constant sharing and interaction among participants, who benefit from one another's experiences and ideas.

- **Focused on developing knowledge and skills together.** It focuses on knowledge about

fundamental principles and rights at work and, at the same time, teaches skills and techniques to apply these principles and rights within companies.

- **Adaptable.** The training materials have been designed as a flexible tool that can fit different situations, different types of manager and different national contexts.

The training materials are composed of four modules and various action-planning exercises. All modules integrate lectures, group work on case studies, exercises and discussions. The modules are as follows:

- **Module 1: Introduction.** This module focuses on the history, objectives and current activities of the Global Compact.

- **Module 2: Why should you care?** This module demonstrates why it is important to undertake initiatives that support the Global Compact and, in particular, its four labour principles.

- **Module 3: What do the principles mean?** This module is designed to ensure that participants understand the meaning of the four labour principles, including their origins.

- **Module 4: From principles to practice.** This module gives participants an understanding of how

the principles can be implemented practically within their company. It primarily uses case studies to demonstrate what other companies have done.

The modules can be delivered independently of each other or combined to offer a full course on the Global Compact labour principles. The ILO is currently working on training trainers who can offer the materials to companies. More specifically, the ILO is conducting training at the following levels:

- Training trainers in national employer organisations
- Training trainers in business schools
- Training managers in companies, who can go back and train and implement the programme in their own company or through the company's supply chain

The ILO also conducts a limited number of training courses with groups of companies to allow for ongoing development of the materials.

FURTHER INFORMATION

Website: www.ilo.org/multi

IMPROVE YOUR BUSINESS. BASICS: PEOPLE AND PRODUCTIVITY

International Labour Organisation, Small Enterprise Development

This training manual is designed for owners and managers of small businesses in developing countries.

As part of the 'improve your business' (IYB) management training programme, the 'people-and-productivity' module links productivity with basic human resource management practices, the working environment and relations with the community. It promotes good working conditions, as well as some of the principles enshrined in the core standards of the International Labour Organisation (ILO), by relating them to what matters most to the entrepreneur — business success. Through stories, action plans, exercises and easy-to-understand illustrations, the manager of a small business is introduced to these issues in a simple and practical way.

The 'people-and-productivity' module includes a trainee's and a trainer's manual, as well as a video. It uses an active, problem-centred learning approach to small business management. The following areas are explored in greater detail:

- Linking people and productivity
- Influencing productivity
- Recruiting productive people
- Encouraging staff productivity
- A safe and productive workplace
- Troubled employees
- Business relations and productivity

The IYB programme — including the six other modules, focusing on different parts of the small business — aims to make small businesses more viable, so contributing to job creation. It originates from a programme developed by the Swedish Employer's Confederation for Swedish small-scale entrepreneurs. The methods and materials were adapted by the ILO to meet the needs of people running small businesses in developing countries. The ILO has enabled organisations, consultants and companies in some 70 developing countries to provide training on the basis of these teaching materials.

FURTHER INFORMATION

International Labour Organisation (ILO) website: www.ilo.org/seed

Publication and video: contact your local ILO office or email vejs@ilo.org

TOOL

ENVIRONMENTAL MANAGEMENT SYSTEMS: TRAINING RESOURCE KIT

United Nations Environment Programme, International Federation of Consulting Engineers, International Chamber of Commerce

AN ENVIRONMENTAL MANAGEMENT SYSTEM

(EMS) is a method of incorporating environmental care throughout an organisation. It is a problem-identification and problem-solving tool, based on the concept of continual improvement, that can be implemented in an organisation in many different ways, depending on the sector of activity and the needs perceived by management. Key elements in an EMS are:

- The undertaking of an initial environmental review
- The definition of an environmental policy
- The development of an environmental action plan and definition of environmental responsibilities
- The development of internal information and training courses
- An audit of the EMS and the conducting of an environmental management review

The EMS training resource kit developed by the United Nations Environment Programme (UNEP), the International Federation of Consulting Engineers (FIDIC) and the International Chamber of Commerce (ICC) is a practical guide to EMSs designed as a 'train-the-trainer' tool to give trainers and company managers the materials necessary to conduct courses in EMSs for companies. Special attention is given to the structure and elements of an EMS that are in common with the EMS standard ISO 14001 of the International

Organisation for Standardisation (ISO). However, the kit goes beyond this standard by giving instructions on how to report on a company's environmental performance and how to integrate the EMS with other systems such as health and safety, and chemicals management.

The materials in the kit have been designed for a variety of training activities. These can take the form of short seminars held over two days, a series of weekly or monthly evening sessions, or training linked to ongoing consultancy advice in the drawing-up and implementation of an EMS within an individual enterprise.

The kit includes examples of an initial environmental review protocol, an EMS audit protocol and case studies. Its 'A–Z of EMS' covers the following:

- An initial environmental review
- The definition of an environmental policy
- The development of an environmental action plan
- The definition of environmental responsibilities
- The definition of environmental procedures
- Training and internal information
- The EMS audit and the management review
- External communication.

The kit, which is available in 15 languages, is complemented by the UNEP/ICC/FIDIC EMS handbook and a guide to ISO 14001 for certification and

registration, making it a perfect tool for practical implementation of an EMS and ISO 14001 registration.

The EMS handbook is intended to be used by participants on training seminars organised by using the EMS training resource kit. The handbook's central feature is a step-by-step checklist, followed by more detailed information on the purpose and objectives of each step and by a series of fact sheets on global environmental issues, for rapid consultation. Like the EMS kit, the handbook can be used as a stand-alone guide or as a training resource.

The ISO 14001 guide is intended for organisations developing their EMS to a level that will enable certification to ISO 14001. The user-friendly guide describes the requirements of ISO 14001, discusses the necessary documents and records, and provides guidance on the various requirements for certification. In addition, it outlines the philosophy behind ISO 14001.

FURTHER INFORMATION

United Nations Environment Programme website: www.uneptie.org

International Federation of Consulting Engineers website: www.fidic.org

International Chamber of Commerce website: www.iccwbo.org

International Organisation for Standardisation website: www.iso.org

Publications: www.earthprint.com

ENVIRONMENTAL MANAGEMENT NAVIGATOR FOR SMALL AND MEDIUM-SIZED ENTERPRISES

Wuppertal Institute, InWEnt, United Nations Environment Programme, United Nations Industrial Development Organisation

THE WUPPERTAL INSTITUTE HAS DEVELOPED a capacity-building package on environmental management tools, the Environmental

Figure 15 WHICH ENVIRONMENTAL MANAGEMENT TOOLS? A NAVIGATOR FOR SMEs

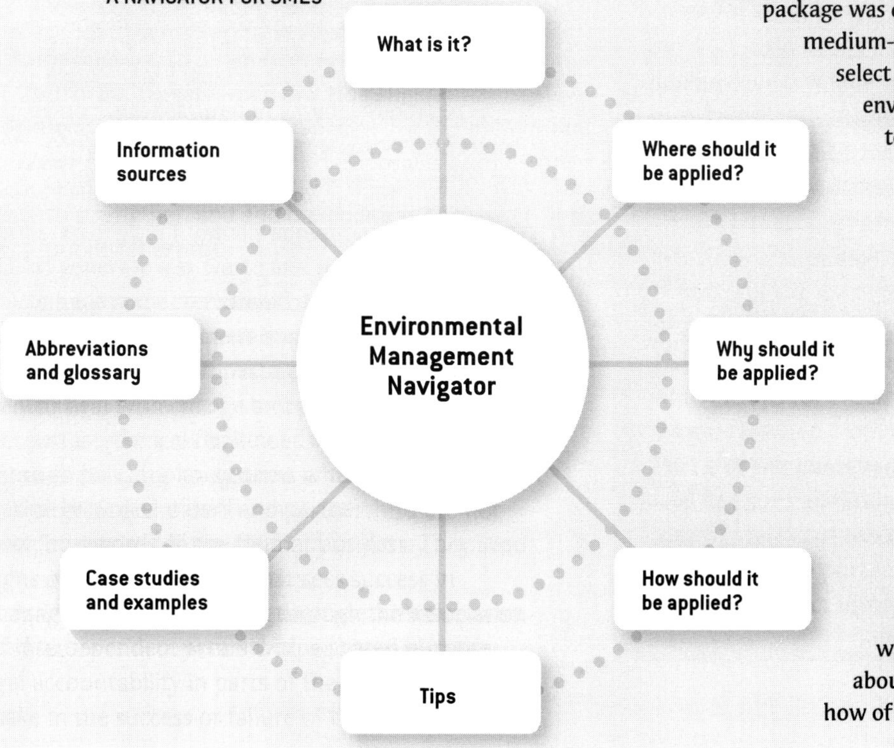

- What is it?
- Where should it be applied?
- Why should it be applied?
- How should it be applied?
- Tips
- Case studies and examples
- Abbreviations and glossary
- Information sources

Environmental Management Navigator

Management Navigator (see Figure 15), on behalf of InWEnt (Internationale Weiterbildung und Entwicklung gemeinnützige GmbH), the United Nations Environment Programme (UNEP) and the United Nations Industrial Development Organisation (UNIDO). The package was devised to help small and medium-sized enterprises (SMEs) select the most suitable environmental management tools according to their internal organisational and external market demands.

The navigator provides a step-by-step guide to tools such as environmental management systems (EMSs), environmental performance evaluation, full-cost accounting, green supply chain management and many more, using the 'knowledge wheel'. Readers of the guide will learn what each tool is about and the where, why and how of applying it. Also featured are 'tips for action', case studies and details of sources of further information.

Available as a handbook for capacity-building, the navigator is suitable for intermediary parties — those positioned between the concept developers and businesses in developing countries or in countries in transition — in order to provide them with guidance on SME training. Such intermediaries include consultants, environmental advisers, organisations bringing together representatives from industry or industry stakeholders, academics and cleaner production specialists. The length and content of the training package can be customised to the needs of the business, but are recommended as 2 day or 3.5 day sessions. All training modules are included in the handbook as PowerPoint presentations.

The navigator has been used for 'train-the-trainer' workshops in Germany, and trainees have further used the material for extended local workshops, in Brazil, Colombia, Cuba, Morocco, Peru, India and Vietnam among others.

FURTHER INFORMATION

Website: www.em-navigator.net

Wuppertal Institute: www.wupperinst.org

TOOL

SUPPLY CHAIN TRAINING

Business for Social Responsibility

BUSINESS FOR SOCIAL RESPONSIBILITY

(BSR) has developed labour-rights training for consumer goods manufacturers producing under contract for multinational enterprises. Excerpts of this training are available on the BSR website.

The objectives of this training are to enhance the awareness of suppliers concerning the application of internationally accepted labour rights principles as well as of applicable laws and codes of conduct consistent with international principles. In addition to awareness raising, the training workshops are designed to provide practical knowledge, tools and resources to implement management policies that promote the fair treatment of workers producing goods being sold in the international marketplace. The training is intended to enhance local capacity to ensure that global supply chains are operated consistent with international principles.

The training is designed to be highly functional. It consists of a mixture of classroom discussions, group exercises and, on occasion, an in-factory module. Participants in the workshops receive tools and information that can be used or adapted for use in conducting self-assessments or creating management policies and practices that enable workers and management to work collaboratively to improve working conditions along the supply chain.

Information and tools provided in these workshops, which have been conducted in more than 20 countries globally, have been identified by participants as having improved their ability to understand and implement the labour-rights principles contained in the UN Global Compact.

Specifically, the workshops usually incorporate the following subject matter:

- The importance of global labour standards

- Information on locally applicable principles

- The business benefits of applying labour standards

- Details of wage and hour principles

- Health and safety

- Labour issues (e.g. child labour, freedom of association and collective bargaining, forced labour, non-discrimination and non-harassment)

- Emerging issues (e.g. migrant labour, and women's health)

- Stakeholder dialogue

- Management practices to promote corporate social responsibility (CSR)

A potential limitation of the tool is the reach of the workshops. Improper labour conditions violating recognised principles may arise from any one of a number of staff, and the workshops do not reach all the managers and supervisors who would benefit from the information offered. In addition, there remains a gap between the availability of local trainers and local needs.

The training itself takes place over one or two days — a substantial amount of time for a busy manager, but not generally excessive. The real commitment comes not during the workshop but afterwards, as the lessons and materials offered in the workshops are incorporated into factory practices. This too will depend on the degree to which changes are suggested by the learning that takes place.

FURTHER INFORMATION

Website: www.bsr.org/BSRServices/CSRTrainings.cfm

DIALOGUE, MOTIVATION AND A CLOTHES LINE . . . AT PALAVRA MÁGICA

PALAVRA MÁGICA (MAGIC WORD) IS A SMALL publisher based in the city of Ribeirão Preto, in the Brazilian state of São Paulo. Palavra Mágica publishes three different lines of books: those covering citizenship for children and teenagers; general fiction and non-fiction; and books focusing on the region of Ribeirão Preto.

Concern about corporate social responsibility (CSR) motivates the company into monitoring how its values are applied in practice. A socially responsible corporation needs to adopt an ethical approach when dealing with clients, suppliers and competitors, but particularly with its own employees, who Palavra Mágica calls 'collaborators'. First-class working conditions are deemed essential if staff is to flourish both professionally and personally.

Since its creation in 1995, Palavra Mágica has encouraged its collaborators to contribute to the process of evaluating and monitoring the company's beliefs and values, starting on their first day. When a person is hired, he or she receives the company manual, which is updated yearly, and is given the opportunity to discuss the company's mission, vision and values. The manual contains an overview of the company's history, a brief profile of all collaborators and their functions, data and goals for the year and an explanation of the internal mechanisms for employee participation in decision-making.

Collaborators are encouraged to enrol for voluntary work. Regular weekly and monthly meetings are held to discuss topical issues and to debate the company's ethical values. A key event is the *projeto boa semana* (the 'good week project'). Every Monday morning, a volunteer chooses and reads a motivational text. Collaborators take turns to volunteer and although participation is optional around 90% of the workforce attends these meetings.

Encouraging collaborators to become involved in monitoring the company's ethical values requires them to have a deep involvement in, and understanding of, those values. The company wants all collaborators to have a say in corporate decision-making, especially relating to CSR. Once a month, the whole workforce meets to discuss the company's financial status and to problem-solve. An annual meeting is held in December to discuss developments and plans for the following year and to outline company objectives. Internal communication is via the company notice board, dubbed the *varal* ('clothes line').

The company believes there is more to life than work. Gatherings such as parties, trips and barbecues are organised outside work, and birthdays are celebrated. Along with internal news and information, the company distributes a cultural guide, giving details of theatre shows, art exhibitions, films and other events .

These initiatives have contributed to maintaining a calm and integrated atmosphere at work, promoting a good work–life balance and increasing productivity. The views of every member of the workforce are respected and taken into account, even to the extent of refusing contracts with alcohol and tobacco firms when the majority of collaborators expressed opposition to working with such companies.

FURTHER INFORMATION

Website: www.palavramagica.com.br

Boosting Employment Through Small Enterprise Development

Type of resource: website

Author organisation: International Labour Organisation

This job quality website from ILO's InFocus Programme on Boosting Employment Through Small Enterprise Development (SEED) gives a brief overview of the ILO's work in improving job quality (the 'decency' in decent work) in micro and small enterprises. It explains the roots of the job quality concept, what its various aspects are, the strategies for promoting job quality and how SEED works on developing a market for services to improve job quality. SEED emphasises the need for linking a better quality of employment to productivity improvement and demonstrates how incremental improvements in working conditions can benefit businesses as well as workers.

Tools for enabling small enterprises to improve job quality are downloadable from the site. These include:

- Training manuals for enterprises of different sizes and complexity and for entrepreneurs of diverse educational background
- Training videos
- A tool for assessing the quality of work in a comprehensive manner and for identifying priority areas for improvement

In addition, the website provides access to:

- Job quality assessment reports for ten developing countries
- Enterprise-level case studies (written and on video) that demonstrate that small enterprises can improve their performance through the creation of better working conditions
- SEED's progress report on Decent Employment Through Small Enterprises, including descriptions of some of the work undertaken to improve job quality

FURTHER INFORMATION

Web address: www.ilo.org/seed

The Tripartite Declaration of Principles Concerning Multinational Enterprises and Social Policy: A User's Guide

Author organisation: International Labour Organisation, Multinational Enterprises

Year of publication: 2002

This guide, based on the shared values of the Tripartite Declaration (see page 39), offers practical suggestions on building relationships among business, government and labour that encourage profits while caring for workers' rights and socioeconomic development. The guide was developed on the basis of consultations with governments, business and workers' organisations and provides illustrations on how to set common expectations, maintain dialogue, and sustains partnerships. It provides a handy reference to business, labour and government for the coordination of roles and responsibilities across global and local markets to ensure that workers' rights are respected, workplaces made safe, and skills and competencies built. Many of its practical examples draw from experiences reported by ILO constituents around the world as reported in the periodic surveys on the effect given to the Tripartite Declaration.

FURTHER INFORMATION

Website: www.ilo.org/multi

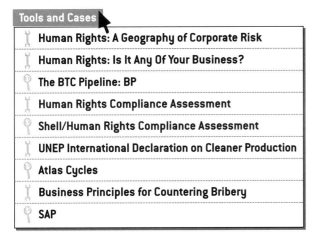

CHAPTER EIGHT

POLICIES AND STRATEGIES

IN AN EFFICIENT ORGANISATION, EMPLOYEES cannot continuously guess and make up the right way of doing things. As we have seen before, empowerment is enabled by clear policies that specify a number of decision criteria that are fundamental to the organisation. A good example is 'safety comes first'. In any business situation, such a policy requires employees to perform their work in ways that do not compromise their safety or that of their fellow employees or the public. If necessary, they are expected to stop production or a shipment, regardless of the impact on profits, until the conditions are safe. No deliberations are needed. They have been given power to do this. Experience has proven that a 'safety first' policy drives outstanding safety performance without penalising profits. At any point of time the policy allows consistent decisions in favour of safety while delegating authority and leaving freedom for initiative and creative solutions.

This goes for policies in general. They provide decision rules that the company sets to steer towards the vision and away from particular risks. They get people to be proactive rather than wait for someone else to work out the right way to handle a situation. Policies create the distinctive company culture — the 'way we do things around here'. Yet they should also link this culture to the broader expectations of society. The Global Compact principles offer and imply a number of policies: they create a framework not only to guide a company towards optimum shareholder value but also to bring social and environmental benefits to those who will probably never read the company balance sheet. In the ideal scenario, the company defines and adopts a set of policies that connect at minimum to each of the Global Compact principles.

Although each policy is demanding in own right, policies should not be placed in opposition to each other in a manner that compromises individual policies. For example, a company committed to excellence may have established the following policies:

- Policy 1: safety always comes first
- Policy 2: quality is defined by the customer
- Policy 3: we will maintain premium prices and not discount them
- Policy 4: we will operate to the same highest standards in all matters of people, technology and accounting throughout the world
- Policy 5: our resources will be allocated to the projects with highest five-year discounted cash flow

Such a set of policies empowers employees to use creativity and initiative. They are not mutually exclusive per se, but there will be instances when they just do not add up, or where the values in each will need to be balanced. For example, raising the environmental and labour standards of a potential acquisition to serve the expanding East Asian market may put a company's operations at a perceived cost disadvantage *vis-à-vis* its competitors that do not bother about local compliance. Policy 4 seems therefore to clash with policy 5. Yet the project team is required to find a way to look at all options to meet both policy objectives. It may look at partnerships, seek capacity development credits or bundle products with other lucrative lines. It is by refusing the easy trade-off that companies achieve technological and management breakthroughs. When all options are exhausted the team can present a final optimum proposal to management.

A set of policies is not meant to be an automatic pilot system. It also helps to identify significant exceptions that should be resolved only at the appropriate level of management. The management, if it is characterised by the sort of foresight possessed by companies dedicated to excellence in the long haul, may well decide in favour of strong social and environmental standards. Alternatively, it may relax the timing for the improvement of standards in favour of shorter-term financial performance. Determining how to balance the application of policies in exceptional cases is a critical management responsibility. It is up to management to balance risks and trust with other business goals.

A framework of rules or policies and a list of leadership priorities are a good start to ensure success towards the vision. It is the basis of the 'plan' phase in the Deming cycle (see Chapter 3, page 57) that involves the formulation of a detailed strategy. But we would be hard pressed to unlock now the secrets of the perfect strategy design. As referred to in Chapter 3 (page 54) Henry Mintzberg,[1] professor of management studies at McGill University and professor of organisation at INSEAD, found five major definitions for strategy and ten schools of thought. The choice of methodologies offered by multiple textbook models is huge.

We believe, however, that it is vital for leadership to take time to link the company vision to current reality with a credible story of change. That story combines the skills, the knowledge and material assets, and the natural and financial resources accessible to the company in a way that creates a durable competitive advantage. This story is a strategy. A strategy should always be about competitive advantage and vision. It enfolds within it the set of rules that define how the company operates — the policy framework — and a sharp focus on the elements that drive value. Those elements may be technology, access to natural resources, customer preference or employee creativity. Or they may derive, as in the SIGMA Management Framework presented in Chapter 5 (page 79), from the five capitals: natural capital, human capital, social capital, manufactured capital and financial capital. The point is that they must be combined in ways that make the company unique and hard to imitate.

A good strategy is almost obsessed with those elements that create value. It nurtures, combines and promotes them with extreme care. Proprietary know-how, access to raw materials, distribution networks, quality performance and others are among classic value drivers. Everyone knows a great deal about them. But there is also growing evidence of some generally unsuspected, intangible value drivers that could well make a clear difference over time: A commitment to the common good and a better world, a precautionary and caring approach to environmental, labour and social issues,

---

1 H. Mintzberg, B. Ahlstrand and J. Lampel, *Strategy Safari* (London: Pearson Education, 1998).

accountability and openness and an engagement in dialogue have also sustained the value creation for the group of companies analysed in Chapter 15. These drivers are certainly no substitute for good product innovation or cost management, but they are still unusual in the business world at large.

The company strategy is a story of progress. It is a shared story. It must be shared and understood, first of all by the employees who make it happen. It must also be integrated in the dialogue and learning sessions. There is a trend in many of our tools and cases to involve stakeholders in strategy formation and communication. But this is a new approach, and one that companies and stakeholder groups still approach warily. Where is the line between openness and preservation of competitive advantage? How much time can some stakeholders take to discuss strategy before finding they neglect their own organisation? Should they be compensated, like consultants, for their time to provide advice that improves business strategies? Although we recommend without reservation the need for discussion with outside stakeholders, we also suggest it be remembered that employees too are citizens, often engaged in community or social interests. As such they have questions and opinions that are often similar to the range of stakeholders who are aware of company activities. Therefore there is not necessarily a need to expose all strategy details outside. Strategy reviews by employees should encourage their reactions from the perspective of citizen-stakeholders — this will be another empowerment dimension that can only

strengthen the quality of strategy formation and the strength of ownership for implementation.

In Chapter 3 we described, in a 'four-shelf' model (see Figure 8, page 61), how principles, codes and standards relate to each other. We suggested that the second shelf from the top was the place to inspire leadership priorities and topics for policies. The international codes, declarations and conventions serve the leadership perspective of what should most count for the organisation and illuminate the need to adopt rules that delineate what the company should stand for. This chapter therefore continues with more information and sources that can reveal areas where a company should articulate a specific policy. These areas would be those where current policies provide insufficient guidance to live up to the principles of the Global Compact in all the situations that employees are likely to experience.

Given what we have stated about strategy, in particular the multiplicity of approaches and the search for the unique combination of those elements to drive value creation, it would be naïve to offer simple recipes for strategy formation; however, in the next section we present a few tools that address the search for intangible value drivers, helping companies to reflect beyond the business textbooks and find new performance factors that enhance competitiveness. This category of tools often use the vocabulary of navigation — radars, compasses, maps — for they try to clarify and organise a still hazy territory of business performance.

BUSINESS AND HUMAN RIGHTS: A GEOGRAPHY OF CORPORATE RISK

Amnesty International and The Prince of Wales International Business Leaders Forum

THIS TOOL CONSISTS OF A SUITE OF SEVEN detailed world maps, covering diverse industrial sectors, that are designed to illustrate and help companies identify the situations and contexts in which they may be exposed to business risks related to human rights. This publication complements *Human Rights: Is It Any of Your Business?* (see page 108).

Published in 2002, the maps are targeted at operational and company managers to enable them to recognise the particular human rights challenges their business may face in given locations and the vulnerability of their company to allegations of complicity in human rights abuses. Each map highlights the particular violation types prevalent in the featured countries in which they may find themselves entangled.

Text accompanying each map also helps companies better comprehend the nature of those critical human rights dilemmas that have confronted their industry peers and to which they may also be exposed. Digests of leading industry-related initiatives are also profiled, together with web links to assist managers in locating expert advisers and partners. The maps also equip managers with the means by which to identify industry peers with whom to share insights and explore avenues for collective action.

The seven colour-coded pull-out maps (listed below) are straightforward to use and feature over 30 countries with well-documented records of human rights abuse, and 129 leading multinational companies with operations in the featured countries. The compilers of the maps do not imply that featured companies are complicit in human rights violations, nor do they encourage companies to disinvest, but rather they attempt to make the business and moral argument for appropriate company policies and implementation strategies. The maps are as follows:

- Composite map (see opposite)
- Extractive sector (oil and gas, mining)
- Food and beverages (beverage producers, food producers and processors)
- Pharmaceutical and chemical (pharmaceutical, chemical, health)
- Infrastructure and utilities (construction and building materials, electricity, gas, gas distribution and water, diversified industrial)
- Heavy manufacturing and defence (automobiles and parts, aerospace and defence, engineering and machinery)
- Information technology hardware and telecommunications

FURTHER INFORMATION

Map: www.humanrightsrisk.com

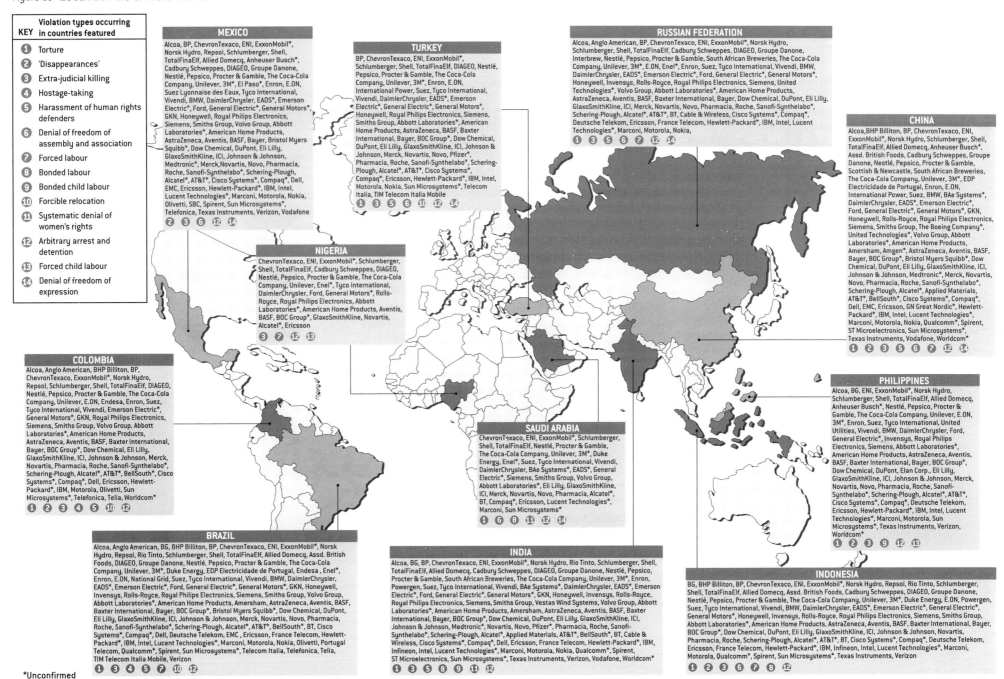

KEY — Violation types occurring in countries featured

1. Torture
2. 'Disappearances'
3. Extra-judicial killing
4. Hostage-taking
5. Harassment of human rights defenders
6. Denial of freedom of assembly and association
7. Forced labour
8. Bonded labour
9. Bonded child labour
10. Forcible relocation
11. Systematic denial of women's rights
12. Arbitrary arrest and detention
13. Forced child labour
14. Denial of freedom of expression

*Unconfirmed

MEXICO
Alcoa, BP, ChevronTexaco, ENI, ExxonMobil*, Norsk Hydro, Repsol, Schlumberger, Shell, TotalFinaElf, Allied Domecq, Anheuser Busch*, Cadbury Schweppes, DIAGEO, Groupe Danone, Nestlé, Pepsico, Procter & Gamble, The Coca-Cola Company, Unilever, 3M*, El Paso*, Enron, E.ON, Suez Lyonnaise des Eaux, Tyco International, Vivendi, BMW, DaimlerChrysler, EADS*, Emerson Electric*, Ford, General Electric*, General Motors*, GKN, Honeywell, Royal Philips Electronics, Siemens, Smiths Group, Volvo Group, Abbott Laboratories*, American Home Products, AstraZeneca, Aventis, BASF, Bayer, Bristol Myers Squibb*, Dow Chemical, DuPont, Eli Lilly, GlaxoSmithKline, ICI, Johnson & Johnson, Medtronic*, Merck, Novartis, Novo, Pharmacia, Roche, Sanofi-Synthelabo*, Schering-Plough, Alcatel*, AT&T*, Cisco Systems*, Compaq*, Dell, EMC, Ericsson, Hewlett-Packard*, IBM, Intel, Lucent Technologies*, Marconi, Motorola, Nokia, Olivetti, SBC, Spirent, Sun Microsystems*, Telefonica, Texas Instruments, Verizon, Vodafone
2 3 6 12 14

TURKEY
BP, ChevronTexaco, ENI, ExxonMobil*, Schlumberger, Shell, TotalFinaElf, DIAGEO, Nestlé, Pepsico, Procter & Gamble, The Coca-Cola Company, Unilever, 3M*, Enron, E.ON, International Power, Suez, Tyco International, Vivendi, DaimlerChrysler, EADS*, Emerson Electric*, General Electric*, General Motors*, Honeywell, Royal Philips Electronics, Siemens, Smiths Group, Abbott Laboratories*, American Home Products, AstraZeneca, BASF, Baxter International, Bayer, BOC Group*, Dow Chemical, DuPont, Eli Lilly, GlaxoSmithKline, ICI, Johnson & Johnson, Merck, Novartis, Novo, Pfizer*, Pharmacia, Roche, Sanofi-Synthelabo*, Schering-Plough, Alcatel*, AT&T*, Cisco Systems*, Compaq*, Ericsson, Hewlett-Packard*, IBM, Intel, Motorola, Nokia, Sun Microsystems*, Telecom Italia, TIM Telecom Italia Mobile
1 3 5 6 10 12 14

RUSSIAN FEDERATION
Alcoa, Anglo American, BP, ChevronTexaco, ENI, ExxonMobil*, Norsk Hydro, Schlumberger, Shell, TotalFinaElf, Cadbury Schweppes, DIAGEO, Groupe Danone, Interbrew, Nestlé, Pepsico, Procter & Gamble, South African Breweries, The Coca-Cola Company, Unilever, 3M*, E.ON, Enel*, Enron, Suez, Tyco International, Vivendi, BMW, DaimlerChrysler, EADS*, Emerson Electric*, Ford, General Electric*, General Motors*, Honeywell, Invensys, Rolls-Royce, Royal Philips Electronics, Siemens, United Technologies*, Volvo Group, Abbott Laboratories*, American Home Products, AstraZeneca, Aventis, BASF, Baxter International, Bayer, Dow Chemical, DuPont, Eli Lilly, GlaxoSmithKline, ICI, Merck, Novartis, Novo, Pharmacia, Roche, Sanofi-Synthelabo*, Schering-Plough, Alcatel*, AT&T*, BT, Cable & Wireless, Cisco Systems*, Compaq*, Deutsche Telekom, Ericsson, France Telecom, Hewlett-Packard*, IBM, Intel, Lucent Technologies*, Marconi, Motorola, Nokia,
1 3 5 6 7 12 14

CHINA
Alcoa, BHP Billiton, BP, ChevronTexaco, ENI, ExxonMobil*, Norsk Hydro, Schlumberger, Shell, TotalFinaElf, Allied Domecq, Anheuser Busch*, Assd. British Foods, Cadbury Schweppes, Groupe Danone, Nestlé, Pepsico, Procter & Gamble, Scottish & Newcastle, South African Breweries, The Coca-Cola Company, Unilever, 3M*, EDP Electricidade de Portugal, Enron, E.ON, International Power, Suez, BMW, BAe Systems*, DaimlerChrysler, EADS*, Emerson Electric*, Ford, General Electric*, General Motors*, GKN, Honeywell, Rolls-Royce, Royal Philips Electronics, Siemens, Smiths Group, The Boeing Company*, United Technologies*, Volvo Group, Abbott Laboratories*, American Home Products, Amersham, Amgen*, AstraZeneca, Aventis, BASF, Bayer, BOC Group*, Bristol Myers Squibb*, Dow Chemical, DuPont, Eli Lilly, GlaxoSmithKline, ICI, Johnson & Johnson, Medtronic*, Merck, Novartis, Novo, Pharmacia, Roche, Sanofi-Synthelabo*, Schering-Plough, Alcatel*, Applied Materials, AT&T*, BellSouth*, Cisco Systems*, Compaq*, Dell, EMC, Ericsson, GN Great Nordic*, Hewlett-Packard*, IBM, Intel, Lucent Technologies*, Marconi, Motorola, Nokia, Qualcomm*, Spirent, ST Microelectronics, Sun Microsystems*, Texas Instruments, Vodafone, Worldcom*
1 2 3 5 6 7 12 14

NIGERIA
ChevronTexaco, ENI, ExxonMobil*, Schlumberger, Shell, TotalFinaElf, Cadbury Schweppes, DIAGEO, Nestlé, Pepsico, Procter & Gamble, The Coca-Cola Company, Unilever, Enel*, Tyco International, DaimlerChrysler, Ford, General Motors*, Rolls-Royce, Royal Philips Electronics, Abbott Laboratories*, American Home Products, Aventis, BASF, BOC Group*, GlaxoSmithKline, Novartis, Alcatel*, Ericsson
3 7 12 13

COLOMBIA
Alcoa, Anglo American, BHP Billiton, BP, ChevronTexaco, ExxonMobil*, Norsk Hydro, Repsol, Schlumberger, Shell, TotalFinaElf, DIAGEO, Nestlé, Pepsico, Procter & Gamble, The Coca-Cola Company, Unilever, E.ON, Endesa, Enron, Suez, Tyco International, Vivendi, Emerson Electric*, General Motors*, GKN, Royal Philips Electronics, Siemens, Smiths Group, Volvo Group, Abbott Laboratories*, American Home Products, AstraZeneca, Aventis, BASF, Baxter International, Bayer, BOC Group*, Dow Chemical, Eli Lilly, GlaxoSmithKline, ICI, Johnson & Johnson, Merck, Novartis, Pharmacia, Roche, Sanofi-Synthelabo*, Schering-Plough, Alcatel*, AT&T*, BellSouth*, Cisco Systems*, Compaq*, Dell, Ericsson, Hewlett-Packard*, IBM, Motorola, Olivetti, Sun Microsystems*, Telefonica, Telia, Worldcom*
1 2 3 4 5 10 12

SAUDI ARABIA
ChevronTexaco, ENI, ExxonMobil*, Schlumberger, Shell, TotalFinaElf, Nestlé, Procter & Gamble, The Coca-Cola Company, Unilever, 3M*, Duke Energy, Enel*, Suez, Tyco International, Vivendi, DaimlerChrysler, BAe Systems*, EADS*, General Electric*, Siemens, Smiths Group, Volvo Group, Abbott Laboratories*, Eli Lilly, GlaxoSmithKline, ICI, Merck, Novartis, Novo, Pharmacia, Alcatel*, BT, Compaq*, Ericsson, Lucent Technologies*, Marconi, Sun Microsystems*
1 6 8 11 12 14

PHILIPPINES
Alcoa, BG, ENI, ExxonMobil*, Norsk Hydro, Schlumberger, Shell, TotalFinaElf, Allied Domecq, Anheuser Busch*, Nestlé, Pepsico, Procter & Gamble, The Coca-Cola Company, Unilever, E.ON, 3M*, Enron, Suez, Tyco International, United Utilities, Vivendi, BMW, DaimlerChrysler, Ford, General Electric*, Invensys, Royal Philips Electronics, Siemens, Abbott Laboratories*, American Home Products, AstraZeneca, Aventis, BASF, Baxter International, Bayer, BOC Group*, Dow Chemical, DuPont, Elan Corp.*, Eli Lilly, GlaxoSmithKline, ICI, Johnson & Johnson, Merck, Novartis, Novo, Pharmacia, Roche, Sanofi-Synthelabo*, Schering-Plough, Alcatel*, AT&T*, Cisco Systems*, Compaq*, Deutsche Telekom, Ericsson, Hewlett-Packard*, IBM, Intel, Lucent Technologies*, Marconi, Motorola, Sun Microsystems*, Texas Instruments, Verizon, Worldcom*
1 2 3 9 12 13

BRAZIL
Alcoa, Anglo American, BG, BHP Billiton, BP, ChevronTexaco, ENI, ExxonMobil*, Norsk Hydro, Repsol, Rio Tinto, Schlumberger, Shell, TotalFinaElf, Allied Domecq, Assd. British Foods, DIAGEO, Groupe Danone, Nestlé, Pepsico, Procter & Gamble, The Coca-Cola Company, Unilever, 3M*, Duke Energy, EDP Electricidade de Portugal, Endesa, Enel*, Enron, E.ON, National Grid, Suez, Tyco International, Vivendi, BMW, DaimlerChrysler, EADS*, Emerson Electric*, Ford, General Electric*, General Motors*, GKN, Honeywell, Invensys, Rolls-Royce, Royal Philips Electronics, Siemens, Smiths Group, Volvo Group, Abbott Laboratories*, American Home Products, Amersham, AstraZeneca, Aventis, BASF, Baxter International, Bayer, BOC Group*, Bristol Myers Squibb*, Dow Chemical, DuPont, Eli Lilly, GlaxoSmithKline, ICI, Johnson & Johnson, Merck, Novartis, Novo, Pharmacia, Roche, Sanofi-Synthelabo*, Schering-Plough, Alcatel*, AT&T*, BellSouth*, BT, Cisco Systems*, Compaq*, Dell, Deutsche Telekom, EMC, Ericsson, France Telecom, Hewlett-Packard*, IBM, Intel, Lucent Technologies*, Marconi, Motorola, Nokia, Olivetti, Portugal Telecom, Qualcomm*, Spirent, Sun Microsystems*, Telecom Italia, Telefonica, Telia, TIM Telecom Italia Mobile, Verizon
1 3 4 5 7 10 12

INDIA
Alcoa, BG, BP, ChevronTexaco, ENI, ExxonMobil*, Norsk Hydro, Rio Tinto, Schlumberger, Shell, TotalFinaElf, Allied Domecq, Cadbury Schweppes, DIAGEO, Groupe Danone, Nestlé, Pepsico, Procter & Gamble, South African Breweries, The Coca-Cola Company, Unilever, 3M*, Enron, Powergen, Suez, Tyco International, Vivendi, BAe Systems*, DaimlerChrysler, EADS*, Emerson Electric*, Ford, General Electric*, General Motors*, GKN, Honeywell, Invensys, Rolls-Royce, Royal Philips Electronics, Siemens, Smiths Group, Vestas Wind Systems, Volvo Group, Abbott Laboratories*, American Home Products, Amersham, AstraZeneca, Aventis, BASF, Baxter International, Bayer, BOC Group*, Dow Chemical, DuPont, Eli Lilly, GlaxoSmithKline, ICI, Johnson & Johnson, Medtronic*, Novartis, Novo, Pfizer*, Pharmacia, Roche, Sanofi-Synthelabo*, Schering-Plough, Alcatel*, Applied Materials, AT&T*, BellSouth*, BT, Cable & Wireless, Cisco Systems*, Compaq*, Dell, Ericsson, France Telecom, Hewlett-Packard*, IBM, Infineon, Intel, Lucent Technologies*, Marconi, Motorola, Nokia, Qualcomm*, Spirent, ST Microelectronics, Sun Microsystems*, Texas Instruments, Verizon, Vodafone, Worldcom*
1 3 5 8 9 11 12

INDONESIA
BG, BHP Billiton, BP, ChevronTexaco, ENI, ExxonMobil*, Norsk Hydro, Repsol, Rio Tinto, Schlumberger, Shell, TotalFinaElf, Allied Domecq, Assd. British Foods, Cadbury Schweppes, DIAGEO, Groupe Danone, Nestlé, Pepsico, Procter & Gamble, The Coca-Cola Company, Unilever, 3M*, Duke Energy, E.ON, Powergen, Suez, Tyco International, Vivendi, BMW, DaimlerChrysler, EADS*, Emerson Electric*, General Electric*, General Motors*, Honeywell, Invensys, Rolls-Royce, Royal Philips Electronics, Siemens, Smiths Group, Abbott Laboratories*, American Home Products, AstraZeneca, Aventis, BASF, Baxter International, Bayer, BOC Group*, Dow Chemical, DuPont, Eli Lilly, GlaxoSmithKline, ICI, Johnson & Johnson, Novartis, Pharmacia, Roche, Schering-Plough, Alcatel*, AT&T*, BT, Cisco Systems*, Compaq*, Deutsche Telekom, Ericsson, France Telecom, Hewlett-Packard*, IBM, Infineon, Intel, Lucent Technologies*, Marconi, Motorola, Qualcomm*, Spirent, Sun Microsystems*, Texas Instruments, Verizon
1 2 3 6 7 8 12

Source: Reproduced with permission of Amnesty International and The Prince of Wales International Business Leaders Forum

HUMAN RIGHTS: IS IT ANY OF YOUR BUSINESS?

Amnesty International and The Prince of Wales International Business Leaders Forum

THE PURPOSE OF THIS HUMAN RIGHTS

management 'primer' is to equip companies with the terms of reference to deal with a wide range of human rights dilemmas and challenges and to assist them in developing policies in keeping with Principles 1 and 2 of the Global Compact. It helps companies analyse the interface between their business and the social operating environment, and to prioritise actions around human rights.

The primer is targeted at those who formulate policy at the corporate level, as well as at operational managers of transnational corporations. It is designed to enable them to address human rights issues across functions and operations.

The primer offers:

- A rationale and a guide to companies to develop and implement human rights policies
- Practical recommendations for good corporate practice, drawing on case studies from selected transnational companies, including BP, Levi Strauss, Pentland, Rio Tinto and Shell
- A survey of the human rights landscape facing companies where a wide range of influences are having an impact on the company's reputation with regard to its human rights performance

- An overview of useful initiatives, codes and guidelines that may help a company wanting to put into practice a commitment to uphold human rights standards

As a tool for company managers, the primer features recommendations on how to develop a global company-wide human rights strategy, as well as checklists on how to tackle particular human rights and labour standards challenges. These include guidance on how to:

- Devise and implement policies when operating in conflict zones
- Safeguard human rights when using state or private security forces
- Operate in areas inhabited by indigenous peoples
- Build the right to freedom of association into a company's labour practices
- Deal with the problem of child labour
- Address poor working conditions
- Tackle instances of bonded and forced labour

The primer is an easily accessible information tool for those needing to identify the human rights challenges facing their company, and for those embarking on the development of group-wide human rights policies and

implementation strategies. It does not claim to be a definitive guide to this field but does offer a comprehensive and practical introduction.

To get the most out of the primer, a company or operational manager will need to acknowledge the human rights challenges the business faces and be prepared to invest sufficient time to read and digest the material on offer. Having done so, there will also be a need to invest the necessary resources to work through the recommendations provided in order to move towards developing a rigorous human rights policy and implementation strategy.

FURTHER INFORMATION

The Prince of Wales International Business Leaders Forum (IBLF)
website: www.iblf.org

Amnesty International UK website: www.amnesty.org.uk

The primer can be ordered by calling +44 (0)1788 545553, quoting product code PB179.

THE BTC PIPELINE: FOLLOWING THROUGH WITH GLOBAL COMPACT COMMITMENTS — BP

Scope and History of Project

The Baku–Tbilisi–Ceyhan (BTC) oil and gas pipeline project, when completed in 2005, will carry up to a million barrels of oil a day over a thousand miles across Azerbaijan, Georgia and Turkey. It is of great regional significance because it represents the first direct transportation link between the Caspian and the Mediterranean Seas, and its anticipated operation is at least 40 years. The pipeline will be the primary conduit for oil from a field off the coast of Baku which has an estimated 5.4 billion barrels of recoverable resources. With an estimated construction cost of $2.95 billion, the BTC project is expected to meet up to 10% of incremental global oil requirements over the next decade.

The remarkable scope of the project raises questions regarding how oil companies can best integrate human rights protections in keeping with commitments outlined in Principles 1 and 2 of the Global Compact. In designing the BTC project, BP plc ('BP'), the project operator, on behalf of itself and the ten other shareholders (collectively, 'BTC Co.'), sought to establish a new benchmark for a major infrastructure project with respect to the promotion of internationally recognised human rights and environmental standards. To this effect, BTC Co. incorporated into core project documents a commitment to respect applicable standards articulated in major international treaties and guidelines, adopted a precedent-setting level of transparency, and comprehensively engaged local populations. In November 2003, the International Finance Corporation (IFC) and the European Bank for Reconstruction and Development (EBRD) approved loans of up to $250 million for the BTC project.

Consultations with stakeholders

At an early stage in the project, BTC Co. undertook to ensure that the more than 450 communities and 30,000 land-owners and land-users affected by the pipeline were consulted over a 20 month period. The objective behind such extensive consultation was to secure significant community involvement and support at the outset of the project by dealing with concerns proactively and supporting sustainable community development.

Based on its consultations, BTC Co. produced a 'Regional Review', which serves as a comprehensive socio- and macro-economic assessment of the project's impact on the region. No other extractive-sector project has undertaken a more extensive multidimensional assessment of its impact on surrounding communities. Additionally, detailed consultations were undertaken as part of the integrated environmental and social impact assessments (ESIAs), including in-depth reports for each of the participating nations. Part of the consultation process with local communities included developing a comprehensive Public Consultation and Disclosure Plan (PCDP) for each of these countries. BTC Co. must now ensure that it continues its outreach to the communities including, perhaps, by facilitating the creation of citizens' advisory groups to counsel the project regarding ongoing issues.

Transparency

The BTC project sets a new industry benchmark for transparency. Over 11,000 pages of project documents are accessible on the BTC website, www.caspiandevelopmentandexport.com, which makes public more information than any previous extractive-sector

project. The publication of this information provides stake-holders with a broad understanding of the project and its implications.

Social and environmental concerns:

In selecting the pipeline route, BTC Co. sought a commercially viable option that minimised risk, avoided the displacement of communities, and incorporated long-term security arrangements. The pipeline route that was adopted avoids the permanent dislocation of any people and the destruction of any buildings. The pipeline will be buried, with land reinstated for use following construction. Economically displaced land-owners and -users are to be compensated using a transparent and consultative process that provides opportunities for economic enhancement. The pipeline was routed away from conflict zones and areas with known security concerns to minimise the need for security interventions.

With regard to environmental issues, the creation of the pipeline avoids additional tanker traffic in the congested and narrow Turkish Straits. The pipeline circumvents internationally and nationally designated protected areas, including the Borjomi–Kharagauli National Park. Some non-governmental organisations (NGOs), including Friends of the Earth and WWF, are nonetheless concerned that the pipeline's proximity to the park poses an unacceptable risk to the Borjomi region. As a consequence, these groups sought to delay or halt financing for the project.

Legal framework

Legal regimes must provide clarity, certainty and high international standards to attract complex and long-term infrastructure projects, and the transitional economic and

continued over →

THE BTC PIPELINE: FOLLOWING THROUGH WITH GLOBAL COMPACT COMMITMENTS — BP

→ *from previous page*

political nature of the three host governments — in particular, those of Azerbaijan and Georgia —presented obstacles to BTC Co. and the international investment community. Accordingly, the parties created a Prevailing Legal Regime (PLR), a special legal framework for the project, which supplements the existing structure of local laws and regulations. The PLR ensures that human rights, labour, health, safety and environmental standards applicable to the project will in no event be less stringent than the highest of applicable European Union standards (including EU Directives), World Bank Group standards, and standards under international labour and human rights treaties. BP's policies on ethical conduct, relationships and security, which set out commitments and responsibilities for all BP employees and their contractors, were also incorporated into the PLR.

Joint Statement

In an effort to respond to concerns that BTC Co. needed to clarify its commitment to international standards, the company drafted and orchestrated the signing of a 'Joint Statement' on 16 May 2003 by the three host governments and itself. The Joint Statement guarantees adherence to internationally recognised human rights, labour rights and environmental standards. These standards include explicit support for the principles in such documents as the Universal Declaration of Human Rights (see page 38), the European Convention on Human Rights,[2] the OECD Guidelines for Multinational Enterprises (see page 41), and, with specific regard to labour standards, ILO Conventions on forced labour, freedom of association and discrimination.[3]

Project security

Security is perhaps the single most important human rights issue to oil and gas companies due to the reputational and legal risks related to the actions of security forces assigned to protect company assets in conflict-prone or conflict-ridden countries. The Joint Statement specifically ensured that the Voluntary Principles on Security and Human Rights (see page 119) became part of the PLR, marking the first time that the Voluntary Principles were incorporated into legal contracts governing a project. Other security-related international principles committed to in the Joint Statement include the United Nations Basic Principles on the Use of Force and Firearms by Law Enforcement Officials,[4] and the United Nations Code of Conduct for Law Enforcement Officials.[5]

Response to NGO concerns

Some NGOs expressed concern that the project could undermine the human rights of local residents, endanger the environment, and spark conflict in the region. In particular, Amnesty International published a report in May 2003 which concluded that the legal agreements 'undermined the protection of human rights and created disincentives for the three states to fulfil their current and future human rights obligations'.[6]

BP and BTC Co. entered into a dialogue with representatives of Amnesty International soon after this report was released. As a result, BTC Co. drafted and signed a Deed Poll — a legally binding contract designed to protect the rights of the three host governments to promote and regulate human rights and environmental issues. BTC Co. also committed to publishing a 'Citizen's Guide' to the BTC project on its website in local languages.

BTC Co. may have been able to avert some of the NGO concerns by undertaking a Human Rights Assessment and proactively engaging with these stakeholders at an earlier juncture. In light of the project's anticipated lifespan, the primary challenge facing BTC Co. at this juncture will be to effectively operationalise and implement the standards it has set through the development of monitoring and compliance mechanisms. In this process, BTC Co. should continue to benefit from the relationships that it forged with Amnesty International and other NGOs.

FURTHER INFORMATION

BTC website, www.caspiandevelopmentandexport.com

---

2 For more details of this Convention, see www.hri.org/docs/ECHR50.html.

3 For more details of the ILO Conventions, see www.ilo.org/ilolex/english

4 Adopted by the UN Congress on the Prevention of Crime and Treatment of Offenders, 7 September 1990: www.unhchr.ch/html/menu3/b/h_comp43.htm.

5 Adopted by the General Assembly, 17 December 1979: www.unhchr.ch/html/menu3/b/h_comp42.htm.

6 'Human rights on the Line: The Baku–Tbilisi–Ceyhan Pipeline Project', www.amnesty.org.uk/business/btc *and* www.amnestyusa.org/business/humanrightsontheline.pdf.

HUMAN RIGHTS COMPLIANCE ASSESSMENT

Danish Institute for Human Rights

THE HUMAN RIGHTS COMPLIANCE ASSESSMENT (HRCA) is the result of a joint venture between the Danish government and Danish business and human rights groups. All parties recognise that human rights are an increasingly important area for business, but many Danish companies are too small to provide adequate in-house expertise. The need was to find a widely accessible resource that would help these companies help themselves to deal with human rights issues. The result was the HRCA.

The HRCA has been developed over a five-year period, from 1999 to 2004, by a team of researchers at the Danish Institute for Human Rights, who drew on the input and expertise of many of the 120 other human rights specialists at the Institute. The researchers worked in direct cooperation with the Confederation of Danish Industries, the Danish Industrialisation Fund and a number of affiliated companies to ensure that the resulting tool met the needs of businesses.

The tool runs on a database containing over 350 questions and 1,000 human rights indicators, developed from the UN Declaration of Human Rights and over 80 other major human rights treaties and conventions. An interactive web-based computer programme allows each company to select and modify the information in the database to suit its type of business and area of operation. The standards and indicators are updated on an annual basis, based on feedback from company and human rights groups users, to reflect changes and developments in international human rights law.

After the tool is run, a computerised report is produced that identifies the user company's areas of compliance and non-compliance with human rights generally, and these results are cross-referenced with another 'country risk' database at the Danish Institute for Human Rights, so that the results are adapted to the particular political and cultural environment of company operations. In addition, where there are weaknesses, the HRCA proposes ways of avoiding the main cultural and legal pitfalls and offers suggestions on how to strengthen the rights at greatest risk. The company's overall performance is quantified, so that continued improvements can be measured and tracked on a regular basis.

The tool itself can be downloaded free but to run a full HRCA one needs to invest, on average, 40 hours. However, a 'quick check' can be completed in less than a day.

The development of the HRCA involved a year-long consultation process funded by the European Union, involving 45 companies and human rights groups from ten European countries. Each review team included one business and one human rights representative so that the resulting standards and indicators represented practical and economic concerns as well as community and rights interests. In particular, Shell International served as the test company for the tool (see over). Field tests were run in relation to two distinct Shell companies: one in a country with a poor human rights record generally; the other in a society suffering racial conflict.

FURTHER INFORMATION

Human Rights and Business Project website:
www.humanrightsbusiness.org

Danish Institute for Human Rights website: www.humanrights.dk

The following brochures may be obtained free of charge from the Danish Institute for Human Rights:

M. Jungk, *Defining the Scope of Business Responsibility for Human Rights* (2001)

M. Jungk, *Building a Tool for Better Business Practice: The Human Rights Compliance Assessment* (2003)

SHELL PILOTS THE HUMAN RIGHTS COMPLIANCE ASSESSMENT

SHELL IS A GLOBAL GROUP OF ENERGY AND petrochemicals companies, operating in over 145 countries and employing more than 115,000 people. For the past three years, Shell and the Danish Institute for Human Rights (DIHR) have been working closely together to develop a human rights analysis system that could be used to assess Shell's human rights compliance in the countries in which it operates. Being a multinational company, Shell is faced with a number of human rights issues that vary depending on the country of operation and the type of business activity. The major challenge was to develop a system that is systematic, easy to apply and yet flexible enough to address adequately the variety of human rights issues that Shell encounters.

The main objective of the cooperation was to develop an integrated human rights analysis system capable of addressing human rights concerns within Shell in a systematic way. This system is based on the Human Rights Compliance Assessment (HRCA), a tool developed by the DIHR and consisting of more than 350 questions and 1,000 indicators (similar to an environmental impact assessment) that can be applied to all the specific areas of the company's operations. Indicators were developed from a variety of sources, including the International Labour Organisation (ILO) Conventions and the United Nations human rights treaties and declarations. Two field tests on Shell companies have been undertaken so far, in South Africa and in Oman. The field tests were undertaken to answer the following three questions:

- Does the HRCA identify most of the important potential violations?
- Are the guidelines and indicators straightforward and easily applied by non-specialists?
- Can the system be easily integrated in Shell?

The first test on Shell South Africa showed that the tool works well and is highly beneficial but could be streamlined. These lessons were then used to improve the second test, on Shell Oman, where an integral human rights analysis system was developed based on Shell's particular needs. This system comprises six steps:

- A country risk analysis on human rights is carried out to examine the level of risk in the particular country.
- The results of this analysis are used to identify major human rights focal areas for contractors.
- Appropriate questions and indicators from the HRCA are then selected and analysed.
- These results are used in a SWOT (strengths–weaknesses–opportunities–threats) analysis providing an overview of the company's major strengths and weaknesses in relation to human rights protection.
- In order to facilitate stakeholder dialogue on the weaknesses detected, recommendations are made concerning individuals or organisations to contact in the country of operation.
- The results are reported to the public.

The two HRCA tests showed that the tool is capable of detecting the most important human rights concerns in relation to each company's location and type of operation. They also provided good practice worth disseminating across Shell. By combining the HRCA with a country risk analysis, as was done in relation to Oman, it was possible to limit the number of questions investigated to 48 out of a total of 350, and the SWOT analysis provided a clear and concise assessment of the overall human rights performance of the company.

FURTHER INFORMATION

Shell website: www.shell.com

Human Rights and Business project website:
www.humanrightsbusiness.org

INTERNATIONAL DECLARATION ON CLEANER PRODUCTION

United Nations Environment Programme

LAUNCHED BY THE UNITED NATIONS

Environment Programme (UNEP) in October 1998 at Phoenix Park, South Korea, the International Declaration on Cleaner Production outlines a set of principles that, when implemented, will lead to increased awareness, understanding and, ultimately, greater implementation of cleaner production techniques and methods.

Cleaner production is a strategy for increasing the efficiency of natural resource use and for minimising waste. Pollution and risk to human health and safety are reduced at source rather than at the end of the production process (i.e. rather than at the 'end of pipe'). The adoption of cleaner production typically involves improving maintenance practices, upgrading or introducing new technology or changing production processes. It results in meeting consumers' needs with more environmentally compatible, quality products and services. As well as reducing pollution, this strategy also generates tangible economic savings for a business enterprise by improving the overall efficiency of production.

The Declaration text is essentially an outline of what signatories can say and do to advance cleaner production in their organisation. It is broken down into two sections: the introduction and the principles (leadership; awareness, education and training; integration; research and development; communication; implementation). The principles section of the text generally presents the actions to be undertaken and is the core of the Declaration commitment. Each principle has one or more action points that help the signatory understand what specific activities are required to meet the commitment.

The potential benefits of implementing the Declaration, by principle, are as follows:

- **Leadership:**
  - Improved dialogue along the supply chain
  - Increased confidence from consumers, suppliers and users
- **Awareness, education and training:**
  - Increased confidence from consumers, suppliers and users
  - Achievement of a long-term change in company culture, resulting in greater motivation in the industry
  - Strengthened internal capacity
- **Integration:**
  - The integration of a cost-effective environmental strategy
  - The creation of linkages with international conventions
- **Research and development:**
  - The spurring of innovation
  - Creation of the potential for new markets
- **Communication:**
  - Improved public perception
  - Creation of the potential for new partnerships
- **Implementation:**
  - Improvement of due diligence
  - Reduced risk and liability
  - The realisation of economic savings
  - An improved local, regional and global environment

Only by implementing the Declaration can the potential benefits listed above be realised. Implementation of the Declaration principles can be greatly facilitated by consulting UNEP's implementation guidelines for companies. These guidelines provide implementation activity suggestions, as well as a practical planning and progress measurement methodology to assist signatories implement the Declaration's six principles.

The guidelines present each principle with an activity 'toolbox' for each action point. More than 100 activity suggestions are listed. The activities range from those that are easily implemented to those that are more involved, requiring increasing effort (i.e. in terms of human or financial resources) or increasing involvement of external stakeholders.

In addition to the activity toolbox, the guidelines provide a methodology for planning implementation activities over time. The planning tool, dubbed the 'implementation horizon', shows five progressive steps allowing signatories flexibility in timing and in activity selection and offer a means to indicate activities that are one-off, ongoing or progressive. It also acts as a record for tracking progress, which is useful when responding to the biennial 'signatory implementation questionnaire', issued by UNEP to measure signatory implementation progress.

To further assist the implementation efforts of signatories in the various world regions, UNEP has published an initial 18 case studies. Additional cases will be added on a monthly basis to the Declaration's website. An example is provided in the following case.

FURTHER INFORMATION

Website: www.uneptie.org/cp/declaration

CLEANER PRODUCTION MAKES CLEANER BICYCLES: ATLAS CYCLES

STARTING WITH THE PRODUCTION OF ONLY

bicycle saddles in 1951 in India, Atlas Cycles Ltd is today ranked among the largest bicycle manufacturers under one roof in the world. Atlas has been involved in setting up large manufacturing plants in countries such as Tanzania, Iran, Zambia and others and has an annual turnover exceeding Rs3.5 billion (US$77 million). As a signatory of the International Declaration on Cleaner Production since October 2000, Atlas has undertaken the following activities to uphold its commitment to cleaner production:

- **Leadership.** Atlas has taken a lead among northern Indian industries as a 'change agent', demonstrating effective implementation of cleaner production in production activities. Atlas has conducted workshops and training programmes in schools, colleges and institutes around Haryana and Delhi. Atlas takes the precautionary approach and actively pursues cleaner production measures to prevent environmental deterioration.

- **Awareness, education and training.** Atlas spreads awareness among local stakeholders about the effects of environmental damage in the Indian context via workshops and training programmes. Since signing the Declaration, Atlas has held 52 courses aimed for various audiences (e.g. students, small entrepreneurs and government officials), reaching approximately 1,700 persons.

- **Integration.** Atlas has integrated several cleaner production techniques into production facilities, including:

  - A surface hardening process that eliminates sodium cyanide (NaCN) effluent and the use of sodium hydroxide (NaOH)
  - Use of high-speed diesel (replacing residual furnace oil) for brazing furnaces, reducing the emission of particulates, energy use and emissions to air
  - Electrostatic spray-painting, doubling the efficiency of paint absorption and improving air quality

- **Research and development.** Atlas has made the following innovations:

  - *Dust collection.* A newly installed magnetic plate on polishing machines more effectively captures steel particles that were once airborne and widely dispersed during cleaning.
  - *Hazardous waste.* A new process for converting hexavalent chrome to trivalent chrome by using sodium metabisulphite reduces the generation of hazardous sludge, and the treated effluent is colourless.

- **Communication.** In addition to improved internal communications within the systemic framework of the cleaner production strategy, Atlas has regular two-way communications for sharing knowledge and skills with the following organisations:

  - National Cleaner Production Centre, New Delhi, India
  - National Productivity Council, New Delhi, India
  - Central Pollution Control Board, New Delhi, India
  - Confederation of Indian Industries, New Delhi, India
  - Haryana State Pollution Control Board, Punchkula, India
  - Other national and international organisations engaged in this field

- **Implementation.** Noise pollution is a major challenge, which the company is addressing as part of its commitment to environmental responsibility as a new participant in the UN Global Compact. Acoustic enclosures have been constructed along with an exhaust muffler to meet the specified decibel level norms for diesel generators.

Achievements since signing the declaration have been:

- Awareness, education and training programmes reaching 1,700 persons
- Cleaner production measures, resulting in:
  - Elimination of NaCN effluent and related NaOH use
  - A great improvement in indoor ambient air quality
  - Reduction in energy use and improvement in process energy efficiency
  - Improvement in employee health
- Improved relations with local residents, pollution control boards, and other stakeholders.
- Engagement in other international initiatives (e.g. the UN Global Compact)

FURTHER INFORMATION

International Declaration on Cleaner Production website: www.uneptie.org/cp/declaration

BUSINESS PRINCIPLES FOR COUNTERING BRIBERY

Transparency International

TO ASSIST COMPANIES IN ADDRESSING THE difficult issue of bribery, Transparency International in partnership with Social Accountability International has facilitated the development of the Business Principles for Countering Bribery, a practical tool that provides a comprehensive model of good practice in the area of anti-bribery.

The Business Principles were developed by an international steering committee drawn from business, academia, trade unions and non-governmental organisations (NGOs). They are specific to the area of bribery and are therefore in no way expected to replace a full code of conduct. Instead, they represent a detailed elaboration of one aspect of a code of conduct.

The two key tenets of the Business Principles state that:

- The enterprise shall prohibit bribery in any form, whether direct or indirect.
- The enterprise shall commit to implementation of a programme to counter bribery.

The Business Principles focus on bribery only and not on the broader manifestations of corruption. The working definition of bribery adopted for the purposes of the Business Principles covers abuse of office, breach of trust or illegal acts by an employee or a third party on behalf of the enterprise. Beyond the strict prohibition of bribery, the Business Principles make it a fundamental requirement to implement a programme to counter bribery, indicating that this programme can be tailored to the special needs and vulnerabilities of a company and should, at the very least, cover areas such as bribes, political contributions, charitable contributions and sponsorships, facilitation payments, gifts and hospitality.

The Business Principles also set out how businesses should apply the programme to business relationships and how the programme should be implemented. They require:

- The board of directors and senior management to play a leadership role
- A culture of anti-bribery to be developed among employees
- Effective communication of the programme, provision of appropriate training, and the maintenance and auditing of effective internal controls
- A regular review

The Business Principles attempt to strike a balance between a compliance-based approach based on detailed rules and an approach that rests on clearly articulated values, without which companies are likely to fail in implementing anti-bribery policies and systems. They are pitched at a good, rather than best, practice level to attract the widest possible acceptance. It is expected, however, that as a 'living document', the Business Principles will evolve over time to reflect changes in anti-bribery practice as well as the lessons learned from their use and application by business.

Transparency International has produced a guidance document to provide additional background on the Business Principles and practical information for those wishing to implement them or to review their own practices.

The Business Principles are now being communicated worldwide through a series of workshops. Future developments are expected to include a range of tools to support them.

FURTHER INFORMATION

Transparency International website: www.transparency.org

Publication: www.transparency.org/building_coalitions/
private_sector/business_principles.html

SAP ENABLES THE CONVENTION ON BUSINESS INTEGRITY IN NIGERIA

SAP AG IS THE WORLD'S THIRD LARGEST independent software company, with headquarters in Walldorf, Germany. In 2002, SAP had €7.4 billion in revenue. The company operates in over 120 countries and has 29,000 employees worldwide. SAP sells software, but in the process also produces tools that help make business processes more transparent.

Established in Lagos, Nigeria, in 1997, the Convention on Business Integrity (hereafter referred to as the Convention) is a voluntary initiative to challenge corruption within the private sector in Nigeria. The Convention is a covenant among businesses operating in Nigeria to build a private-sector coalition against corruption and corrupt practices. It does not impose a legal obligation but represents a moral contract among signatories to promote integrity in the conduct of business. The Convention was the first initiative of its kind to make responsible governance an issue of focus in the Nigerian business world. SAP's financial support enables the Convention to fund its secretariat in Nigeria and pave the way for a potentially pan-African roll-out of the initiative.

Among the founding signatories are Accenture, Cadbury, Dunlop and Pfizer. The Convention promotes ethical conduct, transparency and accountability. Its founding members are: Integrity, an anti-corruption non-governmental organisation (NGO) set up by Nigerian business people; Transparency in Nigeria, a national chapter of Transparency International; and numerous local and multinational businesses. The Convention seeks to increase the level of business confidence in Africa by certifying its members' integrity.

The Convention works on a rating system that seeks to answer the following questions for each signatory:

- **Fitness for purpose.** How do the processes in a particular entity work?
- **Ethics and morals.** What credos, codes or policy statements are made by the organisation?
- **Transparency and accountability.** How are the disclosure processes to stakeholders organised?
- **Will and power to do the right thing.** How is an audit of organisation compliance undertaken?
- **A proven track record.** How can one confirm the commitment of an organisation?

FURTHER INFORMATION

SAP AG website:
www.sap.com/company/publicaffairs/citizenship/cbi.asp

Convention on Business Integrity website:
www.integrity.kabissa.org

Human Rights Principles for Companies

Type of resource: principles

Author organisation: Amnesty International

Year of publication: 1998

Amnesty International's principles for companies are complementary to the UN Global Compact in that they provide a brief introduction to companies' human rights responsibilities with the aim of raising awareness of the moral obligations that should be taken into account when forming company vision and policy. They also incorporate a nine-point 'introductory checklist' and an appendix listing the articles of international law relevant to each point.

The Human Rights Principles are applied in practice through the following introductory checklist:

- Adopt an explicit company policy on human rights
- Ensure that any security arrangements protect human rights and are consistent with international standards of law enforcement
- Take reasonable steps to ensure that company operations do not impact negatively on the human rights of the communities in which it operates
- Ensure that all company policies and practices prevent discrimination
- Ensure that any form of slavery (e.g. forced labour) is prohibited
- Ensure safe and healthy working conditions are provided
- Ensure that all employees can exercise their rights to freedom of association and collective bargaining (even if these rights are not protected in national law)
- Ensure working conditions are fair, including the provision of reasonable job security and adequate remuneration
- Establish monitoring mechanisms to check compliance of all operations with codes of conduct and human rights standards, ensuring that reports are credible and allowing all stakeholders to participate

FURTHER INFORMATION

Website: http://web.amnesty.org/library/Index/engACT700011998

Transnational Corporations in Conflict-Prone Zones: Public Policy Responses and a Framework for Action

Type of resource: publication

Author organisation: International Alert

Year of publication: 2003

The aim of this document from International Alert is to link corporate social responsibility (CSR) and conflict-prevention goals at the level of corporate strategy and to map the existing and emerging policy initiatives.

All human rights (Principles 1 and 2 of the UN Global Compact) are jeopardised in conflict situations, and this document suggests a three-level approach:

- Compliance
- 'Do no harm'
- Peace building

It also provides a basic diagram of specifics to be borne in mind by companies at different stages in conflict zones:

- Conflict prevention
- Post-conflict reconstruction and reconciliation
- Crisis management

The document summarises the CSR and conflict-prevention strategies of six governments and four intergovernmental organisations, potentially assisting a business in predicting likely government reaction to their activities. There are brief details of some existing strategies and codes to engage business in conflict prevention. The document also contains a useful bibliography.

The overriding message is the importance of linking CSR with conflict-prevention goals at the level of corporate strategy. A framework for action is presented through which this can be achieved.

FURTHER INFORMATION

International Alert website: www.international-alert.org

Publication: www.international-alert.org/policy/business/docs/BP_policy_Complete.pdf

Integrated Environmental and Economic Accounting: An Operational Manual

Type of resource: publication

Author organisation: United Nations Environment Programme and United Nations Statistics Division

Year of publication: 2000

This publication provides hands-on guidance for implementation of the System of Integrated Environmental and Economic Accounting (SEEA). It is aimed at policy and decision-makers, as well as environmental economists, statisticians and environmental accountants.

FURTHER INFORMATION

http://unstats.un.org

Contemporary Environmental Accounting: Issues, Concepts and Practice

Type of resource: publication

Authors: Stefan Schaltegger and Roger Burritt

Year of publication: 2000

This book has been written by two of the world's leading experts in the field in order to provide the most comprehensive and state-of-the-art textbook on environmental accounting yet attempted. The book is suitable for students, professional accountants and corporate and organisational managers. No prior knowledge of environmental accounting is necessary to understand the critical issues at stake. The book covers all key issues and includes questions that are answered in a separate and free-of-charge 147-page *Solutions Manual*.

FURTHER INFORMATION

Publication: S. Schaltegger and R. Burritt, *Contemporary Environmental Accounting: Issues, Concepts and Practice* (Sheffield, UK: Greenleaf Publishing, 2000; www.greenleaf-publishing.com/catalogue/cea.htm)

Environmental Management Accounting Research and Information Centre (EMARIC)

Type of resource: website

Author organisation: Environmental Management Accounting Research and Information Centre

Environmental accounting is a broad term that is used in several different contexts, such as management accounting, financial accounting and national accounting. This comprehensive website — packed with resources — focuses on the application of environmental accounting for internal organisational decisions (i.e. environmental management accounting [EMA]). The site is run by the Boston, US-based Tellus Institute and is funded by the US Environmental Protection Agency (EPA), with support from the UK Environment Agency, the Association of Chartered Certified Accountants and the UN Sustainable Development Environmental Management Accounting Expert Working Group.

FURTHER INFORMATION

www.emawebsite.org

CHAPTER TEN
PROCESSES AND INNOVATION

IF WE USE AN ANATOMY METAPHOR, THE BODY is now in shape to make a variety of purposeful moves. Processes are a number of tasks connected to get a planned result. They turn vision, leadership priorities, policies and strategy, and resources into the desired outcomes. Processes are therefore the crux of performance; they must have two qualities — effectiveness and efficiency.

To be effective they must actually produce the desired results on target. This implies, in the first place, that the organisation knows what it wants and that it has set targets. These targets should emerge from a reflection on the best variables that express the strategic intent of the company, in ways that are also understood by its employees, customers and other commercial partners, investors, public authorities and social stakeholders:

- Financial standards, laws and regulations already provide an obvious set of compliance indicators.
- A deep understanding of client needs produces a number of performance variables that define value from the client's perspective, such as on-quality product specifications and on-time delivery.

- A dialogue with stakeholders and integration and understanding of the UN Global Compact principles add further performance indicators.

A number of other indicators are also of key importance to a company's own management. For instance, energy efficiency or employee turnover may not be of immediate importance to clients, investors or stakeholders, but, by making improvements in such areas, other variables — labour and energy costs, emissions and waste — can also be affected favourably.

A selection of meaningful performance variables is fundamental in the drive for quality excellence and effective processes: 'You only improve what you measure'.

Let us take a simplistic example — the basketball players practising real free throws for Alan Richardson's experiment (see Chapter 5, page 72<x>). The performance variable is clear — the ball falls through the basket or it misses. The perfect shot follows from alignment of the ball's path with the centre of the basket. The ball measures nearly half the diameter of the basket. This allows quite a bit of variability in the throws — at least half a diameter left and right of centre before the ball touches the rim and risks rebounding outside. The players must learn to control their grip on the ball, hand–eye coordination, breathing, the impulse and the release of the ball to achieve a scoring effectiveness or a process capability index of at least . . . 1.33! This is how quality experts would redefine the free throw scoring challenge with a single number — a process capability index (C_p).

They would first record the distance of the ball's centre from the centre of the basket at each shot (see Figure 17). With sufficient data, they would then analyse the pattern in the distribution of those misalignments to reach the process variability. They may find that the player missed one-third of his or her shots. This just happens to approximate the lowest unit of a standard measure for variability used by statisticians. They call it sigma, σ. They would recommend improving the performance to a capability of at least $\pm 4\sigma$ — a dramatic progress to narrow the scoring variability to only around 60 misses in 1 million shots; in statistical control this defines a process capability index C_p of 1.33. Such free throw effectiveness would protect the player

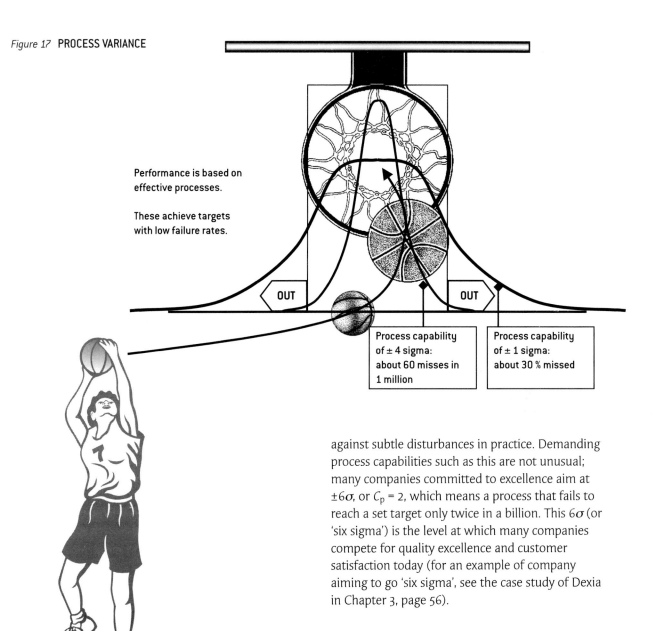

Figure 17 **PROCESS VARIANCE**

Performance is based on effective processes.

These achieve targets with low failure rates.

OUT

OUT

Process capability of ± 4 sigma: about 60 misses in 1 million

Process capability of ± 1 sigma: about 30 % missed

against subtle disturbances in practice. Demanding process capabilities such as this are not unusual; many companies committed to excellence aim at $\pm 6\sigma$, or $C_p = 2$, which means a process that fails to reach a set target only twice in a billion. This 6σ (or 'six sigma') is the level at which many companies compete for quality excellence and customer satisfaction today (for an example of company aiming to go 'six sigma', see the case study of Dexia in Chapter 3, page 56).

Process effectiveness is therefore not just a subjective concept; it is backed by a serious management discipline.[1] Moving from basketball to the domain of sustainable development, we could look at some typical process targets. These remain rare — particularly outside the environmental area. The management of customer satisfaction processes and the management of progress towards sustainable development are still different worlds. Even if they may define them internally, companies hardly ever publish performance targets. Table 6 presents a sample of performance variables extracted from recent company reports.

To meet such targets, managers need to understand the processes that can produce this level of performance; they must control and possibly redesign their processes. Tracing the movements of all quantities of hazardous materials from first occurrence to final waste disposal or following the recruitment and career paths of women towards executive management positions are complex processes, and the complexity grows when it comes to analysing the root causes of real accidents and the larger number of 'near misses' that must be understood to create the conditions for an accident-free workplace.

The same is true when one starts to trace all the sources of emissions of carbon dioxide (CO_2) in a network of worldwide operations. The nature of the targets strongly influences the degree of

QUANTITY	TARGET	ACTUAL VALUE IN 2001	PROCESS CAPABILITY
Diversity: percentage of women in senior executives positions	20 by 2008	7.9	Target is the lower limit of a range that could be defined in line with process variability.
Recycling: percentage use of recycled raw materials for plasterboard	45 by 2005	49 (exceeded target)	Target is the lower limit of a range that could be defined in line with process variability
Emissions of carbon dioxide (CO_2): percentage reduction from 1990 level of CO_2, in kg per tonne of production	20 by 2010	10.7	Target is the lower limit of a range that could be defined in line with process variability
Hazardous waste: kg per tonne of production	0.40 by 2006	0.50	Target is the upper limit of a range that could be defined
Accidents: number of lost-time accidents and restricted work cases per 100,000 hours	0 (always)	0.41	Target is an upper performance limit but allows no range; extremely high process effectiveness is required
Compliance: number of environmental infringement fines	0	9	Target is an upper performance limit but allows no range; extremely high process effectiveness is required
Resources: percentage of from a sustainable source	100 by 2005	On track	Target is an upper performance limit but allows no range; extremely high process effectiveness is required

Table 6 **EXAMPLES OF PERFORMANCE VARIABLES**
Source: excerpts from 2001 reports of Unilever and Shell and the 2002 report of Lafarge

---

1   F. Breyfogle III, J. Cupello and B. Meadows, *Managing Six Sigma* (New York: John Wiley, 2001).

effectiveness required. Many targets that appear as a single number actually imply a range — for example, more than 20% women in executive positions, or less than 0.40 kg of hazardous waste per tonne of production. They allow for some process variability as long as the minimum targets are met. Thus, some targets that seem absolute can be redefined as a range.

Processes that should produce results within a lower or upper set of limits can be designed and managed to a capability that delivers stable and reliable performance, but 'zero accidents' or '100% of fish from sustainable fish stocks' are absolute targets that allow no process variability — any lesser achievement would be a compromise towards lower performance. Such targets mean that the organisation has committed never to rest in its quest for ultimate control and improvements. We will see later, in our discussion of innovation, the value of such uncompromising targets.

Can an organisation improve its processes without targets? In other words, what comes first, the process or the target? The reality is that there is always a process, chaotic and uncharted as it may be. Improvement is cyclical. One first step could be to look around and adopt a process better intended and tested for the purpose. In this chapter and other parts of the book we propose a large choice of processes that have evolved from the drive of a number of organisations to improve performance. Most of them have proved their worth through published case studies.

Although it is acknowledged that one size does not fit all, such processes go a long way to providing clear and documented templates that necessarily induce a higher level of control and performance. The ISO 14000 series of environmental management systems and tools is based on the rationale that if one gets the process right one also gets the output right.[2] This rationale has supported a new approach to compliance that verifies the evidence of a process or management system in place rather than a systematic and costly check of the multiple outputs of this system.

But when it comes to strategy and competitive advantage we recommend pressing along the improvement cycle. The company should move to the stage where processes are re-evaluated in the light of specific performance targets that are valued by the company's customers and stakeholders. A well-maintained car and a driver's licence allow you to drive on public roads. But a life on the road without accidents and with the lowest fuel bill for your mileage and your highest driving pleasure demand a higher mastery of both vehicle and driving habits. The point is that acquired processes are an excellent basis for achieving these goals, provided you continue to drive them well. A licence to operate is not yet a competitive advantage.

It is now time to remember the other crucial quality of a process — it must be efficient as well as effective. *Efficiency means achieving results with the lowest effort and resources in the shortest time.* Effectiveness and efficiency are paired qualities. But effectiveness comes first. Customers, public authorities and other stakeholders would reject a company that fails to meet their demands and jointly agreed targets. Then again, investors and bankers would have little tolerance for an inefficient albeit effective company. Therefore, when aiming at a certain level of process effectiveness, one must also work on the choice or design of the most efficient process.

In their 1990 book, *Improving Performance*,[3] Geary Rummler and Alan Brache provided a comprehensive framework that addresses effectiveness and efficiency. They particularly stress the importance of seeing the organisation as a system of processes. Although many processes are internal, others extend to suppliers and customers and, therefore, are also affected by competitors. Public authorities and public opinion are other key influences on the system, as are the financial institutions. This system view has become familiar to anyone involved in quality and corporate citizenship debates, but Rummler and Brache insist than any process improvement must deal with the interfaces with the other processes in the system. The system always wins, and a good process will not make it in a poor system. Therefore a

---

2 For more details on the ISO 14000 series, see www.iso.ch/iso/en/prods-services/otherpubs/iso14000/index.html.

3 G. Rummler and A. Brache, *Improving Performance: How to Manage the White Space on the Organisation Chart* (San Francisco: Jossey-Bass, 1990).

comprehensive approach is in order. Performance happens at three simultaneous levels: **people** doing jobs in **processes** that are joined as an **organisation** or system. Efficiency and effectiveness at all three levels are influenced by three factors:

- **Goals and targets.** Goals or targets reflect customer and societal expectations, but they must be translated into actionable goals at the employee level, at the process level and for the company as a system. When it comes to the Global Compact principles, the major integration step relies on the definition of a set of goals that are coherent throughout the company at the process and employee level. The integration work that started with vision and leadership choices must crystallise at this level into goals and targets.
- **Design.** The design of job responsibilities, process steps and process interactions must achieve the highest degree of effectiveness to reach these goals with the lowest combination of resources and cycle times.
- **Management.** Management must address ongoing practice, measurement and control at each performance level.

According to Rummler and Brache, performance improvement requires more than just working with good processes; it requires the thoughtful integration of targets, design and management at the three levels where performance takes shape.

They also propose a methodology to make this happen.[4]

This clearly supports the underlying thinking of the Global Compact performance model. The multitude of tools and processes offered here will create value only when employees embrace them in the context of company-wide management and leadership priorities.

In 1993, a 'manifesto for business revolution' was published by two business experts, Michael Hammer and James Champy. *Reengineering the Corporation*[5] remains one of the most portentous business books published in the past few decades because it turned some traditional business thinking about processes and organisation on its head:

- It throws out the notion that processes must be complex strings of elementary tasks because employees can reliably perform only simple tasks. On the contrary, it proposes the enrichment of jobs by compressing all the tasks that can be performed meaningfully by one person and then delegating all the necessary decision power to let that 'case worker' move ahead without waiting for supervision. As a result:
  - Case workers form multi-skilled empowered teams with close alignment to the company's purpose through policies and targets.
  - Checks and controls are reduced because case workers also apply process controls in order to directly design defects out of their own work.
- Direct contact with clients is recommended to ensure that customer needs remain at the forefront of the team's objectives.
- Processes must also be designed for adaptability because not all customers have identical needs.
- The work is to be performed in a sequence and in locations that make most sense to save time and costs, not to fit an existing organisational chart. The system and the organisation must adapt to the re-engineered process, not the other way around.

This revolution is significantly enabled by the progress in information technology that continues to hold the company together while many of the physical connections are wiped out. It continues to change many companies and procures significant cost savings while product and service qualities improve. The operating model has become one of small enterprises associated into a bigger whole. Jobs are enriched, hierarchies are flattened and managers become mentors.

There is also a flipside: job loss is sometimes part of the revolution. Many enthusiastic re-engineering workshops have concluded with an awkward

---

4 Rummler and Brache, *op. cit.*: Part 3.
5 M. Hammer and J. Champy, *Reengineering the Corporation: A Manifesto for Business Revolution* (New York: HarperCollins, 1993).

moment when participants realise they have just outsourced or crossed out, with a tip of a felt marker, the process that used to be their job. Corporations that create value mainly by downsizing in fact externalise the costs of superfluous human resources. A growing economy easily re-employs this pool of skilled labour. A stagnant economy does not. The associated social costs cannot be ignored. They must be redistributed somehow; corporations will share the burden through their taxes, and legislation will set hurdles for further outplacement. In the context of the Global Compact, the next section shows how companies can re-engineer while being attentive to this issue of responsible downsizing and outplacement.

The success of re-engineering demonstrates the capacities of corporations to change, innovate and reinvent themselves. Innovation is also at the core of implementing the Global Compact. Indeed, we make the case that the Global Compact principles are a major source of innovative ideas because they pose a variety of dilemmas to the core of the 'business-as-usual' course of action. For example:

- Internal forecasts are up for the next five years but you are expected to decrease your total emissions of greenhouse gases and your total water usage.
- Purchasing needs the lowest price for polished brass door handles but it must also ensure that absolutely no children are employed in the hazardous processes of casting, sand blasting and polishing at the Indian suppliers.

- You are equipped to serve the fertiliser market of large African plantations; the market is flat, and fierce competition erodes margins. In contrast, there is a huge market of poor small farmers who could use and pay for no more than 10 kilos of product, but nobody is willing to supply them such small packages.

Innovation is to bridge two conflicting realities with a new behaviour that generates value and that can be implemented. If there is no implementation we have only a creative idea, not an innovation, because the value is lost and the two realities remain in conflict. Innovators reject the choice or trade-off of one reality for another, of principles for profit. They also use radical targets, such as the 'zero accidents' or '100% compliance' of Table 6, highlighted above, to stimulate new ideas.

The designer Craig Frazier once said that 'discomfort is almost a prerequisite for a great idea'.[6] At the start of every innovation are creative people who respond to this discomfort, dilemma or the impossibly stretched objective and, somehow, combine their repertoires of ideas and behaviour in an unusual way that creates a new possibility. The rest becomes a process of improving the feasibility and economic viability of the idea or killing it where it fails to meet certain success conditions. More ideas die than make it to market; a common rule of thumb is that only one out of a hundred ideas is

---

6 C. Frazier, *Thoughts on Design* (Hong Kong: Chronicle Books, 1998): 62.

good enough to go all the way to implementation. It is all the more important for companies to stimulate a large stream of ideas based on real customers and social needs. And if the challenge of sustainable development is not an innovation challenge, nothing is.

The Global Compact principles not only present a moral imperative. Companies can also turn them into an engine for innovation and encourage everyone's ingenuity in designing new products, services and business models that unite excellence and responsibility. For this to work the combination of two operating modes is required. One is the tight discipline of quality, process effectiveness and efficiency and the never-ending quest for improvements. The other is the apparently softer engagement with principles with desirable but long-range and ambiguous outcomes. Over the past few decades some companies have slowly — sometimes under public pressure — learned how to make the most of this combination and have begun to align the principled approach with the discipline of excellence. This has generated a number of standard practices, performance assessments and management systems — first in the environmental area and then in the areas of labour, human rights and corruption. Next, we will look at some developments in this area, as well as examples from companies that have documented how they go about bringing the process and innovation disciplines within the sphere of the Global Compact principles.

THE SOCIAL ACCOUNTABILITY 8000 STANDARD SYSTEM

Social Accountability International

SOCIAL ACCOUNTABILITY INTERNATIONAL (SAI)

is an organisation founded in 1997 that seeks to improve workplaces and communities around the world by developing and implementing socially responsible standards.

SAI's first social accountability system, Social Accountability 8000 (SA8000), is a way for retailers, brands, suppliers and other organisations to maintain just and decent working conditions throughout their supply chains. The SA8000 standard and verification system is a comprehensive tool for ensuring workplaces are humane. It includes:

- A standard that covers all key internationally accepted labour rights based on International Labour Organisation (ILO) Conventions,[7] the Universal Declaration of Human Rights (see page 38) and the UN Convention on the Rights of the Child

- A factory-level management system requirement for ongoing compliance and improvement

- Independent, expert verification of compliance, with certification carried out by auditing bodies accredited by SAI, ensuring that auditors have the procedures and resources needed to conduct thorough and objective audits

- Involvement of all stakeholders, with participation by all key sectors — workers and trade unions, companies, socially responsible investors, non-governmental organisations (NGOs) and government — in the SA8000 system, including on the advisory board, with the drafting and revision of the standard and auditing system, at conferences, with the guidance document, with training and in the complaints system

- Public reporting, with SA8000-certified facilities posted on the SAI website; companies that join the SA8000 corporate involvement programme at level 2 release annual progress reports verified by SAI

- The SA8000 certification and corporate involvement programme, helping consumers and investors identify and support companies that are committed to ensuring human rights are respected in the workplace

Companies can implement SA8000 through the following:

- **The SA8000 Corporate Involvement Programme.** Companies that focus on selling goods or that combine production and selling can join the SA8000 Corporate Involvement Programme (CIP). The CIP is a two-level programme that helps companies evaluate SA8000, implement the standard and report publicly on implementation progress.

- **Certification to SA8000.** Companies that operate production facilities can seek to have individual facilities certified to SA8000 through audits by one of the accredited certification bodies. After the initial workplace inspection and certification, the company is monitored for

---

7   For more information on the ILO Conventions, see www.ilo.org.

continued opposite →

THE SOCIAL ACCOUNTABILITY 8000 STANDARD SYSTEM

Social Accountability International

→ *from previous page*

continued compliance. As of November 2003, SA8000 certificates had been issued in 38 countries to over 300 facilities.

There are four basic types of out-of-pocket costs associated with SA8000:

- The cost associated with taking corrective and preventative actions in order to qualify for compliance; after this a firm would seek verification of its compliance
- The cost of preparing for the audit
- The cost of an independent audit, which includes the cost of retaining an accredited organisation to conduct audits
- If there are non-conformances, there are costs associated with taking corrective action in order to resolve problems identified by the auditors (e.g. the company may need to install or repair health and safety equipment, wages may need to be increased or child labourers may need to be enrolled in a remediation programme)

The first three costs are usually borne by the company being certified but can be shared with other parties, such as a customer that prefers SA8000-certified suppliers or has made certification to SA8000 a qualification for its business partners.

For a company, the benefits of adopting SA8000 standards are significant. Improvements in working conditions can lead to significant advantages, including improved staff morale and fewer accidents, leading to a better reputation, greater consumer and investor confidence and enhanced product quality. Close monitoring of contractors and suppliers also leads to better management, production control and product quality.

The benefits of SA8000 to workers include:

- Fewer accidents
- Enhanced opportunities to organise trade unions and to bargain collectively
- A means to address and improve working conditions

- Increased worker awareness about core labour rights
- An opportunity to work directly with employers on labour rights issues
- Creation of evidence that labour rights are good for society and business
- Improved business practices leading to financial growth and new job opportunities

FURTHER INFORMATION

Social Accountability International website: www.sa-intl.org

CASE STUDY

SA8000 TRIGGERS A QUALITY PROCESS AT BEAUTY ESSENTIAL

BEAUTY ESSENTIAL CO. LTD IS A MEDIUM-sized clothing factory in Thailand with two manufacturing sites and over 600 employees. In order to ensure continued success in its relationship with important customers and to maintain the company's export market in the long run, Beauty Essential applied for SA8000 certification. The company was able to demonstrate compliance with the standard on child labour, forced labour, health and safety, freedom of association and right to collective bargaining, discrimination, disciplinary practice and compensation, but it faced issues relating to worker overtime. In order to comply with SA8000, the company had to reduce overtime from 36 hours to 12 hours per week.

The company understood that reducing overtime would be likely to lead to resistance from employees facing reduced take-home pay, as well as an initial drop in overall production. In order to manage these challenges, the strategy was to increase productivity. In doing so, the company hoped to improve the working environment, save on overtime costs and maintain employees' income with fewer working hours.

The internal SA8000 team began by inspecting work practices and workstation design at each stage of the production process. The supervisor and SA8000 team explored ways of improving the working method for each task. Once agreed, the supervisor demonstrated the new methods to workers and encouraged them to ask questions and discuss the changes. There was also discussion about the employees' earning capacity in the long and short term.

The company was able to decrease overtime by nearly 30% within three months of implementing the new work processes. The company attained SA8000 certification and has passed the first surveillance audit.

This case study highlights an often-overlooked benefit of the SA8000 standard — its role as a total quality management tool. In complying with the standard, the company was able to improve its business processes, so achieving better-quality products and enhanced productivity.

FURTHER INFORMATION

Social Accountability International website: www.sa-intl.org

SA8000 TO MANAGING CHANGE IN PARTNERSHIP: SWITCHER

SWITCHER IS A CLOTHING DISTRIBUTOR WITH a head office in Mont-sur-Lausanne, Switzerland, employing over 100 workers. Annual revenue in 2001 was over US$48 million. Prem Durai Exports (part of the Prem Group) is an Indian manufacturer–exporter with a production capacity of 0.5 million units per year and a workforce of 100 employees. Prem Group signed an exclusivity agreement with Switcher to be its supplier. The Group specialises in cotton churning, spinning, knitting and dyeing. The company is fully integrated at the production level, with the exception of the supply of raw materials.

As a result of the agreement with Switcher, and growing concerns about quality and environmental protection, the Prem Group applied for SA8000 certification. The process required the Group to evaluate and review its management structure, work environment, human development, working conditions and general labour relations. Through the process of certification the Prem Group recognised the need for greater control of upstream activities, which led to a strategy of vertical integration.

In 2000, Switcher took part in a pilot audit of its own code of conduct. The audit included a requirement to grade partner companies on working conditions. As part of the process, Switcher was required to support any partner or supplier, such as the Prem Group, in improving working conditions and social performance.

From the beginning, the Switcher–Prem Group partnership focused on the success of a long-term relationship based on efficient business practices through positive social performance. Both companies used the SA8000 workplace standard as a key tool to achieve this goal.

During preparation for SA8000 certification, the Prem Group:

- Developed a complete set of social accountability procedures
- Appointed a social accountability representative
- Distributed the social accountability systems policy to workers, trade unions, active non-governmental organisations (NGOs) and local and regional political authorities
- Provided a free canteen for workers, which also provided a space for socialising and contributing to workers' sense of belonging
- Introduced ongoing work skills training at all levels
- Developed programmes on conflict resolution, problem solving and safety principles
- Ensured compliance with SA8000 standards relating to work conditions, freedom of association, occupational health and safety, non-discrimination, child labour and forced labour

Management review meetings take place twice a year to evaluate the effectiveness of the company's social accountability systems. A corrective action committee has also been established.

The results have been as follows:

- Absenteeism has dropped, from 20% in 2000 to 9% in 2001.
- Employee turnover has decreased, from 8.5% to 4.7%.
- Average monthly overtime has reduced, from 46 hours in 2000 to 22 hours in 2001.
- Production has increased 1.5-fold .
- Quality has improved, with the average re-work level decreasing from 20.4% to 8.3% over the period 2000–2001 and the average rejection level decreasing from 10.6% to 4.8%.
- Equipment and technology upgrades and new management practices (e.g. leading to improved communication processes, online monitoring and a focus on customer satisfaction) have been introduced.

Both Switcher and the Prem Group believe in a partner–supplier relationship and employee empowerment. Workers are continuously encouraged to make suggestions and to take the initiative. This has been encouraged through training and effective communication between management, workers and trade unions. The partnership between these two companies has become a benchmark in the Indian garment industry.

FURTHER INFORMATION

Switcher website: www.switcher.com

Social Accountability International website: www.sa-intl.org

ISO 14001: ENVIRONMENTAL MANAGEMENT SYSTEM

International Organisation for Standardisation

FOLLOWING THE DEMING CYCLE OF

plan–do–check–act (see Chapter 3, page 57), the ISO 14001 standard is designed for establishing and maintaining a certified or registered environmental management system (EMS). ISO 14001 includes core elements in five categories:

- Environmental policy
- Environmental assessment
- Objectives and targets
- Training and communication
- Review and auditing

It includes 52 action requirements. Under the core element, 'check' (checking and corrective action), it includes for example the element 'monitoring and measurement', with the requirement that the 'organisation shall establish and maintain documented procedures to monitor and measure, on a regular basis, the key characteristics of its operations and activities that can have significant impact on the environment'.

ISO 14001 makes an important distinction between environmental aspects and impacts. Environmental **impact** refers to any change to the environment that results wholly or partially from an organisation's activities, products or services. The environmental management system does not directly influence the environmental impacts. It is focused on the causes of the environmental impact, for which ISO 14001 uses the term environmental **aspect**. This is defined as an 'element of an organisation's activities, products or services that can interact with the environment'.

ISO 14001 does not require an organisation to consider all its aspects, but only those that are significant. Adding some guidance, ISO 14004 states that significance is associated with environmental concerns such as the scale, severity, duration and probability of the impact as well as with other business concerns such as potential regulatory or legal exposure. Some of the aspects may not be directly caused by the organisation but by suppliers or contractors or by clients when using the products. In this respect, ISO 14001 requires that an organisation include in its management system not only the aspects of its own operations but also those that it can influence.

In practice the ISO 14001 registration program allows company facilities to:

- Install a management system that over time generates significant advantages, including lowered emissions or waste and risks
- Conform to new approaches or methods for environmental management and new environmental legislative requirements
- Send a signal to stakeholders that the operator of the facility is showing commitment to environmental responsibility
- Help the company to retain or gain new consumers

The ISO 14001 standard has been written to accommodate diverse geographical, cultural and social conditions. The aim is also to be flexible to be applicable to any size of public or private organisation. The system is arguably easier for large companies, as opposed to small and medium-sized enterprises (SMEs), to adopt. In principle, it is applicable to any organisation that, in addition to implementing and improving an environmental management system, wishes to:

- Assure itself of its conformance with its stated environmental policy
- Demonstrate such conformance to others
- Seek certification or registration of its management system by an external organisation
- Make a self-determination and self-declaration of conformance with the international standard

continued opposite →

ISO 14001: ENVIRONMENTAL MANAGEMENT SYSTEM

International Organisation for Standardisation

→ *from previous page*

The environmental management system is part of the broader system of management in the company, with other subsystems on, for example, quality, occupational health and safety, security and economy. This faces the company with the challenge of integration and coordination as the company seeks to find appropriate connections between its physical system boundaries and organisational or functional system boundaries.

In countries that do not have a tradition of environmental legislation, or that have weak enforcement of legislation, the introduction and registration of the standard would probably require a greater number of physical process changes from companies. The cost of investing in the implementation of ISO 14001 — which may range from US$25,000 to US$128,000 — is rewarded by savings generated, provided the right regulatory framework exists. The International Organisation for Standardisation (ISO) has suggested a number of conditions that may determine how quickly and how effective the return on an organisation's investment in ISO 14001 will be. These conditions include:

- The status and level of sophistication of its existing management system
- The degree of environmental challenges it faces
- The amount and quality of resources it has access to
- Its state of preparedness
- The knowledge, skill and ability of its staff
- The expectations of its stakeholders
- Its current status of compliance with legal requirements
- The level of verification required by the organisation to meet market requirements or the expectations of stakeholders

Although ISO 14001 has been criticised for being mainly a process standard that is weak in addressing performance, its strength is in laying the basis for improvement, with the establishment of procedures, documentation and operational control. It also embeds environmental care in the company through training and puts in place an integrated system. ISO 14001 has made its mark with a total of almost 50,000 registrations at the end of 2002 following its launch in 1996.

FURTHER INFORMATION

International Organisation for Standardisation (ISO) website: www.iso.org

See also *ISOFocus*, a bimonthly journal with a worldwide overview of developments related to the ISO 9000 and ISO 14000 series

In addition, see: L. Piper, S. Ryding and C. Henricson, *Continual Improvement with ISO 14000* (Amsterdam: IOS Press, 2003)

TOOL

SUSTAINABILITY FRAMEWORK FOR PRIVATE-SECTOR INVESTMENTS

The International Finance Corporation

THE INTERNATIONAL FINANCE CORPORATION

(IFC), the private-sector arm of the World Bank Group, is the largest multilateral provider of long-term finance to the private sector in developing countries. Its mandate is to support poverty reduction in member countries through increased private-sector investment. For years, the IFC has applied a set of required environmental and social compliance standards to its investments. In early 2001, it began to explore ways in which it could help clients identify opportunities to enhance their environmental, social and governance performance while improving their bottom line.

In order to build evidence for the business case for sustainability, the IFC analysed the relationship between the components of sustainable development and the financial benefits to companies operating in emerging markets. It developed tools to evaluate expected impacts of projects, including 'Measuring Sustainability: A Framework for Private-sector Investments' to encourage clients to 'move beyond compliance', thus increasing their contribution to sustainable development.

The development of the framework reflects a logical evolution for the IFC and builds on its experience in ensuring the financial and economic sustainability of its investments. It is applicable across sectors. Rather than just 'raising the bar' on the required standards, which would be counterproductive in low-income and high-risk markets where meeting the IFC's required standards adds significant value, the framework measures how improvements by private firms in environmental and social management contribute to broader development. Based largely on existing industry standards and codes of best practice, the framework assesses corporate social responsibility performance with regards to impacts of projects. It brings together both quantifiable and non-quantifiable elements.

The framework assesses whether expected project performance goes significantly beyond compliance with the IFC's safeguard policies and associated guidelines in three broad areas, broken down into eight factors, as follows:

- Management commitment and governance:
  - Factor 1: environmental management, social development commitment and capacity
  - Factor 2: corporate governance
  - Factor 3: accountability and transparency
- Environment:
  - Factor 4: eco-efficiency and environmental footprint
  - Factor 5: environmental performance of products and services
- Socioeconomic development:
  - Factor 6: local economic growth and partnerships
  - Factor 7: community development
  - Factor 8: health, safety and welfare of the labour force

continued opposite →

SUSTAINABILITY FRAMEWORK FOR PRIVATE-SECTOR INVESTMENTS

The International Finance Corporation

→ *from previous page*

A high positive impact in environmental, social and corporate governance areas is more than a simple 'yes or no' issue. It is in this respect that the framework can be most useful, enabling better, more nuanced impact assessments than can a pure standards approach on its own. The four performance levels indicate a progression of sustainable practices:

- Level 1 shows compliance with the IFC's required standards where they exist.

- Level 2 indicates creation of local or global environmental, social or corporate governance value, either by reducing resource use, emissions or waste, by broadening the beneficiaries of economic activity or by positively affecting the views of potential investors.

- Level 3 signifies that a project's positive impact influences the behaviour of other firms, creating a farther-reaching demonstration impact at a national level.

- Level 4 describes a leadership position in which a project or firm has a wide influence in driving best practice at a global level.

The framework tool can be used in a number of ways. At the IFC it provides:

- An objective, comparable and credible basis for assessing the value that clients add in the long run to sustainable development

- Guidance for investment teams on 'high-impact' public goods and on what forms added value might take in specific projects

- Guidance for investment teams on how to identify opportunities for the business case for sustainability (i.e. strengthening a project's contribution to sustainable development in the long term while enhancing financial performance)

From a performance perspective, the framework provides:

- A snapshot of the total contribution of IFC projects to long-run sustainable development

- A resource for use in the IFC's performance measurement and incentive systems

---

FURTHER INFORMATION

The International Finance Corporation (IFC) website: www.ifc.org

Document: www2.ifc.org/sustainability/docs/measuring_sustainability.pdf

LEVEL 3 BANANAS FOR FAVORITA FRUIT COMPANY

FAVORITA FRUIT COMPANY, THROUGH ITS various subsidiaries, is the second largest exporter of bananas in Ecuador. The company's commitment to environmental and social responsibility is confirmed in part by its certification to the Rainforest Alliance's sustainable agriculture programme and the ISO 14001 standard and by its efforts to combat child labour in the banana fields through Ecuador's export-promotion association. This commitment has served the company well in that the company has preserved its role as the primary Ecuadorian supplier to Chiquita, thanks to the certifications it has achieved.

When returning to the International Finance Corporation (IFC) for a second round of financing, company representatives noted that progress on environmental and social issues would have to continue for Favorita to retain its leadership position. One area of concern was in Favorita's supply chain. Though all its owned farms were Rainforest Alliance-certified, and plans were in place to certify the new farms to be purchased with the IFC's second loan, even after expansion an estimated 45–50% of Favorita's exports would still come from independent banana growers.

Most of these smaller independent growers' farms did not operate anywhere near certification levels of performance. The IFC's Sustainability Framework proved instrumental in guiding the IFC and Favorita as they set about implementing an action plan to improve practices on these supplier farms.

The four levels of performance enumerated for each of the eight sustainability factors are stratified largely according to impact. Programmes that have an impact on company operations will score at level 2, those that impact the community or suppliers will score at level 3, with level 4 indicative of a global leadership position. Favorita was already a solid level 2 firm on several factors in the framework — namely, environmental management, commitment and governance, local economic growth and partnerships, and labour force health, safety and welfare.

The IFC's environmental and social development specialists assigned to the project team used the framework to identify what sort of action would move the project to level 3 scores. Conveniently, the surest way for the project to move to level 3 was to begin programmes of outreach and training with suppliers. Though the company was already somewhat motivated to tackle issues in the supply chain, having the framework to help guide the discussion and lend credibility to the proposal acted as an additional encouragement to the company to take this course of action.

Also key was the way in which the framework helped the IFC identify how best it might assist Favorita in this effort. The Environment and Social Development Department at the IFC had recently put in place new sources of grant funding to assist borrowers in taking on sustainability projects. By identifying that Favorita's greatest opportunity for improvement was in its supply chain, the framework acted as a screen to help facilitate a decision by the grant manager on where to put grant funding to best use. A grant of US$75,000 was provided to bring in training experts and to cover facility fees for an extensive programme of supplier training.

Typically, the framework is applied to projects at the loan-commitment stage. In the case of Favorita, the environmental and social specialists assigned to the project consulted the framework independently of the aforementioned process. This is indicative of the framework's flexibility — it can be used as a tool to generate better development impact through projects as well as being the metric for such impacts.

FURTHER INFORMATION

International Finance Corporation (IFC) website: www.ifc.org

Favorita Fruit Company website: www.favoritafruitcompany.com

ECODESIGN AND PRODUCT SERVICE SYSTEMS: RECOMMENDATIONS FOR SUSTAINABLE PRODUCTS AND SERVICES

United Nations Environment Programme

THERE ARE THREE MAIN APPROACHES TO providing a sustainable quality of life. Take the example of mobility. One approach is to provide better and cleaner products such as low-emission and fuel-efficient car engines. The next is to provide the same mobility outcome in different and more sustainable ways, perhaps by decreasing individual use of cars by encouraging the use of public transportation or encouraging car sharing. The third approach challenges the need for traditional functions such as mobility and provides different systemic solutions, such as urban planning of mixed residential, working and shopping areas or teleworking. All three approaches use specific evaluation, design and planning tools.

Ecodesign addresses the relationship between a product and the environment. It means that the environment becomes a 'co-pilot' in product development with the same status as more traditional industrial values, such as profit, functionality, aesthetics, ergonomics, image and overall quality. Ecodesign implies that there is a need to balance ecological and economic requirements in the development of products.

Ecodesign therefore looks at environmental impacts at all stages of the product development process in order to design products that have the lowest environmental impact throughout their life cycles. Financially, this means reduced generation of waste and the creation of savings on disposal costs and also on the costs of raw materials and production resources.

Other terms referring to the same approach as ecodesign are 'design for environment', 'life cycle design' and 'environmentally conscious design and manufacturing'.

An ecodesign checklist provides support for a qualitative environmental analysis by listing all the relevant questions that need to be asked to establish the product's critical impacts during its entire life cycle.

The process of planning and design typically involves:

- Analysis of the environmental product profile
- Analysis of the internal ecodesign drivers
- Analysis of the external ecodesign drivers
- Generation of improvement options
- A feasibility study of the improvements options
- Definition of the ecodesign strategy

A product service system is the result of an innovation strategy, shifting the business focus from designing and selling physical products only, to selling a system of products and services that are jointly capable of fulfilling specific client demands.

Shifting from products to a product service system enables the company to move progressively towards a new way of interacting with its clients. What the company or an alliance of companies conceives, produces and delivers is not simply material products but, in fact, a more integrated solution to customer demands.

The product service system approach takes as its starting point the goal of achieving an integrated functional solution to meet client demands. It moves away from discrete resource optimisation efforts in various phases of the product's life cycle. It looks for resource optimisation at the complete system level to satisfy the functional needs of the users. Working on broad system optimisation often generates cascades of savings, such as when a house-builder discovers that a high standard of insulation saves heating and cooling energy to a point that a simple reversible heat pump can replace both the entire fuel system and the air conditioner, cutting more emissions and costs while providing additional storage space. Product–service approaches can produce synergies in profit, competitiveness and environmental benefits (see the outer ring arrow of Figure 18 overleaf). They need to associate in the same design and optimisation effort all those who have a stake in the system.

Meeting consumers' needs with a mix of products and services is not a new concept. House rental, hotels, taxis and restaurants are good examples of product service systems based on economic interest. However, there are other new and innovative applications of product service systems that have developed as a response to make business more sustainable. The main difference between product service systems and the classic examples is that

continued over

ECODESIGN AND PRODUCT SERVICE SYSTEMS: RECOMMENDATIONS FOR SUSTAINABLE PRODUCTS AND SERVICES

United Nations Environment Programme

→ *from previous page*

the preference of consumers is influenced by environmental as well as economic interests.

Product service systems can be seen as strategic innovations that companies may choose in order to decouple resource consumption from its traditional link to profit and standard-of-living improvements. Such systems may also help companies find new profit centres as service providers and enable them to compete and generate value and social quality while decreasing (directly or indirectly) total resource consumption. In brief, product service systems can present win–win solutions for the producers or providers, the users and the environment.

FURTHER INFORMATION

Eco-ReDesign, National Centre for Design, website: www.cfd.rmit.edu.au

Centre for Sustainable Design website: www.cfsd.org.uk

O2 Global Network website: www.O2.org

Sustainments website: www.edf.edu.au

United Nations Environment Programme (UNEP) website: www.uneptie.org

Document (*Product Service Systems and Sustainability: Opportunities for Sustainable Solutions*): www.uneptie.org/pc/sustain/design/pss.htm

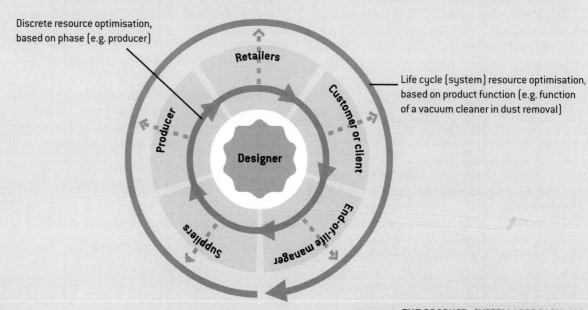

Figure 18 THE PRODUCT–SYSTEM APPROACH: ALL SYSTEM STAKEHOLDERS ARE INCLUDED IN A SHARED DESIGN AND OPTIMISATION PROJECT

ENVIRONMENTAL ASSESSMENT TOOLS

SETTING IMPROVEMENT OBJECTIVES AND

assessing progress require a number of processes that have been developed and standardised over the past two decades for the environmental dimension of sustainable development. Owing to their analytical character the different assessment tools have the same structure:

- Problem identification
- Data gathering
- Evaluation
- Selection of best alternative (with interpretation and documentation)

However, their scope is different. The following tools can be distinguished.

- **Cleaner production assessment.** Cleaner production is the continuous application of an integrated preventative environmental strategy to processes, products and services to increase efficiency and reduce risk to humans and the environment. Cleaner production assessment (CPA) is a structured methodology to systemically identify and evaluate cleaner production opportunities and facilitate their implementation. Initially, it may be alluring to work on a piecemeal basis as the benefits might be faster. However, interest would drop if long-term sustainable benefits were not realised. A structured methodology helps to institutionalise the cleaner production programme and integrate it with day-to-day business practice.

- **Environmental impact assessment.** Environmental impact assessment (EIA) is used to identify the environmental impacts of a project prior to decision-making. It aims to predict environmental impacts at an early stage in project planning and design, find ways and means to reduce adverse impacts, shape projects to suit the local environment and present the predictions and options to decision-makers. Environmental and economic benefits can be achieved through EIA, such as reduced cost and time for project implementation and design, avoidance of treatment and clean-up costs and ensuring compliance with laws and regulations. EIA is often required by national regulations for major projects; it is a legal requirement for such projects in EU member states.

- **Environmental risk assessment.** Environmental risk assessment (ERA) is a process that enables the probability of adverse environmental effects caused by exposure to one or more physical, chemical or biological agents to be determined. ERA requires knowledge about the negative effects of exposure to chemical substances or materials as well as knowledge about the intensity and duration necessary for these to cause negative effects. Decision-making, within sound risk management, entails examining the various choices for risk reduction. The US National Academy of Sciences has published a widely accepted structure for ERA.

- **Environmental technology assessment.** Environmental technology assessment (EnTA) is a tool to help decision-makers understand the likely impact of the use of a new or existing technology. The assessment process looks at the costs of the technology, its monetary benefits and at the environmental, social and political impacts.

- **Life cycle assessment.** A product's life cycle starts when raw materials are extracted from the earth, followed by manufacturing, transport and use, ending with waste management, including recycling and final disposal. At every stage of the life cycle there are emissions and consumption of resources. Life cycle assessment (LCA) is a tool for the systematic evaluation of the environmental *aspects* (see ISO 14001, on the definition of aspects, on page 140) of a product or service through all the stages of its life cycle. LCA has been standardised within the ISO 14040 series.

FURTHER INFORMATION

UNEP Cleaner Production Programme website: www.uneptie.org/pc/cp/understanding_cp/home.htm

European Commission, environmental impact assessment website: europa.eu.int/comm/environment/eia/home.htm

US Environmental Protection Agency (EPA), integrated risk information system website: www.epa.gov/iris

International Environmental Technology Centre (IETC) workbook for EnTA training for decision-makers: www.unep.or.jp/ietc/Publications/TechPublications/TechPub-5/index.asp

ISO standards on LCA: www.iso-14001.org.uk/iso-14040.htm

UNEP and the Society of Environmental Toxicology and Chemistry (SETAC), life cycle initiative website: www.uneptie.org/pc/sustain/lcinitiative/home.htm

Publication: National Academy of Sciences, *Risk Assessment in the Federal Government* (Washington, DC: National Academy Press, 1983)

A SMALLER FINGERPRINT FOR THE MOROCCAN DYEING INDUSTRY: BASF

IN MOROCCO, THE DYEING INDUSTRY PLAYS A VITAL ROLE,
providing significant employment in many small and medium-sized
enterprises (SMEs). In order to stay competitive and environmentally sound,
companies must continuously modernise their production systems. This
requires access to methods of analysis and production processes at the highest
international standard. However, these technologies and methodologies are
difficult to obtain and to apply at the SME level. It is in this context that the
United Nations Industrial Development Organisation (UNIDO), the United
Nations Environment Programme (UNEP) and BASF AG, a major manufacturer
of chemicals, have initiated a pilot Eco-efficiency Programme for seven SMEs.
A second phase, launched in January 2003, will disseminate the methodology
to 27 developing countries via the network of UNIDO and UNEP Cleaner
Production Centres.

The eco-efficiency analysis focuses on each phase of a product's life cycle,
'from cradle to grave', beginning with the extraction of raw materials from the
earth up to the recycling or waste treatment after use. The basis of the
analysis is a life cycle analysis according to the ISO 14040 sequence of
standards. The analysis allows, for example, the measurement of pollution
from the products used. The usage behaviour of the final consumer together
with the various possibilities for re-use and disposal are also analysed. The
economic and ecological advantages and disadvantages of process changes are
compared. The results can be pictured in a 'balanced fingerprint' diagram (see
Figure 19).

continued opposite ➔

Figure 19 THE BALANCED FINGERPRINT

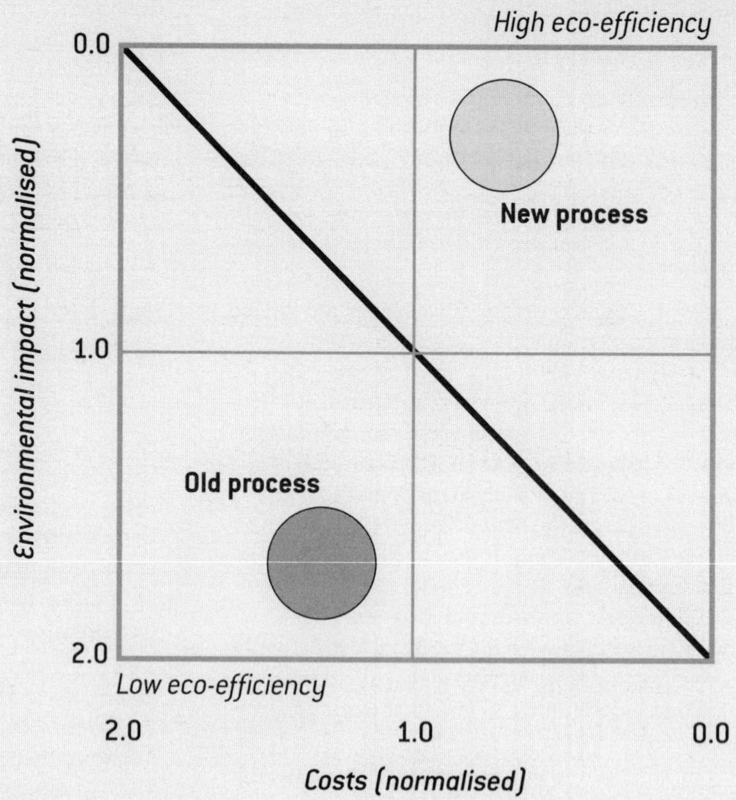

High eco-efficiency

New process

Old process

Low eco-efficiency

Environmental impact (normalised)

Costs (normalised)

A SMALLER FINGERPRINT FOR THE MOROCCAN DYEING INDUSTRY: BASF

→ *from previous page*

The ecological side of the balanced fingerprint has six indicators:

- Consumption of raw materials
- Consumption of energy
- Land use
- Emissions to air, water and soil (waste)
- Toxic potential of the substances employed and released
- Potential for misuse and hazard potential

Each of these six categories covers a large number of detailed individual criteria, which are assessed by so-called relevance factors. These state how strongly individual criteria contribute to the overall environmental pollution (i.e. how ozone destruction potential is weighted relative to greenhouse warming potential). The availability and natural occurrence of raw materials is also included in the calculation. The overall pollution of the environment by a product or process is given by the combination of the individual categories. In parallel, the economic data is put together. For this purpose the material and energy flows, including all relevant incidental flows, are taken into consideration. Labour and machine costs are also included. Weak points, driving costs and areas affording potential for cost reduction can therefore be readily identified.

In the textile dye works industry, three important production steps take place:

- Pre-treatment of the yarn or fabric
- Dyeing
- Post-treatment

For each step, chemicals, energy and water are needed, and emissions and solid waste possibly occur. The analysis makes it possible to identify weaknesses in this process. The impact of a current process, of which companies are often only vaguely aware, is presented in visual terms. Alternative fingerprints can be simulated as a basis for the selection of the most viable production process.

In a nutshell, with fingerprinting, SMEs are able to:

- Capture, calculate, evaluate and then transparently depict even complex matters within the production process
- Improve their decision-making relating to alternative production processes
- Communicate with customers and consumers
- Increase acceptance of defined solutions to problems
- Promote understanding for thinking in overall contexts
- Prove and illustrate acceptance of corporate responsibility principles

FURTHER INFORMATION

United Nations Industrial Development Organisation (UNIDO) document: www.unido.org/userfiles/timminsk/ecoefficiency_Morocco_aug2002.pdf

BASF AG website: www.basf.de

SAFE: SUSTAINABILITY ASSESSMENT FOR SMALL AND MEDIUM-SIZED ENTERPRISES

Wuppertal Institute

THE AIM OF SAFE IS TO HELP SMALL AND medium-sized enterprises (SMEs) improve their competitiveness and tackle the difficult task of increasing their eco-efficiency. SAFE operates through an effective and straightforward staff involvement process to optimise energy and economic resources. Thus, the use of materials, energy and economic resources can be optimised by harnessing the potential of employees in order to increase the success of the entire enterprise.

An additional benefit of SAFE is that it increases the competence, motivation and commitment of employees. As employees are actively involved in the process, they become aware of their skills, expertise and knowledge and so come to realise how to apply these in a more effective way.

SAFE analyses the organisational structure of an enterprise and helps to determine and assess those environmental, economic and social aspects that are relevant to the company's future success. A company profile is drawn up and potential areas for improvement identified. An action plan is developed and a monitoring system is introduced to assess progress. A central element of SAFE is that employees initiate a process of continual improvement. In this way the instrument offers the possibility of examining and optimising the various aspects of the company's leadership as well as its different management systems. SAFE can be used in all sectors and across geographical boundaries. Today, it is used for example in Germany, the Netherlands, Spain, Costa Rica, Latvia, Finland and Russia.

SAFE is carried out in six steps:

- Setting up the SAFE team of about 6–20 employees
- Status quo analysis in terms of a first sustainability check, by using a questionnaire that is completed by all employees
- Evaluation of the questionnaire, with the team analysing and assessing the results and presenting the overall findings as feedback to the employees
- Discussion of the results in a workshop, involving employees and the management, with suggestions for improvement being made and discussed by employees and management and with areas of action and measures for improvement being agreed
- Implementation of concrete measures
- Monitoring of results

Enterprises are benefiting from the SAFE tool in many ways. The tool is easy to use and produces good results in a very short time. The results can be differentiated into 'hard' and 'soft' facts. Hard facts are actual results achieved, consisting of the profile of the enterprise, a strengths–weaknesses profile and a list of improvement options suggested by employees. These suggestions are in the field of economic and environmental aspects, social affairs and communication. Soft facts are the more subtle, subjective outcomes experienced by employees such as increased competence, improved communication and capacity for communication, increased confidence, better teamwork, increased self-initiative and motivation, a stronger sense of being involved in the group or company, greater identification with the enterprise, better understanding of operational problems and improved job satisfaction and self-esteem.

FURTHER INFORMATION

Wuppertal Institute website: www.wupperinst.org/safe

BREWING ENVIRONMENTAL QUALITY AT MORITZ FIEGE

APPROXIMATELY 70 EMPLOYEES WORK IN THE private brewery Moritz Fiege (hereafter referred to as Fiege) in Bochum, Germany. The brewery had an annual turnover of €18.6 million in 2002. It supplies restaurants and pubs as well as retailers.

In the 1990s, Fiege introduced several quality and environmental management tools, notably ISO 9001 and ISO 14001. Unfortunately, the commitment and enthusiasm for these tools has decreased over time. For example, suggestions for improvements made by employees fell from 83 in 1992 to only 4 in 1999.

Following the suggestion of the Wuppertal Institute, in March 2000 management decided to initiate the SAFE process, which consisted of four phases:

- Phase 1: the SAFE team was established, representing all hierarchical levels and departments within the company.
- Phase 2: following an introduction to the subject by two external moderators, employees, trainees and managers assessed the business situation, its environmental compatibility, the social developments made and the existing communication channels. This was done by answering multiple-choice questions and formulating personal

comments and suggestions for improvements, which took about 45 minutes.

- Phase 3: the operations manager and quality officer evaluated the questionnaires.
- Phase 4: the operations manager and quality officer then presented their findings, including a strength and weakness profile for the company, at a workshop.

At the workshop, small groups were formed to develop suggestions on:

- Eliminating weaknesses
- Building on strengths
- Responsibilities
- Time-budgets
- Monitoring

Finally, the SAFE team decided which of the suggestions should be put into action.

The results of the SAFE process at Fiege site can be differentiated into hard and soft facts. The most important hard fact is savings of approximately €40,000 annually from decreased consumption of energy and water as a result of technical alterations in the

production process. The necessary investments are to be amortised within four years. Furthermore, several improvements in different areas were achieved that also resulted in higher cost efficiency. With regard to soft facts, there have been improvements in terms of more effective communication, better motivation and improved working atmosphere. Brewery manager, Jürgen Fiege, concludes:

SAFE improved cooperation generally, not just concerning the environment, because methods are used which are suitable to our employees. Furthermore, projects were established, and some even completed, which led to cost savings.

FURTHER INFORMATION

Wuppertal Institute website: www.wupperinst.org/safe

Moritz Fiege website: www.moritz-fiege.de

MONITORING GUIDANCE AND COMPLIANCE BENCHMARKS

Fair Labor Association

THE FAIR LABOR ASSOCIATION (FLA) IS A

non-profit organisation combining the efforts of industry, non-governmental organisations (NGOs), colleges and universities to promote adherence to international labour standards and improve working conditions worldwide.

Members of the FLA must check compliance with the FLA Workplace Code of Conduct, based on the FLA's 'principles of monitoring'. This tool, designed to assist FLA members in fulfilling this requirement, is made up of two parts:

- Information that should be gathered at the monitoring stage (the comprehensive list of questions and observations is such that the information could be quickly formalised into an easily formatted checklist system)

- Basic benchmarks to designate compliance or non-compliance with the Workplace Code of Conduct, correlating directly to the system of information-collection in the first part of the tool

There are seven main ways in which information should be gathered and observations made:

- Knowledgeable local sources
- Worker interviews
- Management interviews
- A capacity review
- A records review
- Visual inspection
- Analysis and reporting

The first part of the tool is a comprehensive list of questions to be asked (and of whom), observations to be made and areas to be investigated, in each of the ways listed above. Reference is made to seven specific issues:

- Forced labour
- Child labour
- Harassment or abuse
- Non-discrimination
- Health and safety
- Freedom of association and collective bargaining
- Wages and benefits, hours of work and overtime compensation

Particular care is taken over context-specificity (e.g. over the identification of locally appropriate forms of investigation). The need for confidentiality is emphasised, focusing on areas of particular importance (although ensuring there are enough open-ended questions to allow those involved to volunteer information important to them).

The next section of the document takes each of the seven specific issues and provides a set of compliance benchmarks for each. Benchmarks are necessary in order to compare the observations made to conditions at other places of work and/or earlier visits to the same site.

The tool is very detailed and requires considerable resources in terms of time (training monitors and taking observations) and financial input (applying it to as many places of work as possible). However, successful monitoring is predicated on just such a detailed approach, and the benchmarks ensure that the focus will be on areas most open to abuse. The tool is seen as being potentially useful in the designing of a business code of conduct.

FURTHER INFORMATION

Fair Labor Association (FLA), Monitoring Guidance and Compliance Benchmarks website: www.fairlabor.org/all/monitor/compliance.html

FLA Workplace Code of Conduct website: www.fairlabor.org/all/code/index.html

BASING SUPPLIER RELATIONSHIPS ON THE UN GLOBAL COMPACT AT BAYER

BAYER HAS REORGANISED ITSELF INTO A strategic holding, with headquarters in Germany and sales in 2002 of €29.6 billion. Its 350 subsidiary companies operate in the areas of healthcare, crop protection, polymers and materials science chemicals, employing, in 2002, 117,500 people in Europe (58%), North America (20%), Asia–Pacific (12%), Latin America (8%) and Africa and the Near East (2%).

An essential part of Bayer's commitment to work for the common good and contribute to sustainable development is securing and maintaining a sustainable supply chain. The annual procurement of half a million different material groups, including raw materials, packaging, services, technical goods and plants, represents a substantial portion of Bayer's total operating costs. It has therefore decided to focus on suppliers who share its corporate values, including the chemical industry's Responsible Care programme[8] and the Principles of the UN Global Compact.

Recognising that companies need to make their own assessment of their suppliers, Bayer introduced a programme called 'supplier relationship management' (SUPREME) in Spring 2003. Among other things, SUPREME consists of a database of suppliers that have been evaluated by Bayer staff. The evaluation protocols are available to procurement personnel worldwide in six different languages, enabling procurement to be channelled to the best suppliers. Furthermore, following the principle of 'no evaluation without consequences', Bayer and its suppliers have agreed on measures to continuously improve the suppliers' performance, with suppliers acting either alone or with help from Bayer. This raises the benchmark performance of all parties.

Suppliers are evaluated according to business-specific criteria. For existing suppliers, health, safety and environment performance criteria based on Responsible Care and Global Compact Principles 7–9 are evaluated. By accepting an order, a supplier also confirms its compliance with all regulatory requirements applicable to the country of manufacturing and sale. For new suppliers, the evaluation will be extended to include human rights and the International Labour Organisation (ILO) core labour standards according to Global Compact Principles 1–6. In all cases, use of child labour is grounds for the immediate termination of business transactions.

Bayer aims to cover 80% of its total procurement volume with the evaluation module of SUPREME, with listed suppliers being evaluated at least once a year. Currently, the tool is being rolled out, with priority evaluation assigned according to purchasing volume, strategic importance of the materials or services, critical markets and suppliers and potential for improvement. A strategic review is planned for 2004.

FURTHER INFORMATION

Bayer, Supplier Management Portal website: www.bayer-srm.com

---

8 www.icca-chem.org/section02a.html

A STRATEGIC INTEGRATION OF ENVIRONMENTAL MANAGEMENT: SAMARCO

SAMARCO MINERAÇÃO SA (HEREAFTER referred to as Samarco) is a Brazilian company engaged in mining, milling, pelletising and exportation of iron ore. It is the second largest world exporter of iron ore pellets by sea, selling all its products to more than 15 countries in Europe, Asia, Africa, the Middle East and the Americas.

The task of establishing a sustainable mineral extraction process imposes high demands on the company's environmental management and provides an incentive to search for the best environmental and operational practices. The environment is seen as a priority and the company is committed to achieving the triple bottom line of sustainable development.

One of the innovative aspects of Samarco's approach to environmental protection is its management pattern. The environmental division supplies knowledge and techniques for environmental action and results but, because Samarco is aware that its environmental performance does not rely purely on its environmental experts, decisions are shared with other divisions within the company.

Another aspect is the independence of the environmental division, so that this division is not subordinated to the production departments. In addition, environment is integrated with health, safety and quality.

Samarco's approach to environmental management has evolved in two stages. In the first stage, between the 1970s and mid-1990s, the company adopted values and introduced practices and processes that brought environmental benefits. In order to develop a safe transportation system for iron ore — both from a logistical and an environmental point of view — the company built a 396 km ore pipeline to take the ore extracted at the Germano plant to Ponta Ubu to be upgraded into iron pellets and delivered to the port. In addition, sewer treatment systems were installed at both plants.

During the second phase of the project, between 1990 and 1998, Samarco consolidated its management system, creating an environmental, health and safety area. In 1998, Samarco became the first mining company in the world to receive the ISO 14001 certificate for the whole of its production process. In 2000, it received the OHSAS 18001 certificate and established a specific environmental division, autonomous of the production area, that was to coordinate the environmental, safety and occupational health functions, as noted above.

The company has formed many partnerships, with goods and service suppliers, governments, non-governmental organisations, shareholders, community leaders, environmental agencies, schools and teachers (for environmental education projects), independent researchers, universities and environmental institutions. Samarco invests approximately 3% of its annual budget in environmental projects.

The results of the project to date have been as follows:

- Reduction of power consumption, generating an annual saving of more than US$4 million

- A 13% reduction of waste generation (in kilograms of waste per tonne of pellets produced) compared with 2000 values

- Control of atmospheric emissions, with a 90% reduction in particulates, keeping the emissions within the legal requirement

- Improved company image

A company's proactive and ethical attitude towards society and the environmental entities makes effective actions feasible. Environmental improvements must be taken as a strategy that enhances the company's global results. The company's leadership to establish better practices is essential but also needed is investment in qualified and prepared people to enable them to deal with challenges and to see mistakes as an opportunity for improvement.

FURTHER INFORMATION

Samarco Mineração SA website: www.samarco.com

Designing a CSR Structure

Type of resource: publication

Author organisation: Business for Social Responsibility

Year of publication: 2002

Designing a CSR Structure sets out the necessary stages for a business to consider and set up an internal management system aimed at integrating corporate social responsibility (CSR) into the entire company's organisation and culture. The tool is designed to provide easy-to-understand steps that can be adapted by different companies according to their own decision-making structures and processes. It provides examples of how various companies have applied the stages outlined in the document and relies on a straightforward step-by-step process to lead users through the processes outlined in the document.

FURTHER INFORMATION

Business for Social Responsibility (BSR) website: www.bsr.org

Sustainability Trend Guide

Type of resource: publication

Author organisation: Sept ou 8

Year of publication: 2004

The Sustainability Trend Guide focuses on consumption trends. It provides companies with the means to integrate sustainability into marketing, products and service development, packaging and presentation, customer relations and communication strategies.

The guide will enable companies to anticipate consumer expectations and to identify major trends relating to sustainable consumption. It covers the following sectors: food, retailing, textiles, cosmetics, healthcare, mobility, households products, and electronic appliances

The guide is divided into three parts:

- **Part 1.** This part is an analysis of sustainable consumption patterns, including relevant regulatory developments, findings of research and focus groups on consumer behaviour, and the role of non-governmental organisations (NGOs) in influencing consumer behaviour and business attitudes.

- **Part 2.** This part identifies four major trends likely to affect company and consumer behaviour, based on the findings of part 1. It includes scenarios illustrating new consumption patterns, materials, products and services.

- **Part 3.** This part contains client-specific research to answer concerns relating, for example, to product development and communications strategies.

The Sustainability Trend Guide 2004 is available in print form and on CD-ROM and includes short video clips. It applies to international markets but has a specific focus on Europe.

FURTHER INFORMATION

Sept ou 8 website: www.septou8.com

Eco-efficiency: Creating More Value with Less Impact

Type of resource: publication

Author organisation: World Business Council for Sustainable Development

Year of publication: 2000

This report is an essential compendium of information and a reference source for all those wishing to understand eco-efficiency. It highlights some of the ways in which eco-efficiency has been interpreted by companies in different sectors. The political dimension of eco-efficiency is also examined, and recommendations are made on how governments can measure eco-efficiency and make it work for society by creating the right framework conditions.

FURTHER INFORMATION

World Business Council for Sustainable Development (WBCSD) website: www.wbcsd.org

Measuring Eco-efficiency: A Guide to Reporting Company Performance

Type of resource: publication

Author organisation: World Business Council for Sustainable Development

Year of publication: 2000

This practical guide offers companies advice on how to select, use and report on eco-efficiency indicators, thereby helping them to measure their progress toward sustainability. The results of a special one-year pilot programme by 24 companies are documented.

FURTHER INFORMATION

World Business Council for Sustainable Development (WBCSD) website: www.wbcsd.org

Environmental Consumer Information for Products and Services

Type of resource: labelling and certification schemes

Author organisation: United Nations Environment Programme

Environmental consumer information tools for products and services include the conventional eco-labels (environmental product declarations) and certification schemes such as the Forest Stewardship Council (FSC) and the Marine Stewardship Council (MSC). The International Organisation for Standardisation (ISO) established the ISO 14020 series on labelling in order to classify the different environmental information schemes:

- Type I (ISO 14024) claims are based on criteria set by a third party and, ideally, the criteria should be based on the key life cycle impacts. The awarding body may be either a governmental organisation or a private or non-commercial entity. Well-known eco-label icons include the EU Flower, the Nordic Swan and the German Blue Angel.
- Type II (ISO 14021) claims are based on specific declarations by manufacturers or retailers.
- Type III (ISO/TR 14025) claims consist of quantified product information based on a life cycle assessment.

Type I eco-labelling, the identification that products and services meet a minimum environmental criterion, has been available and further developed for three decades now. These types of label have gained much importance in certain markets for communication from businesses and retailers to consumers.

Type III labelling has moved to the centre of attention in the form of the Environmental Product Declaration scheme, which includes third-party verification. An environmental product declaration is defined as quantified environmental data for a product with pre-set categories of parameters (e.g. emissions of carbon dioxide, or global warming potential) based on the results of a life cycle assessment study carried out according to the ISO 14040 standards series but not excluding additional environmental information. Environmental product declarations are increasingly being used in business-to-business communication.

FURTHER INFORMATION

Global Eco-labelling Network website: www.gen.gr.jp

Global Type III Environmental Products Declarations Network website: www.environdec.com/gednet/info.html

Forest Stewardship Council (FSC) website: www.fscoax.org

Marine Stewardship Council (MSC) website: www.msc.org

EU Flower website: http://europa.eu.int/comm/environment/ecolabel/index_en.htm

Nordic Swan website: www.svanen.nu/Eng/default.asp

German Blue Angel website: www.blauer-engel.de

Developing Countries and Technology Cooperation, Volumes 1 and 2

Type of resource: publication

Author organisation: United Nations Industrial Development Organisation/World Business Council for Sustainable Development

Year of publication: 2002

This publication examines ten case studies of innovative technology cooperation and draws lessons for businesses and governments on ingredients to promote successful partnerships.

FURTHER INFORMATION

United Nations Industrial Development Organisation (UNIDO) website: www.unido.org

World Business Council for Sustainable Development (WBCSD) website: www.wbcsd.org

Document website: www.unido.org/en/doc/5171

Analytical Tools for Environmental Design and Management

Type of resource: publication

Editors: Nicoline Wrisberg and Helias A. Udo de Haes

Year of publication: 2002

In 1998 and 1999 the European Union Environment and Climate Programme commissioned a group of environmental experts to produce a toolbox of life cycle management methods. The network of experts also defined the ideal domains of application, the linkages between the tools and provided peer-reviewed definitions and comments on strengths and limitations. A number of case studies illustrate their applications. The resulting book is a good source for business people when it comes to a choice of assessment process.

FURTHER INFORMATION

Publication details: N. Wrisberg and H.A. Udo de Haes (eds.), *Analytical Tools for Environmental Design and Management in a Systems Perspective* (Dordrecht, The Netherlands: Kluwer Academic, 2002)

Part 3

CHAPTER ELEVEN

IMPACT ON EMPLOYEES

EMPLOYEES ARE ONE OF THE MOST

important assets that a company has. It is a mutually beneficial relationship. It sounds simple. However, as any human resource person will tell you, it is not. For a start, employees have many rights that, when respected, lay the foundation for job satisfaction and high performance. Some of these rights are reflected in the UN Global Compact's four labour principles (Principles 3–6). Others are directly related to basic human rights, reflected in the two human rights principles of the Compact (Principles 1 and 2). In addition to these basic rights, other issues such as empowerment of employees, training, career development and volunteering are just some of the things that affect professional development, as well as the personal development of employees.

Consider the following research that highlights the treatment and respect of employees both as a way to save costs and as a way to reinforce the idea that respecting the basic rights of workers matters and is good for business:

- **Health and safety.** Work injuries cost Americans US$146.6 billion in 2002. That amounts to US$1,060 per worker.[1] Worldwide, there are 1.2 million fatalities on the job each year (about 3,300 each day). Moreover, it is estimated that for each fatality there are 1,200 accidents resulting in three or more days off work each year.[2]

- **Hours of work.** Extensive research in the USA showed that continuing scheduled overtime has a strong negative effect on productivity, which increases in magnitude proportionate to the amount and duration of overtime.[3]

---

1 National Safety Council, 'Report on Injuries in America' (2002), www.nsc.org/library/report_injury_usa.htm.
2 J. Takala, 'Life and Health are Fundamental Rights for Workers', *Labour Education* 126 (ILO Bureau of Workers' Activities [ACTRAV], 2002): 1.
3 Associated General Contractors of America, 'Guideline on Overtime, Construction Costs and Productivity' (2003), www.constructionguidelines.org/pdf/ D3iOvertimeCostsProd.pdf.

- **Freedom of association.** The World Bank concluded in a recent study that economies with coordinated labour markets perform better. More specifically, it found that, at the macroeconomic level, high unionisation rates lead to lower inequality of earnings and can improve economic performance in the form of lower unemployment and inflation, higher productivity and speedier adjustment to shocks.[4]

- **Discrimination.** More active equal opportunity policies have a greater positive effect on productivity.[5]

- **Employee participation.** According to a study of the Fortune 1,000 companies, satisfaction and performance levels are notably higher at companies that have implemented power-sharing programmes.[6]

These are just some of the many available statistics and research that highlight the positive relationship between respecting employee rights and running a successful enterprise. But what about

personal development? Some of the more enlightened companies have long recognised that employees look to their job not only as a way to make a living but also as a way to develop themselves intellectually, socially and professionally. Susan Bowick, senior vice president of human resources for Hewlett-Packard (HP), explains:

> Our employees have passion about wanting to make a difference. We have an opportunity to align HP's activities with that employee energy and have a significant impact in the world.[7]

This finds an echo in the 2002 Social Review[8] of Unilever, an organisation with 265,000 employees:

> To succeed as a business in competitive markets, Unilever must attract and retain the best people. Competitive rewards linked to performance and more opportunities for personal development are increasingly important elements of our business strategy.

People are a key factor of success — this is the *leitmotiv* of a majority of company statements around corporate social responsibility (CSR): they also underline the commitment of the company to foster the welfare and personal development of its employees.

This is not just rhetoric for public reports. It is confirmed by extensive practices and progress assessments. For example, Danone, the Paris-based food group with worldwide product lines in mineral water, dairy products and biscuits (in 2002, sales were €14.237 billion, with 92,209 employees), demands that working groups throughout the company's facilities conduct self-assessment discussions to evaluate the degree of implementation of the core values and policies of the company. This 'Danone Way' programme[9] covers 130 criteria, of which 27 address human resources management. The workgroups make a four-level assessment, where level 1 is the lowest implementation level, and level 4 represents the achievement of best company practice for each criterion. Such a methodology stimulates a company-wide discussion that deepens the understanding of policies at the operational level while sharing good ideas on how to improve implementation at the next level. Other companies conduct systematic employee satisfaction surveys or hold work forums to receive feedback.

Commitment to CSR and engagement with the Global Compact has encouraged a stream of performance reports and communications from the most active companies. Whereas a few years ago the section on social standards mentioned only health and safety, the number of aspects covered

---

4 World Bank, *Unions and Collective Bargaining: Economic Effects in a Global Environment* (Washington, DC: World Bank, 2003).

5 V. Perotin and A. Robinson, 'Employee Participation and Equal Opportunities Practices: Productivity Effect and Potential Complementarities', *British Journal of Industrial Relations* 38.4 (December 2000): 557-93.

6 N. Rogovsky and E. Simms, *Corporate Success through People: Making International Labour Standards Work for You* (Geneva: International Labour Organisation, 2002): 64.

7 Hewlett-Packard, 'Social and Environmental Responsibility Report' (2002), www.hp.com.

8 Unilever, 'Listening, Learning, Making Progress: 2002 Social Review' (2002), www.unilever.com.

9 Groupe Danone, 'Social and Environmental Responsibility: The Danone Model of Action' (2001), www.danone.com.

now is much broader, although quantitative data and targets are often wanting. However, such reports are an ideal source of examples of good practice. They suggest a range of indicators that reflect impacts on employees directly or indirectly connected to the Global Compact principles. We looked at a number of reports published in 2002 by active supporters of the Global Compact to draw up a list of such practices and indicators (see Table 7). The list of practices and indicators in Table 7 shows how companies are ensuring their employees' well-being and job satisfaction. Not every company embraces all these practices or indicators, nor does this sample of indicators cover all possible issues in relation to the Global Compact principles. Nonetheless, it offers a spectrum of options for measurable practices and specific indicators of progress.

Table 7 also shows that remuneration is only one part of the job-satisfaction equation. This is borne out by numerous studies. One such study was undertaken by Tom Terez,[10] a consultant and motivational speaker on job satisfaction and performance excellence. Seeking the key features for a fulfilling workplace, he conducted hundreds of interviews on the subject with focus groups. His website continues to collect this information through online assessment tools. He concluded that he could not reduce the answers to just a few easy features. He retained 22 keys to creating a

---

10   T. Terez, '22 Keys to Creating a Meaningful Workplace' (2002), www.BetterWorkplaceNow.com.

ISSUE	PROGRESS INDICATORS
Personal safety	Provide all employees with a safe and secure workplace. Make zero occupational injury a goal, underpinned by comprehensive policies, safety equipment and technical and behavioural training.
Health	Extend responsibilities from the obvious protection against occupational health hazards to the more complex issues of stress. Include access to healthcare services, from the provision of flu shots and medical check-ups to comprehensive drug dispensaries and HIV/AIDS treatment where appropriate.
Travel risk assistance	Focus on road accidents and risks, which erode safety performance, as well as concentrating on making workplaces safer.
Working hours	Set a maximum contractual working time where local legislation does not exist. Also give attention to the upward creep in working hours during travel or at home because of its correlation with stress, safety and general work–life balance.
Harassment	Ensure that all employees are treated with dignity, respect and courtesy by fostering a culture of openness and by providing proper reporting structures.
Privacy	Ensure the protection of employee records in line with a company-wide standard and, as a minimum, in compliance with the most stringent local legislation.
Labour and social standards	Avoid geographical disparities that could appear as discrimination or that could create difficulties for expatriates and their families. Demonstrate an equal appreciation of employees, wherever they work, and set harmonised, transparent standards that comply, as a minimum, with local legislation.
Staff forum, help-lines	Foster dialogue on working conditions through staff meetings and the provision of specific grievance facilities such as independent counsellors, help-lines, doctors or ombudsmen, in addition to allowing union membership and legal workers' committees.
Compensation	Provide transparent compensation systems that are best in class. Align individual and team performance rewards with company goals.
Insurance and pension	Manage risk insurance and pension benefits with a view to enhancing employees' personal financial security above the national or business-sector average.

Table 7 **PRACTICES AND INDICATORS ADOPTED BY ACTIVE SUPPORTERS OF THE GLOBAL COMPACT** (continued over)

Source: authors' survey of company reports for 2002

ISSUE	PROGRESS INDICATORS
Restructuring	Handle downsizing in a way that enables employees to transfer as smoothly as possible to other paid work with acceptable conditions.
Recruitment	Create a clear understanding of, and commitment to, the objectives and culture of the company through targeted campus programmes, interviewing approaches and introductory and mentoring programmes for new staff.
Training	Ensure skills development and continuous learning. Cement alliances with professional institutes and business schools.
Career development	Encourage internal mobility, promotion and job opportunities, and offer career and succession planning.
Share ownership	Reward outstanding performance through share options. Provide access to share ownership through employee purchase schemes.
Well-being	Set up company programmes to support employees' fitness and well-being.
Integrity standards	Enable employees to operate with integrity in all business situations on the basis of clear business standards in an open and honest environment. Provide help and advice to clarify the company position in the case of conflicting demands.
Diversity and inclusion	Embrace diversity of background as an opportunity to gain a competitive advantage. Give all employees the opportunity to participate and achieve personal growth (in many global companies this is a priority issue overseen by a dedicated top management 'champion'). Give employees' family members access to certain company programmes and facilities.
Tough choices	Support employees in making tough choices against local practices that allow or encourage fraud and bribery, child labour or forced labour, or discriminate against ethnic, caste or religious groups. Tough choices may also include issues such as stem cell research or animal testing that may conflict with an employee's personal morals.
Leadership dialogue	Associate employees to leadership issues through dialogue and listening.
International exchange	Foster management diversity through international project teams, leadership and competence networks. Promote international job postings and moves from foreign subsidiaries to headquarters and major business units.
Volunteering	Foster employee involvement in the community with time allowances, sabbaticals and other material support and recognition.

Table 7 (continued)

meaningful workplace and also analysed the most frequent mentions. They are:

- Purpose
- Ownership
- Fit
- Oneness
- Relationship-building

Employees do not just expect material advantages from their job, but rather an enhancement of meaning and community in their lives.

Readers now familiar with the Global Compact principles will no doubt recognise the correlations and multiple connections between these timeless foundations of human excellence and fulfilment and the universal framework of human rights, dignity in the workplace, integrity and conservation of our common environment.

GIVING STREET CHILDREN A FUTURE: AN EMPLOYEE INITIATIVE AT VOLKSWAGEN

VOLKSWAGEN (VW), WHICH PRODUCES and distributes passenger cars and small trucks worldwide, employed 324,402 people in the year 2000; it was from this workforce that the company's successful street children project, One Hour For The Future, has grown.

The project, begun in September 1999 in partnership with the children's rights organisation Terre des Hommes, aims to supply continuous, long-term financial support for street children projects run by local institutions and initiatives near VW sites around the world (Mexico, Brazil, South Africa and Germany). The project was initiated by the employee's General and Group Works Council, which in mid-1999 encouraged every employee at VW's German factories to donate the equivalent of an hour's pay every year. The rate of participation was extremely high, with factories outside Germany also joining the initiative.

The campaign was repeated in 2000, and employees were encouraged to make donations on a regular basis to guarantee long-term support for the projects. In the meantime, many suppliers and business partners of VW began to make regular donations, as well as many retired employees and various clubs and action groups involving VW employees. By the beginning of 2001, over DM4.2 million (US$1.9 million) had been donated.

FURTHER INFORMATION

Volkswagen (VW) website: www.volkswagen-environment.de

TOOL

SOCIALLY SENSITIVE ENTERPRISE RESTRUCTURING

International Labour Organisation, Management and Corporate Citizenship

THIS TRAINING COURSE, DEVELOPED BY THE

Management and Corporate Citizenship Unit of the International Labour Organisation (ILO), is intended for businesses that face the unenviable task of restructuring their enterprises. It examines, in logical steps, the process of restructuring within companies, starting with preparation and finishing with evaluation. Particular emphasis is placed on the impact of restructuring on employees, including morale, and on issues such as discrimination and freedom of association in the workplace, in accordance with international labour standards.

Enterprises all over the world are faced with fluctuations in the marketplace and increased competition owing to:

- Globalisation of markets, commerce and financial flows
- Deregulation and trade liberalisation
- Rapid technological changes
- The shift from an industrial to a knowledge-based and information-based economy
- Threats to environmental sustainability
- Changing expectations and value systems

Enterprises need to be prepared for these new challenges in order to be able to address them with maximum economic benefits and minimal social costs.

Restructuring is not necessarily downsizing. In fact, it can be done in a variety of different ways. The course invites managers to address the following questions:

- Can restructuring be done without cutting labour costs (portfolio restructuring, mobility, etc.)?
- If cutting labour costs is the only solution, can it be done without layoffs (through management accepting pay cuts, outsourcing, etc.)?

- If cutting labour costs is not possible without downsizing, could this process be carried out in a socially sensitive way?

The training emphasises that, in any case, restructuring should take into account, as much as possible, all stakeholder concerns. Evidence is presented that such an approach results in improved competitiveness.

While business is dealing with outside pressures, the problems and challenges it faces also affect governments and employers' and workers' organisations, as in many countries — and even globally — entire sectors have had to restructure. This tool addresses what enterprises *and* policy-makers can do to tackle the restructuring challenge. More specifically, the following areas are explored in greater detail:

- Enterprise-level strategy, policies and practices
- Government assistance in facilitating the restructuring process

Enterprises should:

- Explore all restructuring options
- If downsizing is the only option, carry out the downsizing in the most socially sensitive way
- Create a system of functional flexibility, which allows the enterprise to be continuously prepared to face outside challenges
- Enter into dialogue and communication between workers and managers

Tools that may be used by enterprises and that contribute to socially sensitive enterprise restructuring include:

- Use of voluntary redundancies
- Provision of severance packages
- Provision of psychological help
- Provision of help with internal job searches
- Provision of help with external job searches
- Provision of help in the creation of small businesses
- Use of internal mobility
- Use of pre-retirement options
- Provision of vocational training
- Use of alternative work-schedules (e.g. restructuring to create part-time jobs, to allow job sharing, to create a compressed working week and so on)
- Use of workforce leasing
- Use of outsourcing

Government should:

- Play a legal and macroeconomic role
- Create appropriate labour-market institutions
- Enter into social dialogue at the national and sectoral level

This course is given in the form of a one-day or two-day seminar for groups of participants that include employees, employers and trade unions as well as for groups of managers from individual companies.

FURTHER INFORMATION

International Labour Organisation (ILO) website: www.ilo.org/mcc

DEALING WITH LAYOFFS AT FLOREAL

FLOREAL KNITWEAR LTD, FOUNDED IN 1971, is the second largest wool knitwear supplier in the world after Benetton. Floreal Knitwear operates 12 production units in Mauritius and one in Madagascar, has a total workforce of 5,700 employees, and a turnover of US$61 million. Its main customers are Armani, Gap, Blue Navy, Zara and Célio.

Floreal knitwear was — like many other companies around the world — adversely affected by the Asian financial crisis that started in 1997. After three years of declining profits, in April of 2000 the company was faced with falling prices for sweaters in the USA and Europe, a Mauritian rupee that had appreciated *vis-à-vis* the euro by 20% in five months and a net loss of €5.8 million in the current operating year (2000). Floreal Knitwear knew it had to act quickly if it was to survive.

As a first step, the company decided to conduct a full review and evaluation of all its departments and production units. After this, the company realised that it needed to restructure in order to gain the necessary increase in productivity. Subsequently, after all other restructuring options were explored, Floreal Knitwear was forced to reduce the workforce from 6,150 to 5,500.

Conscious of its good name among its staff and in the community, the company decided to make the extra effort to restructure in a socially sensitive way. As part of these efforts, the company took the following steps:

- A careful evaluation of all employees that was transparent and fair
- Sensitivity training for managers who had to dismiss people in their departments
- Dialogue and communication with all involved, [11] including with:
  - Employees and their representatives
  - The Ministry of Labour and Industrial Relations
  - The Employers' Federation
  - The Industrial and Vocational Training Board (IVTB)
- The setting-up of a re-skilling and reorientation programme financed by the company and IVTB, including the provision of a hotline for employees to enquire about training

On 2nd June 2000, 376 employees in 20 different units were laid off. As a result of the company's careful planning:

- 90 employees completed training courses in information technology (IT), the hotel business, entrepreneurship and maintenance.
- The commitment of employees to the company remained after the restructuring.
- Team spirit among managers was improved.

Nevertheless, the company admits that the restructuring was a very painful experience and some things could have been done better. For example, many employees were not expecting to be laid off, which increased the level of stress for all involved.

FURTHER INFORMATION

International Labour Organisation (ILO) website: www.ilo.org/mcc

Floreal Knitwear Ltd email: fkl@floreal.intnet.mu

---

11 As a part of this strategy the company hired an expert in communication.

UNIONISATION FOR A BETTER WORKING CLIMATE: DELTA ELECTRONICS

DELTA ELECTRONICS, FOUNDED IN 1971, IS A leading Asian supplier in the field of hardware electronics. With headquarters in Thailand's Samutprakarn Province, Delta Electronics employs more than 11,000 people and has business operations and production sites around the globe. Delta Electronics plc has four affiliated subsidiaries:

- Delta Networks, a major producer of networking products
- Cyntec, a high-technology company specialising in thin-film technology and products
- Delta Optoelectronics, producing large-size colour LED displays and polymer LED displays[12]
- Yuasa-Delta Technology, a company manufacturing rechargeable batteries

Thailand is a founding member of the International Labour Organisation (ILO), which, in turn, has been providing the country with technical assistance in order to strengthen the capacity of employers' and workers' organisations in collective bargaining and dispute settlement, workplace cooperation, social security and wage issues. Although Thailand counts ten trade union congresses, trade unions are rather fragmented. In February 2000, the Thai Parliament passed the State Enterprise Labour Relations Bill, giving workers the right to organise more than one trade union in the same company, as well as the right to join any confederation of private enterprise trade unions and to bargain collectively. However, only 2% of Thailand's total workforce is currently unionised, and collective bargaining is carried out mainly at the company level rather than at industry level.

In 1998, staff turnover at Delta Electronics was more than 8% per month. This high level of turnover not only caused significant administrative expenses but also led to high recruitment and training costs and created an atmosphere of unrest. Rates of sick leave were also too high. The situation was exacerbated by the economic crisis of the late 1990s.

In order to respond to these challenges and to improve the company's competitiveness Delta's management decided to take active measures to reduce staff turnover by improving employees' satisfaction levels and help them identify better with the company's business goals.

The management introduced a policy that actively encouraged unionisation, well aware of the advantages this could create with regard to opinion-building, reliable negotiations, decision-making and improved communication. By providing administrative and financial support, it also helped create a labour union — the Delta Labour Union.

One of the main reasons why the company's management encouraged the creation of the Delta Labour Union was its respect for the right of workers to form and join trade unions as set out in International Labour Conventions 87 and 98. These Conventions are not directly addressed to employers but rather to governments of ILO member countries. However, they can, on a voluntary basis, serve as managerial guidelines and sources of policy and strategy formulation at the company level.

The Delta Labour Union is the first labour union in the EPZ (export-processing zones), the industrial zone where the company is located). Tensions between workers' and employers' representatives diminished significantly after its formation. No formal collective bargaining procedure has taken place so far, but both parties meet on a regular basis to exchange views and ideas. A newsletter is published every two months, a television programme is produced and the 'labour committee', consisting of union members and managers, meets regularly. In addition, the post of labour relations officer has been created, to follow up complaints and questions.

Three years after the unionisation initiative, Delta has improved its competitive position, almost doubled its workforce and gained new customers. The company has also successfully tackled the problems of high rates of staff turnover and sickness absence. The results are impressive:

- Annual turnover is less than 3%, compared with almost 100% when the initiative started.
- 70% of the workforce is 100% present.
- Employee satisfaction has increased dramatically.

FURTHER INFORMATION

International Labour Organisation (ILO) website: www.ilo.org/multi

---

12   LED = light-emitting diode.

LABOUR RIGHTS SELF-ASSESSMENT

Business for Social Responsibility

BUSINESS FOR SOCIAL RESPONSIBILITY (BSR) has developed labour rights training courses for suppliers to multinational enterprises to assist them in the development of operational policies and practices consistent with the labour rights principles contained in the UN Global Compact. These courses have been delivered to several thousand business people in more than 20 countries around the world in the past six years.

As part of the training, BSR has created a range of tools to assist suppliers and buyers in the understanding and implementation of good practice with respect to applicable labour standards.

The aim of this tool is to enable suppliers to self-assess their performance, address any shortcomings and make improvements to achieve and demonstrate implementation of core labour standards. It is intended to promote proactive work by suppliers to address concerns about social and environmental performance that are being expressed more and more frequently in the global marketplace.

The tool is specifically designed to be applied by companies producing goods under contract for multinational enterprises and relies on a basic question-and-answer approach. Companies that use this diagnostic can anticipate the questions asked by their customers and, therefore, manage important labour issues more effectively.

The tool can be implemented in a short period of time by using information that is readily at hand. It is available in English, simplified Chinese and Spanish.

FURTHER INFORMATION

Business for Social Responsibility (BSR) website: www.bsr.com

CASE STUDY

CAPITALISING ON EXPERIENCE: THE GREY REVOLUTION AT B&Q

B&Q PLC IS THE UK'S LEADING DO-IT-YOURSELF (DIY) product retailer, with annual sales of US$3.9 billion and a 13.5% share of the home repair, maintenance and improvement market. Worldwide, the company employs over 35,000 people and has sales of nearly US$6 billion.

One of B&Q's main corporate social responsibility (CSR) initiatives was introduced more than a decade ago. Started in 1989, the initiative was a pilot employment policy to promote the employment of older people and was one of the company's first diversity programmes.

Discrimination against people on the basis of age is not uncommon in the UK. The Institute for Employment Studies (IES) has found that between 25% and 34% of UK employers use explicit age bars on jobs. Whereas other European countries, including France and Spain, have age-related legislation (such as a ban on using age limits in job advertisements), the UK still has no legislation to prevent age discrimination. There are plans to change this policy, with the Department for Trade and Industry drafting new regulations to implement EU legislation on discrimination, which must be implemented by the end of 2006.

B&Q and various non-governmental organisations (NGOs) argue that discriminatory employment practices relating to age pay no attention the rapid growth in Britain's ageing population. More than 40% of the UK workforce is currently over 45 years old. Furthermore, the past 15 years have seen a substantial decrease in the number of 20–24-year-olds in employment. Ageism in the workplace creates physical and mental hardship not only for the over 50s but also for their dependants. Contrary to public assumptions, research conducted by B&Q found that 58% of staff over 50 years old had members of their family that depended on

them financially, and 16% had to care for relatives, mainly parents who were elderly or infirm. Commenting on the survey results, then B&Q chair Jim Hodkinson said that:

> Increased life expectancy, a growing number of people not willing or able to rely on the state to look after dependants and an increasing proportion of older people against a backdrop of a falling number of school leavers; these are all factors which need to be considered in planning recruitment policies.

During 1989, recruiting from the core labour pool became more difficult for the company. B&Q's efforts to promote diversity were therefore strongly rooted in commercial realities. The fact that older people were more likely to have knowledge and experience in the DIY trade, along with an urgent need to address changing UK demographics and the need for well-motivated retail staff, caused B&Q to launch its so-called Grey Revolution in 1989.

Initially, the board of directors did have some concerns regarding older employees working with some of the more physically demanding aspects of the job and with new technology. B&Q therefore decided to test the new programme with an initial job advertisement for 55 new employees at a new store in Macclesfield, Cheshire. When Warwick University evaluated the Macclesfield store against other stores, it topped the list on most measures. In 1993, in her independent review of the Grey Revolution initiative, Mandy Jetter noted the following achievements:

- A massive reduction in unattributable stock loss
- A very low absentee rate
- The best sales record for the whole of B&Q

Other figures cited by B&Q to demonstrate the new over-50s store's success compared with other B&Q retail outlets at the time include:

- Profits 18% higher
- Staff turnover six times lower
- Absenteeism 39% lower
- Shrinkage 59% lower
- Improved customer perception of service
- Increased skill base in the staff team

B&Q has not continued to pursue an only-50s employment policy for specific stores. The company's aim is simply 'to achieve a balance of ages throughout the company to reflect the age profiles of communities in which the stores are based'.

In order to build on the success of the pilot project, the company initially adopted an over-50 target of 10% of the workforce, later revised to at least 15% of staff. Between 1991 and 1998, the percentage of employees that were over 50 years of age in B&Q stores rose from 7.3% to 13% (excluding temporary staff). Today, 18% of B&Q employees are over 50 years old; its oldest employee is 89.

FURTHER INFORMATION

International Labour Organisation (ILO) website: www.ilo.org

B&Q website: www.diy.com

WORKING WITH DISABLED PEOPLE: ALIMCO

ALIMCO IS THE LARGEST MANUFACTURER of artificial limbs in South Asia. An undertaking of the government of India, it employs 72 disabled persons, about 13% of its workforce. It is one of the first organisations in India that has been built on the 'All Access' philosophy. There are no architectural barriers for disabled workers in the factory. By providing ramps with side railings, large-size Western-style toilets, washbasins at a convenient height, special doors and a lift for the three-storey building, wheelchair-bound employees can move easily around and between any of the buildings of the company. A large number of jigs and fixtures have been specially manufactured for disabled workers to achieve the desired level of accuracy in production. The company adapts the work to the worker and provides hands-on training. As a result of minor modifications carried out to suit the disability of a person, the productivity of such disabled employees has been observed to be, by and large, higher than able-bodied employees (in some cases by more than 200%).

Alimco also maintains healthy relations with labour unions authorised to negotiate on issues relating to labour welfare. As a result of healthy industrial relations, the company has achieved 140% capacity utilisation. The concept of 'Workers Participation in Management' is effectively implemented by involving them in shop-level and plant-level committees.

There is a total prohibition on child, forced and compulsory labour in the corporation.

The rights and opportunities of female employees in the company are fully ensured, and they are given equal opportunities for participation and development.

FURTHER INFORMATION

Artificial Limbs Manufacturing Corporation of India, Kanpur, India, website: www.artlimbs.com

Corporate Success through People: Making International Labour Standards Work For You

Type of resource: publication

Author organisation: International Labour Organisation

Year of publication: 2000

This book advocates and promotes the notion that international labour standards (ILS) developed by the International Labour Organisation (ILO) are tools for good managerial practice and that they reflect the principles on which good management systems are based. The book seeks to help managers understand the interrelationship between best management practice and ILS by presenting numerous case studies from large and small companies from different regions and industries.

FURTHER INFORMATION

International Labour Organisation (ILO) website: www.ilo.org/mcc

As One Employer to Another . . . What's All This About Equality?

Type of resource: publication

Author organisation: International Labour Organisation, Bureau for Employers' Activities

Year of publication: 1998

The purpose of this publication is to clarify the issues relating to equality between men and women from an employer's point of view. It also presents a number of business arguments for developing company action in this area and provides an outline of the steps companies can take towards the introduction and management of an equal opportunity policy.

FURTHER INFORMATION

International Labour Organisation (ILO), Bureau for Employer Activities website: www.ilo.org/actemp

Publication: www.ilo.org/public/english/dialogue/actemp/download/1998/equal.pdf

CHAPTER TWELVE

IMPACT ON VALUE CHAIN

COOPERATION AND TRANSACTIONS WITH

suppliers and customers enable a company to realise its added financial value. This is also where it confronts its competition. There is only value added when someone buys from the company at a price that is higher than the company's total cost to produce and deliver the product or service. And that price must be *perceived* as a better deal than buying from a competitor, not buying at all or saving the money for other purposes. This is true between both you and your customers and also between you and your suppliers. Although this is elementary marketing, for the purposes of this book we will show how the UN Global Compact principles can enhance this transaction.

The operative keyword in the above description of the transaction is *perceived*. No matter how much clarity and detail is provided in the technical description of the product, no matter how much standardisation is attained in the market, every product retains a 'cultural footprint'; every buyer

has a cultural sensitivity. So, the perfectly calibrated board of plywood suddenly turns out to contain wood from a virgin forest logged for cash by a dissident army in a faraway poor country. It was a commodity product just a minute ago but now it is perceived as tainted — *if* the buyer cares. And buyers *have* started to care about environmental destruction, human rights abuses, child labour, threatened species, animal testing and other 'evils'. They care more for certain problems at certain times. For example, the problem of child labour in the manufacturing of sporting goods and clothing is perceived to be more widespread than in the processing of scrap metal for chandeliers with a colonial design. Outrage about abuse is uneven — it often depends on the determination and ability of pressure groups to 'represent' the distant victims. The impact also depends on the interest of the public, the mobilisation of the media and the sensitivity of the intermediaries in the supply chain. A high-profile branded company cannot afford to take risks with its reputation when public outrage is based on a plausible cause. This also applies to any company that has made a visible commitment to the Global Compact principles — it must avoid or rapidly resolve any instances of real abuse.

Marketing rule number one remains valid — buyers prefer the product with the perceived better total quality-to-price profile. It is then advisable to understand how customers perceive the issues around the Global Compact principles, particularly if they have not yet articulated a public position. Companies need to ask: 'How aligned are our respective views on social responsibility?' 'Where can we see shared causes?' But tact is needed. It is not easy to change customers' behaviour. Many outside stakeholders wish that companies were agents of change with a strong activist style. However, rather than direct interference, the best approach is to understand customer needs in the context of their unspoken cultural and ethical sensitivities. As for the other quality features, this intelligence is built through an integrated approach to customer and market needs. It is only on this basis that a company can decide how its commitment to the Global Compact can enhance its competitive offerings to those consumers — or how their beliefs and practices may compromise its standing with observers of corporate behaviour. At least a company can work itself out of a relationship with a supplier if it suspects a potential risk to its reputation that it cannot influence or manage within the relationship.

It is somewhat easier to bring suppliers and contractors towards company requirements, as they depend on the company's purchases. However, companies with mature social and environmental performance levels in their own operations have been accused of tolerating their suppliers' or distributors' poorer standards. As stated in a *New York Times* article in December 2003, many companies don't want to violate workers' rights themselves, 'but they are willing to look the other way when their contractors do it'.[1] At the same time, many companies have influenced their contractors to adopt strict environmental, labour, safety and anti-corruption practices identical to their own. They even often include them in their performance indicators and targets. And yet ensuring consistent practice in far-ranging supply chains is complex. Although pressing suppliers to adhere to national legislation is a good starting point, there are growing expectations that the supply chains of companies reflect international norms and conventions. Kaspar Eigenmann, head of corporate health, safety and environment at Novartis, describes the challenge:[2]

> You must bear in mind that we have about 40,000 suppliers. We are thinking of building three elements into our contracts with suppliers — firstly, a clause which obliges suppliers to adhere to the basic principles of law; secondly, a statement in the contracts to the effect that the supplier is as committed as we are to the advances in those areas covered by the Global Compact; and finally, the proviso that, in the event of grossly incorrect conduct, we are also free to terminate any such contract.

As major companies move up the supply chain to disseminate guidelines that reflect their own policies and codes of ethics, and follow-up with compliance audits, they can find it more effective and efficient to join forces in sector-wide initiatives or partnerships with UN agencies or with non-governmental organisations (NGOs). Such initiatives should help raise the level of performance more efficiently than would be the case were the process to be undertaken many times by every major customer. Partnerships with NGOs and UN agencies also facilitate capacity-building and create legitimacy in the eyes of consumers and other observers. They induce ad hoc, voluntary corrections to the market and trade framework. The market otherwise finds it difficult to produce rules that internalise universal principles in ways that reward compliance with favourable price signals. Without support from the main actors — governments and business — this will not happen for a long time. And it is, in any case, complicated. The market at large is still insensitive to most of the issues discussed here, and prices do not yet help to determine under which conditions goods and their raw materials have been produced.

---

1 S. Greenhouse, 'Week in Review: Middlemen in the Low-wage Economy', *New York Times*, 28 December 2003.
2 Novartis 'Corporate Citizenship at Novartis' (2001), www.novartis.com/corporatecitizen.

The creation of specific standards and effective labels of conformity hold some promise. Once customers and consumers have this information, and a significant minority purchase accordingly, market forces will drive further change. In the meantime, forward-looking producers can differentiate their products to nurture the growth of this market through good, honest communication. The Global Compact performance model can help them do that competitively.

The information in this chapter demonstrates the efforts made in recent decades to extend our understanding of impacts and 'upstream' risks, from buyers to suppliers. They also show how to extend the domain of awareness and responsibility 'downstream', from supplier to customers and consumers. Integrated value chains are an important factor of excellence and competitiveness. The best companies have the best suppliers and the best customers. They share knowledge and principles — critical information moves up and down the value chain. Often, therefore, a tool that was developed and used in the 'upstream' direction of the value chain can also be adapted to identify risks and opportunities in the market and to improve the company's product and customer mix accordingly.

CORPORATE SOCIAL RESPONSIBILITY AND CUSTOMER SATISFACTION: BT HAS NUMBERS!

BT HAS OVER 19 MILLION RESIDENTIAL customers in the UK and, for many years, has monitored overall customer satisfaction ratings based on over 3,000 face-to-face interviews every month. A detailed statistical analysis of this mass of data identified four factors strongly correlated with changes in overall customer satisfaction (see Table 8).

The cause and effect modulation (or elasticity) factors for each of the four main drivers of customer satisfaction are best explained by an example: if BT's overall image and reputation goes up by, say, 2%, then it would expect to see a 0.84% (2% × 0.42) increase in its customer satisfaction rating.

	Customer satisfaction			
Direction of relationship	⬆	⬆	⬇	⬆
Elasticity factor	0.31	0.46	−0.06	0.42
Factor	Product and services	Contact and experience	Price and value	Image and reputation

Table 8 **FACTORS OF CUSTOMER SATISFACTION AT BT**

Modulation factors and figures were adjusted by using a process of refined iteration to achieve an optimum fit to the customer satisfaction figures. The model was then allowed to 'free run' to assess its predictive quality. Results to date have been very encouraging.

It is very important to emphasise that the model predicts *changes* in customer satisfaction figures and does not identify absolute proportions. This explains why the principal four modulation figures do not add up to one, and why it would be wrong to say, for example, that BT's reputation delivers 42% of customer satisfaction.

In opinion polls, members of the public often say that ethical issues inform their purchasing decisions. However, given that each consumer makes thousands of purchasing decisions every year, it is only in a relatively small number of cases that the consumer actually makes a

continued over ➔

CORPORATE SOCIAL RESPONSIBILITY AND CUSTOMER SATISFACTION: BT HAS NUMBERS!

→ *from previous page*

conscious consideration of the supplier's environmental, social and ethical performance.

Given that the BT model shows that a company's reputation has a significant influence on customer satisfaction ratings, and given that corporate social responsibility (CSR) is a component part of reputation, this would suggest that there could be an important *subconscious* CSR element to purchasing decisions.

As part of its corporate reputation survey analysis with the general public, BT has, over the years, included a number of CSR-related questions. This has allowed it to apply the same statistical correlation methodology to determine the contribution that CSR makes to the image and reputation modulation factor of customer satisfaction. This analysis is based on 80 months of data, comprising tens of thousands of interviews. Table 9 shows a breakdown of the most significant factors affecting the reputation modulation factor. The figures in bold type relate to CSR and constitute over 25% of the 0.42 reputation modulation factor.

Customer satisfaction

0.42

Sub-factor of image and reputation	Elasticity factor
Cares about customers	0.05
Trust	0.05
Good role model	0.04
Responsible to society	0.04
Technology innovator	0.04
Prefer to buy from	0.03
Meets future needs	0.03
Helps UK business	0.03
Reliability	0.03
Treats employees well	0.02
Environmentally responsible	0.02
Keeps unprofitable payphones	0.02
Supports charities	0.01
More than one phone company	0.01

Note: entries in bold type relate to corporate social responsibility.

Table 9 INFLUENCES ON THE IMAGE AND REPUTATION MODULATION FACTOR

Taking the model to the bounds of reasonable extrapolation, the 25% would indicate that if BT were to cease all its CSR activities (i.e. cease treating employees with respect, ignore environmental issues, no longer emphasise the need to act with integrity [trust], stop non-profitable services and cancel all community activities) then its customer satisfaction rating would drop by about 10% (25% × 0.42).

Evidence of the cause and effect link between improved customer satisfaction and customer loyalty comes from BT's general consumer survey data. Of the most dissatisfied customers, one-third say they will leave BT. This is significant because the most discerning customers are also the most profitable, each delivering an average annual 'earnings before interest and taxes' of roughly £70.

FURTHER INFORMATION

British Telecom website: www.bt.com/betterworld

BAA: BRITISH AIRPORTS LAUNCH INTO SUPPLY CHAIN REVIEW

BAA PLC IS THE OWNER OF SEVEN UK

airports, including the world's busiest international airport, London Heathrow. It also has management contracts or stakes in ten airports outside the UK, plus retail management contracts at two airports in the USA. It has over 11,000 employees and in 2002 generated revenues of £1.9 billion and a group operating profit of £587 million.

BAA plc recognises the importance of managing its supply chain and has been working on supply chain sustainability performance improvements. To kick-start this effort, BAA held a workshop to determine which areas of the purchasing department represented the majority of the organisation's spending with its suppliers and subcontractors. As a result, the following three streams of supply chain activity were prioritised for action:

- Construction materials
- Consultancy
- Cleaning services

From this initial workshop, BAA was able to list its key supply chain risks and opportunities. The logic was: 'where there is a big spend, there is a potential risk'. BAA then developed a simple matrix (see Table 10), with the vertical dimension covering areas of high spend and the horizontal dimension representing the key sustainability indicators (air quality, climate change, noise, waste, water quality, contaminated land, biodiversity, local labour and suppliers, respect for people and use of materials and natural resources).

BAA then rated whether there were any actual or potential low, medium or high sustainability risks to these indicators in any of the high-spend areas it had identified, filling in the cells in the matrix with one, two or three ticks

Areas of high spend	Key sustainability indicators									
	Air quality	Climate change	Noise	Waste	Water quality	Land contamination	Biodiversity	Local labour and suppliers	Respect for people	Use of materials and natural resources
Construction										
Consultants (e.g. architects)										
Waste disposal										
Cleaning services										
⋮										

Sustainability risk
✓ = Low ✓✓ = Medium ✓✓✓ = High

Table 10 **MATRIX FOR A RISK AND OPPORTUNITY ANALYSIS IN THE BAA SUPPLY CHAIN**

respectively. Where areas of high spend generated high sustainability risks, BAA produced management plans for these priority areas that set objectives, goals, strategies and measures (OGSMs) for the company's purchasing managers, suppliers and subcontractors relevant to a specific supply stream. For example, its OGSMs for construction included the determination of the provenance of wood or wood products and a ban on the use of PVC (polyvinyl chloride).

BAA's priorities stem from the combination of high-spend areas in its supply chain and the sustainability indicators under the highest risk from supply chain activity. As management plans are delivered and performance improved, BAA will work on the remaining medium-priority and low-priority issues plus any emerging issues that may arise as it continues its work.

As a result, BAA has developed a range of supply chain management initiatives and approaches, including:

- Supplier and subcontractor questionnaires
- Briefings for purchasing managers
- Sustainable development criteria and targets in contracts with suppliers
- Second-tier supplier training and help for local firms
- Seminars and follow-up meetings with large suppliers

FURTHER INFORMATION

BAA sustainable development website:
www.baa.com/main/corporate/sustainable_development_frame.html

CARREFOUR INITIATES A PARTNERSHIP AGAINST CHILD LABOUR

CARREFOUR IS A FRENCH RETAILER WITH consolidated sales of €68.7 billion at the end of 2002. Operating 9,632 stores in 30 countries, Carrefour manages hypermarkets and supermarkets. The company has 396,662 employees.

Carrefour demonstrates its respect for fundamental human rights throughout its operations through its work with FIDH (Fédération Internationale des Droits de l'Homme), a grouping of 116 human rights organisations from around the world. In conjunction with FIDH, the company established INFANS, a monitoring agency, in 2000, which has helped Carrefour to establish a code of conduct for its suppliers. The purpose of the code is to commit the company's suppliers to recognise and respect international standards regarding working conditions set out in various International Labour Organisation (ILO) Conventions with regard to the abolition of child labour and forced labour, freedom of association and collective bargaining, minimum wages and hours of work, occupational health and safety and non-discrimination. The basic goal of the code is to contribute to the gradual and total elimination of child labour while respecting cultural diversity.

In addition to developing the code, INFANS has also developed a monitoring and verification methodology. This methodology involves local partners as well as the use of internal and external audits. By April 2003, 288 audits were conducted in seven countries, involving 214,265 employees. The audits took place in sectors such as textiles, footwear and food. FIDH helped to identify priorities for action in INFANS and also helped in promoting an understanding of human rights risks in local operational contexts. It involves local non-governmental organisations (NGOs) in monitoring compliance with international human rights standards through, for example, unexpected factory visits. So far, 15% of Carrefour's imports have been covered by detailed audits.

Carrefour's ambition is that the whole of the French retail sector will move to this way of doing things. The Fédération du Commerce et la Distribution currently coordinates the project Clause Sociale, which aims to encourage French retailers to share their experience in supply chain management and to harmonise their efforts in this area. The initiative currently involves 14 French distributors, including Camif, Casino, Carrefour, Cora, Leclerc, Galeries Lafayette and Monoprix. These companies have committed to using the same questionnaire for their social audits, which assess supplier performance on the basis of ILO core conventions. Between 2000 and 2002, the above group of distributors have conducted 670 audits, covering more than 15% of their supply chains abroad.

FURTHER INFORMATION

Carrefour website: www.carrefour.com

Fédération Internationale des Droits de l'Homme (FIDH) website: www.fidh.org

ETHICAL TRADING INITIATIVE WORKBOOK AND CD-ROM

Ethical Trading Initiative

THE ETHICAL TRADING INITIATIVE (ETI)

Workbook is an ethical trading manual for sourcing companies, based on ETI's experiences and learning to date.

Presented as a step-by-step guidance manual, it is intended to be of practical use to staff responsible for ethical sourcing. It covers the key management issues that companies need to address when setting up and implementing an ethical sourcing strategy.

ETI, an alliance of companies, trade union organisations and non-governmental organisations (NGOs), was set up to identify and promote good practice in the implementation of labour codes. The workbook is based on lessons from ETI's tripartite experimental projects and on the day-to-day experiences of ETI member companies that have been implementing the ETI Base Code for several years. The workbook therefore reflects both the 'nuts and bolts' commercial reality in which ethical sourcing must operate and the 'ethical' rigour of the workers' rights and developmental agendas of ETI's NGO and trade union members.

The workbook has been written primarily for sourcing companies that are relatively new to ethical sourcing. It will also be of direct use to:

- Other organisations that have adopted an ethical sourcing policy or code of labour practice (e.g. government departments or large NGOs)
- Companies, organisations or individuals who advise others on ethical sourcing strategy (e.g. consultancy firms or NGO policy advisers)
- Others who wish to develop a practical understanding of what companies need to do to implement an ethical sourcing strategy (e.g. manufacturers that have to implement a customer's code of practice)

It covers:

- An introduction to ethical sourcing and the ETI
- Building support for ethical sourcing strategies
- Understanding supply chains
- Getting suppliers to comply with an ethical sourcing code

- Inspections
- Corrective actions
- Reporting
- Verification
- Contacts and information sources
- Practical resources (e.g. sample inspection checklists and audit report formats)
- Case studies of companies' experience (e.g. a member company's experience of working with its suppliers to implement corrective actions)

It is designed to be a 'living document', and a new edition will be produced annually.

FURTHER INFORMATION

Ethical Trading Initiative (ETI) website: www.ethicaltrade.org

ETI Base Code: www.ethicaltrade.org/Z/lib/base/index.shtml

HEWLETT-PACKARD DEVELOPS A SUPPLIER'S CODE OF CONDUCT

HEWLETT-PACKARD (HP), HEADQUARTERED IN Palo Alto, CA, is a technology solutions provider to consumers, businesses and institutions. It operates in 178 countries and employs approximately 160,000 people across the globe.

This case study describes how HP developed a human rights and labour policy within its global citizenship strategy and is engaged in the complex and unclearly defined issues of human rights within its business. The case also describes ongoing development and challenges, and examines how the company has been implementing the UN Global Compact, specifically the principles that deal with human rights.

The company contractually obliges its top 40 suppliers to commit to its supply chain code of conduct. These cover 100 sites and account for 80% of its spent dollars. HP is in the process of increasing the number of suppliers it involves, making this commitment and strengthening the means by which it ensures compliance with the obligation. Eventually, this code of conduct will be explicit in all new supplier contracts, so compliance will be a necessity to do business with HP.

In developing its supply chain code of conduct, HP did its own extensive benchmarking and research, and worked with Business for Social Responsibility (BSR), a think-tank and consultancy concerned with corporate social responsibility (CSR), based in San Francisco. The director of supply chain services stated that HP scoured the landscape of supplier codes of conduct, and various international standards before developing its own code.

The HP supplier code of conduct professes to focus on compliance with local laws in the areas of environment, worker health and safety, and labour and employment practices and is intended to work in conjunction with management systems to measure, improve and communicate progress in these areas. The treatment of labour issues is fairly comprehensive and, despite the use of headings that refer to compliance with local laws, contains standards, for example, in relation to non-discrimination and prison labour, which may or may not be covered by local legislation. The focus on these issues is positive and its effectiveness will be greatly enhanced by the planned improvements in compliance monitoring (see below).

To meet HP's human rights obligations, the supplier code of conduct should be expanded to cover human rights matters beyond labour issues, matters such as:

- Performance and monitoring of security guards by suppliers
- The impact on the local community of supplier operations
- The penalisation of suppliers with regimes that are corrupt or abusive of human rights

Currently, HP monitors its supply chain by using a self-assessment questionnaire completed by HP's top 40 suppliers. HP then works collaboratively with suppliers to achieve the required standards in any area that is identified as falling below requirements. HP's director of supply chain services reports that HP's suppliers take this process very seriously given the importance to them of their relationship and business with HP. The company is moving to expand and strengthen its supply chain monitoring, extending self-assessment beyond the top 40 suppliers to the suppliers HP regards as 'high-risk'.

At the same time, HP is strengthening the monitoring of the top 40 suppliers by utilising its own procurement auditing capacity to conduct site assessments of supplier performance, moving beyond the self-assessment model. In time, this model will also be extended to the high-risk suppliers. Finally, HP is currently researching appropriate entities to conduct third-party assessment of supplier performance. Selective third-party assessment will be the final stage in the evolution of supply chain monitoring at HP.

FURTHER INFORMATION

Hewlett-Packard website: www.hp.com

Integrating SMEs in Global Value Chains: Towards Partnerships for Development

Type of resource: publication

Author organisation: United Nations Industrial Development Organisation

Year of publication: 2001

This publication surveys the changing role of the private sector in economic development and reviews how the formation of linkages between transnational corporations and small and medium-sized enterprises (SMEs) can integrate SMEs into global value chains, thereby contributing to company development.

FURTHER INFORMATION

United Nations Industrial Development Organisation (UNIDO) website: www.unido.org

Document: www.unido.org/userfiles/PuffK/partnerships02.pdf

SIGMA Supply Chain Strategy and Evaluation

Type of resource: publication

Author organisation: The SIGMA Project

Year of publication: 2001

Two reports on supply chain management, strategy and performance evaluation have been produced in the course of The SIGMA Project. The first report provides an overview of the state of the art in supply chain strategy, management and evaluation. It reviews the approaches used in the following economic sectors:

- Water and power
- Transportation
- Information, consumer electronics and telecommunications
- Retailing
- Leisure and tourism
- The public sector
- Building and construction
- Chemicals

The second report provides a detailed review of the tools and techniques being used by a range of organisations, including the use of:

- Written policies and communications materials
- Supplier performance evaluation questionnaires
- Pre-qualification of suppliers (using environmental and/or social and/or ethical criteria)
- Purchasing guidelines
- 'Shared-goal' partnerships with suppliers
- Contractual specifications that incorporate environmental and social parameters

---

FURTHER INFORMATION

The SIGMA Project website: www.projectsigma.com

Suppliers' Perspectives on Greening the Supply Chain

Type of resource: publication

Author organisation: Business for Social Responsibility

Year of publication: 2001

For this publication, Business for Social Responsibility interviewed representatives from 25 suppliers in four industry sectors:

- Automotives
- Electronics
- Forest products
- Business services

Their insights were sought on the following:

- Current trends in supply chain environmental management
- How these trends are impacting their business
- Their recommendations to customers on effective strategies for addressing environmental issues with suppliers
- Whether and how these suppliers are addressing environmental issues with their own suppliers
- Future trends and directions

The resulting guide provides suppliers' perspectives on how they are able to manage environmental issues affecting or arising from their relationships with customers seeking to ensure positive environmental management throughout their supply chains. The guide also provides useful understanding for companies seeking to apply supplier requirements or requiring guidance on environmental issues.

FURTHER INFORMATION

Business for Social Responsibility (BSR) website: www.bsr.org

Publication: www.bsr.org/BSRResources/Environment/Greening_SupplyChain.pdf

Business and Code of Conduct Implementation: How Firms Use Management Systems for Social Performance

Type of resource: publication

Author organisation: International Labour Organisation

Year of publication: 2003

Business and Code of Conduct Implementation is the first draft of a report on the sports footwear, clothing and retail supplier and buyer inputs for the Business and Decent Work research project funded by the US Department of State, examining the management systems and practices used in the implementation of codes of conduct in global supply chains. The report is based on field research carried out over a two-year period (2000–2002) for the purpose of identifying the key issues involved in the code of conduct implementation process. Visits were made to the headquarters of 20 multinational enterprises (MNEs), located in Europe and the USA. The research team also visited 74 factories, located in Turkey, Sri Lanka, Cambodia, Guatemala, Honduras, China, Vietnam, Thailand and the USA. The findings are based on interviews with over 330 managers at the MNEs and supplier factories visited, with workers and workers' representatives in the companies studied as well as with representatives of government, workers, employers and non-governmental organisations (NGOs) associated with the sectors studied.

In general, the research indicates the need for a broad-based and integrated approach to implementing codes of conduct, with implications for management systems throughout MNEs and their suppliers. It also indicates the importance of a wide-ranging dialogue between various stakeholders, including government, workers' representatives and management.

FURTHER INFORMATION

International Labour Organisation (ILO), Management and Corporate Citizenship Programme website: www.ilo.org/mcc

Strengthening Implementation of Corporate Social Responsibility in Global Supply Chains

Type of resource: publication

Author organisations: Business for Social Responsibility, PricewaterhouseCoopers (Denmark) and the Danish Institute for Human Rights

Year of publication: 2003

Amid the ongoing debate on how best to achieve good social and environmental practices in global supply chains, the World Bank Group commissioned a study on barriers to the achievement of better social and environmental performance in suppliers and also on the options that hold the greatest promise for overcoming those barriers and enabling future improvement.

The report found that individual initiatives are more likely to be successful if undertaken with full regard to other steps than if they are undertaken in isolation. Under the best circumstances, a coherent framework would blend a broad range of public and private efforts: those taken by business alone with those involving partnership between sectors, and those that look both at social issues and at environmental issues. Such an approach would reflect a necessary and natural maturation process as the first generation of efforts to address corporate social responsibility (CSR) in supply chains come to an end and would tend to lead to the more sustainable progress that all parties involved in this debate are seeking.

The study also revealed characteristics of successful approaches that should be considered to help ensure the success of future efforts. These include collaboration between interested parties, local 'ownership', an effort to balance the ongoing need for innovation and experimentation with the desire to achieve scalability, and a renewed effort to identify ways that private and civil society efforts draw on or take note of the potential for government involvement.

FURTHER INFORMATION

Business for Social Responsibility website: www.bsr.org

Danish Institute for Human Rights: www.humanrights.dk

Document website: www.bsr.org/BSRResources/HumanRights/index.cfm

CHAPTER THIRTEEN

IMPACT ON SOCIETY

A COMPANY DIRECTLY SHAPES ITS

surrounding community by providing decent work and income to the citizens who live there. The nature of the working conditions affect family life and the quality of life in the community. The larger the company is in relation to the community, the larger is its impact and responsibility.

The company also affects society at large in many ways beyond jobs and salaries, beyond its purchases and its product sales. Just being there changes the landscape or the urban fabric. It creates new traffic patterns, and perhaps noises or smells. It borrows water from the closest natural reservoirs; it returns that water — maybe better or maybe worse, but never quite the same — or utilises a part of it with its products or emits it as a vapour through its stacks. Its impacts may be obvious or subtle, but they effect all the natural cycles. It generates new molecules that take a ride with its products and, because they are sometimes so stable, continue to drift and accumulate in nature long after the product is consumed.

In the 1970s the techniques of detection began to alert society to the magnitude of the material flux caused by the postwar boom. Its ripple effects on human health, directly or through the food chain, accelerated the environmental movement and the policy infrastructure of environmental ministries and compliance agencies.

An array of legislative instruments and major conventions continues to this day to battle for the elimination or mitigation of the worst effects of our economic activity. Increasingly, companies are coming under scrutiny for their impacts on global governance. Corporate lobbying of governments and intergovernmental bodies (e.g. on the Kyoto Protocol) can be critical to the outcome and is widely seen as a key component of their impact on society.

The generally accepted wisdom is that the producer or supplier, rather than the consumer or citizen, is the most efficient leverage point for change (e.g. through the polluter-pays principle or new legislative requirements on extended product responsibility). There is a strong logic to this view: in the complex production–consumption system of the global economy, business represents concentrations of knowledge, resources and an innovation capacity that give it the power to change while continuing to produce output and value.

Whether this 'supply bias' to environmental policy is sufficiently effective, or whether a 'demand side' responsibility could also enhance our collective ability and speed to progress, may well be the next stage of the sustainability debate. The discussion on sustainable consumption is an example. It is concerned about the evidence that many advances made on the supply side are overtaken by increasing consumer demand and unsustainable consumption patterns. Is new computer technology, praised for its 'dematerialisation' benefits, causing us to use less or in fact more paper? The challenge is to persuade consumers to consume differently. The responsibility of the producer to provide product information that enables consumers to make informed choices is only a part of the answer — necessary, but not yet sufficient to cause an effective shift towards sustainability.

In the meantime, the 'supply bias' is the context that generated corporate social responsibility and the mantra of many business people: 'we hold our licence to operate from society'. Business people

should recognise that this implies a number of tensions or dilemmas that are, as always, best managed through innovation.

First, there is the tension of boundaries.

Suppose you consider yourself an excellent producer of paint, performing beyond any health, environmental or human resources standards that apply to your industry. You are keen to engage with stakeholders. In fact you have invited a group of prominent stakeholders to discuss your strategy to be 'the most responsible supplier of coating materials' and now you are stunned by their feedback:

- We congratulate you for changing all your products from solvent-based to aqueous dispersions; but now 40% of your product weight is water. How can you justify shipping around the world so much good water from the local communities where you operate? How do you defend the low price you pay for water?

- You buy a lot of zinc oxide and other metal-based pigments. How confident are you that they are responsibly mined and not supporting local zones of conflict?

- As much as 15% of paint is generally wasted at its end-use stage. What do you do to avoid improper disposal of this waste?

- What do you do to cause your customers to apply your paint to energy-efficient surfaces? Can you see, beyond coating materials, the

tremendous needs for sustainable construction and affordable housing for the poor?

- We commend you for the high standards of your plants in developing countries, but what will you do about HIV and AIDS? The virus travels with your truck drivers, 'under your badge'. If you think it can't be your problem, think again — no one else educates drivers; no one else provides affordable treatment in those countries.

This is the tension of boundaries. You see your business as making an outstanding-quality paint to satisfy the needs of professional and domestic decorators, but stakeholders may see you causing serious problems that you should be tackling. Their expectations are serious and demanding; they voice the silent anxiety of millions who wish someone would take charge. How far into that space will you set your boundaries of responsible excellence? Which of your stakeholders' concerns could provide real business opportunities?

Lars Rieben Sørensen, president and CEO of Novo Nordisk, the leading producer of insulin and diabetes cures, puts it this way:

Defeating diabetes is not just a business proposition — diabetes is a huge individual and societal problem, the consequences of which the world's leaders are only beginning to understand. As a company we deal with the rapidly growing epidemic of diabetes. We cannot solve the enormous problems of hunger, we cannot overcome illiteracy, or provide housing, sanitation or decently paid work to everyone. But what we can do is to acknowledge these factors and identify where and how we can make a difference.[1]

There is then the tension of expectations.

Your strategic ambition envisions 30% more output in five years, but all your efficiency targets will be lost because of your growth! You will certainly use more water and more pigments; you will release more carbon dioxide (CO_2) and cause more waste in the product chain! You are not sustainable!

In your mind the world needs more paint to ward off corrosion, mould, filth and drabness. Paint is both an enabler and a signal of economic development; it also provides jobs. But the problem is that the collateral impacts of more paint in the world should go down; you cannot get stuck with arguing that waste should go up. This is why many still hold that the term 'sustainable development' is an oxymoron: it defines growth and reduction at the same time. More development, less environmental damage and human rights violations, more work but less cheap labour and discrimination. The very commitment to the UN Global Compact principles and the objectives of sustainable development imply that one resolves the tension of expectations in favour of the absolute

1 Novo Nordisk, 'Sustainability Report 2002', Novo Nordisk, Novo Allé, 2880 Bagsværd, Denmark; www.novonordisk.com.

reduction of negative impacts; for example, you may say:

- We will grow by 30% but our major new product line will have a coating power that will allow consumers to reduce usage by 20%. Combined with other process efficiencies we strive to improve our absolute fuel and waste numbers.

- While we increase output, our product coating power and longevity will increase. Seen over the life cycle from the consumer perspective our customers will get the same surface protection with 40% less paint.

However, this is easier to suggest than to realise. But the point is that society expects and needs bold visions and engagement. They have a strong business value — they prompt creative solutions and drive the innovation process. They also indirectly support the licence to grow because a credible scenario of sustainable growth enhances the access to capital based on trust from a number of financial institutions. A licence to grow is rather more valuable than to be stuck still struggling to maintain the licence to operate.

But if the advice is correct — business should integrate society's needs by redefining the boundaries of corporate responsibility and resolve the tension of expectations by doing more of the good things — why has not everyone already rushed to follow it? The reason is the same one that causes stakeholders to pile on pressure in the first place —

the failure of existing business and government institutions to reach a consensus about the nature of the problem and solution.

Many of our sustainable development problems are just too complex for our existing institutions. They work well only in clear cause–effect situations, such as the case of the destruction of the ozone layer:

1 The ozone layer in the high atmosphere gets thinner and thinner.

2 Scientists suggest that chlorofluorocarbons (CFCs) are the principal cause.

3 The producers argue for a while but consensus builds.

4 Harmless substitutes are developed by industry.

5 Governments negotiate a compulsory phase-out timetable and, over time, compliance gains momentum.

Conversely, there is the case of global warming:

1 The average global temperature and the frequency of exceptional climate events are rising.

2 Most scientists declare the greenhouse gases, particularly CO_2, as culprits and predict more trouble on the climate front.

3 Every industry and every household is a source of CO_2.

4 There is no easy substitute for the CO_2 technologies that ensure our economic development.

5 Governments are unable to embrace a real collective mitigation strategy; while some are ready to move forward, others even deny that there is a problem.

Here, our institutions look weak in the face of such complex global problems. The same is also true for poverty that pushes young children into work rather than school, for the rush from rural zones to urban centres, for personal mobility without the combustion engine, for trade rules that also work for the poor countries, and for a host of other situations. At best our institutions can monitor the problem and orchestrate some voluntary collective initiatives.

In many respects our institutions are just plainly deficient. The current economic undervaluation of public goods discourages investment into clean water supplies and sanitation; numerous subsidies privilege or shield certain economic actors from change at the expense of others and the consumer. The list of general institutional failures and of obsolete or flawed economic conventions is long. They affect the most developed economies as well as the poorest.

But there are also country-specific handicaps that make some nations the most vulnerable. Each year the Heritage Foundation and the *Wall Street Journal* publish a league table to assess the factors that most influence the institutional framework of economic growth. Called the 'Index of Economic Freedom' it has shown undeniably how clear, stable, policies, instead of continuous government

interference or repression, stimulate prosperity. In 2003, of 156 countries only 71 were assessed to be 'mostly free' or 'free'.[2]

These same conditions put limitations and risks on how far corporations can stretch their boundaries of responsibility. Why invest in water conservation if the price signals encourage every other competitor to use as much as they need? Why worry if the lack of property rights in a majority of regions undercuts legitimate entrepreneurship? How does one gain market share for use of fuel-efficient engines or heaters when the inefficient technologies are offered at a discount? What does one do with bureaucratic red tape when others cut through with sealed envelopes to public officials? Most of the reasons that push human rights and environmental champions to ask companies for change actually handicap companies to change.

Why bother? The answer is, for two obvious, simple, reasons: inertia only makes things worse, not better, and companies and organisations that bother are actually doing better, not worse.

This is the simple idea that drives the Global Compact and its supporters. It leapfrogs the pessimism of framework analysis and relies on the power of innovation and collective action by all willing actors. It proposes a shared virtual framework of accepted universal principles wherever the actual framework fails. It does not let

governments off the hook but it is impatient for action. And action is happening.

In 2003 PricewaterhouseCoopers and the World Economic Forum published an interesting survey of 992 CEOs from all regions. They concluded:[3]

> Perhaps as a consequence of the increased importance of trust issues, more and more CEOs are coming to terms with their responsibilities as good corporate citizens and watchdogs for the environment.
>
> 79% of the CEOs agreed that sustainability — adding economic, environmental and social value through core business functions — is vital for the profitability of their companies.
>
> In fact, 71% agreed that, when implementing a sustainability programme, they would consider sacrificing short-term profitability in exchange for long-term shareholder value.
>
> In looking at these results we find much cause for hope. The world is an uncertain place. But if CEOs remain confident and committed to building trust and to acting responsibly, they and their companies will be uniquely positioned to overcome today's challenges and to play a vital role in fostering global productivity and prosperity.

---

2 The Heritage Foundation and the *Wall Street Journal* 'Index of Economic Freedom' (2003), www.heritage.org.

3 PricewaterhouseCoopers and the World Economic Forum '6th annual CEO Survey: Leadership, Responsibility, and Growth in Uncertain Times' (2003), www.pwcglobal.com.

ETHOS INDICATORS ON CORPORATE SOCIAL RESPONSIBILITY

Instituto Ethos

THE INSTITUTO ETHOS INDICATORS ON

Corporate Social Responsibility (CSR) are a basic instrument for evaluating the current stage of the policies and practices of CSR in Brazil. The work of disseminating this instrument also has the objective of stimulating new companies to join and of helping society to learn about, and appreciate, the best existing practices and policies.

They are an innovative assessment and reference system for corporate social policies and practices. In light of the multiple dimensions of the social role of companies, the assessment covers the following areas:

- Values and transparency
- Workplace
- Environment
- Suppliers
- Consumers
- Community
- Government and society

Ethos indicators are based on an evaluative questionnaire that is a diagnostic tool for the specific situation of a company, indicating its progress in incorporating social responsibility into its activities. The questionnaire also serves as a management and planning tool, using the analysis of the company's current situation to indicate policies and actions aimed at deepening and expanding its commitments to CSR.

The systematisation of the information that Instituto Ethos has collected from companies has enabled the construction of a wide-ranging frame of reference, providing companies with comparative parameters of how social responsibility is practised by a group of leading firms. This knowledge is important in understanding the contribution of social responsibility to the competitiveness and productivity of companies.

The Ethos questionnaire is delivered in two ways:

- In a common format for all industries and economic sectors
- As a set of customised indicators for three specific economic sectors (finance, mining and paper) and for small and medium-sized enterprises (SMEs), focusing on bars and restaurants and on grocers

The indicator questionnaires were designed to be filled out by the participating companies themselves, as a form of self-evaluation. With an appropriate scoring system, the indicators allow a comparison of the level of social responsibility between different companies. The system of self-evaluation also aims to help companies appreciate the full scope and importance of the issue of social responsibility, which is often confused with, and limited to, corporate philanthropy. As a result, its real character as a new management paradigm is often overlooked.

The areas covered by the questionnaire (listed above) are assessed by means of two groups of indicators. The first assesses the company's current stage of social responsibility, with the desired performance increasing on a scale. This method allows the company to easily locate itself on the scale and so identify its position in relation to the stages most frequently found in the market. The scale provides a mechanism for the company to plan how to reach a higher level of social responsibility.

The second group of indicators, composed of binary (yes–no) responses and numerical values, is intended to confirm and give additional details about the stage of social responsibility identified by the company. This second set of information is important because it allows the creation of a database that can be used for making historical comparisons and for identifying best existing practices.

The structure of these two sets of questions is dynamic and can be modified in accordance with the contemporary paradigms of social responsibility. Instituto Ethos intends to continually update the assessment tool as necessary to match corporate realities and social expectations.

The assessment of the level of social responsibility conducted by the company will be consolidated by Instituto Ethos, according to its own methodology. The final results will be scored based on a system of points given to the different indicators and issues, which will allow consideration of:

- The importance and depth of each indicator, in view of its current significance and impact on society
- Sectors in which certain indicators are not relevant
- Sectors where some issues have less weight compared with others

Instituto Ethos ensures that data about companies will be handled in strict confidentiality.

FURTHER INFORMATION

Instituto Ethos, Business and Social Responsibility website: www.ethos.org.br

CASE STUDY

NO IMMUNITY FOR BUSINESS: FIGHTING BACK HIV/AIDS AT ESKOM

ESKOM IS SOUTH AFRICA'S WHOLLY STATE-
owned electricity utility. It has 24 power stations and is one
of the lowest-cost producers of electricity in the world. The
company supplies electricity to over three million
customers, amounting to 95% of South Africa's electricity
supply.

Since the start of the AIDS epidemic 83% of all AIDS
deaths have taken place in Africa. In South Africa, the
estimated prevalence is currently 4.7 million individuals
(2002). As an organisation conducting its businesses mainly
in South Africa, the containment and management of HIV
and AIDS is a strategic priority for Eskom.

Eskom's employees, suppliers and customers have all
been important components of Eskom's HIV/AIDS
programme. The main objective of the programme is to
minimise the impact of HIV and AIDS on Eskom, and thus a
set of programmes have been formulated and implemented
throughout the organisation, and resources have been
dedicated to these programmes:

- **Information management.** Infrastructure has been
  established to help Eskom maintain a strategic focus on
  the developments related to the prevalence of HIV and
  AIDS in the business.

- **Self-awareness.** The level of self-awareness of HIV
  status among Eskom employees has been increased.

- **High risk.** High-risk areas and situations in the
  organisation for contracting HIV have been identified
  and are being addressed by various business units.

- **Communication.** A communication strategy to support
  the strategic management of HIV and AIDS has been
  developed and implemented.

- **Education and training.** Steps have been taken to
  empower all employees with the skills, knowledge and
  information to deal with HIV and AIDS effectively.

- **Care and support.** The programme caters for the
  psychological support of HIV-positive employees, the
  free treatment of sexually transmitted infections and the
  monitoring of tuberculosis treatment.

- **Policies and practices.** The programme ensures that
  Eskom policies and practices do not discriminate against
  those who are HIV-positive.

The actions taken in order to meet the targets are as
follows:

- A dedicated budget of 125 South African Rand per
  employee was spent on HIV/AIDS projects and activities
  in 2000 (excluding the salaries of employees working
  full-time on the HIV/AIDS programme).

- Partnerships were established with national and
  international institutions and organisations working in
  this field.

- Eskom's activities were benchmarked against South
  African businesses and international businesses. Also, in
  1999 a voluntary, anonymous and unlinked surveillance
  study was conducted, commissioning the Harvard
  Institute for International Development (HIID) to
  analyse the economic impacts of HIV and AIDS on the
  organisation. A set of response strategies was
  formulated to meet the challenge highlighted.

- A cycle tour was organised in 2002 to raise funds to fight
  the HIV/AIDS epidemic. An education and awareness
  programme was launched (including induction

programmes for new employees and peer education
workshops).

- Eskom's business units participated in World AIDS Day.

The results have been as follows:

- All Eskom employees have received HIV and AIDS
  awareness messages, so that the challenge is now
  'beyond awareness'.

- Eskom is a member of the Global Business Council
  (GBC) against HIV and AIDS.

- Eskom contributed 30 million South African Rand over
  five years towards vaccine development.

- Eskom chairs the Southern African Power Pool forum on
  HIV/AIDS. The main purpose of this forum is to share
  experiences and assist in capacity-building.

- Eskom shared its experience and assisted more than 20
  companies in the country with information to help
  them start their own programmes.

Lessons learned have been as follows:

- Businesses are not immune to the devastating impact of
  HIV and AIDS.

- New infections were projected to cost Eskom 4-6 times
  the annual salary per individual infected.

- The annual costs of existing HIV infections during the
  period 2006–2010 will average 7% of the payroll.

FURTHER INFORMATION

Eskom Holdings Limited website: www.eskom.co.za

AVENTIS: PARTNERSHIPS FOR HEALTH

PHARMACEUTICAL COMPANY AVENTIS FOCUSES on the discovery and development of products such as prescription drugs, vaccines and therapeutic proteins through its business units Aventis Pharma and Aventis Pasteur.

Aventis's products are increasingly becoming essential tools in dealing with the many emerging and re-emerging epidemics that threaten people the world over. However, in places where many of these epidemics are prevalent, the fight requires more than products. A lack of clinics and skilled personnel, insufficient supply chains, missing health insurance systems and, in some cases, political unrest and violence make provision of health products complex.

However, there are institutions such as the World Health Organisation (WHO) that have the capabilities and regional knowledge required, and it makes sense for companies such as Aventis to share their competence with such bodies. Thus Aventis teamed up with the WHO and other groups to ensure that the products needed to tackle such epidemics reach those in need. Partnerships include the Global Alliance for Vaccines and Immunisation (GAVI), the Global Polio Eradication Initiative and the recently formed partnership to tackle African sleeping sickness.

Concerned about the disparity between the quantity and types of vaccines supplied in developed countries and those made available in developing countries, Aventis has become a partner in GAVI, which includes others in the vaccine industry, the WHO, Unicef, the World Bank, governments of developing countries and many OECD governments. The goals of the alliance are to:

- Improve access to sustainable immunisation services
- Expand the use of safe, cost-effective vaccines where needed
- Accelerate the development and introduction of new vaccines and technologies
- Accelerate research and development efforts for vaccines needed primarily in developing countries
- Make immunisation coverage a centrepiece of international development efforts

Jacques Berger, Aventis Pasteur's senior vice president for corporate public policy, states:

> For Aventis Pasteur, industry participation in the alliance is necessary to help ensure supply for these markets — and to make vaccines available to the 40 million to 70 million children born each year who would otherwise not have access to this preventative intervention.

He points out that the vaccine industry is the only one that supplies large volumes of products to the poorest segment of the population at highly discounted prices. 'This private–public alliance is a model for other basic-needs markets', he adds.

Aventis is also a partner in the Global Polio Eradication Initiative, launched in 1988 by the WHO, Rotary International, the US Centres for Disease Control, and Unicef, with the goal of eliminating polio worldwide. Between 2000 and 2002, Aventis Pasteur donated 50 million doses of oral polio vaccine to Angola, Liberia, Sierra Leone, Somalia and Southern Sudan. Since 1997, Aventis Pasteur has donated nearly 90 million doses of oral polio vaccine to African countries.

Jean-Jacques Bertrand, chairman and chief executive officer of Aventis Pasteur, states:

> Today, when now more than ever polio eradication is within our reach, we believe that we must sustain this momentum and intensify our fight.

There is a dramatic resurgence of African trypanosomiasis, more commonly known as sleeping sickness, in sub-Saharan Africa. The disease is spreading in some of the poorest Central African communities, threatening more than 60 million people in 36 countries. It has become one of the greatest causes of mortality, ahead of HIV/AIDS in some provinces.

Aventis and the WHO, working with medical humanitarian Organisation Médecins sans Frontières (MSF), designed a large-scale programme to combat the disease.

Aventis Pharma committed US$25 million over a five-year period to support the WHO's activities in the field of African trypanosomiasis. This was not a simple donation of products but rather part of a structured partnership that involves three related efforts to tackle the epidemic. Key pharmaceuticals will be provided to the WHO, to be distributed by MSF. Aventis will also finance the acceleration of disease surveillance, control activities and support new research. For any undertaking to be successful, it is necessary to address the integrated considerations of drug manufacturing and provision as well as the ongoing treatment and needs of patients.

Aventis could not have tackled such programmes alone. The company lacks the experience of working with patients in such affected areas; neither does it possess the capabilities to conduct the necessary surveillance and control of activities. The administration of drugs in some cases is also very demanding on the provider. The WHO, however, possesses the capacity and experience and knows the affected regions, but it does not possess the capacity to manufacture the treatment drugs. Clearly, then, partnerships that bring together these necessary skills, experience and capacities are required.

FURTHER INFORMATION
Aventis website: www.aventis.com

AWARENESS AND PREPAREDNESS FOR EMERGENCIES AT LOCAL LEVEL (APELL)

United Nations Environment Programme

THE AWARENESS AND PREPAREDNESS FOR

Emergencies at Local Level (APELL) Programme was developed by the United Nations Environment Programme (UNEP) and partner organisations in 1988 as a way of raising awareness of local communities surrounded by industrial zones of the potential risks to which they are exposed. The initiative came as a response to major accidents in the early 1980s, specifically in Mexico City and Bhopal. It has been developed to minimise the occurrence and the harmful effects of disasters by improving the communication between the interested and affected parties. It provides a well-structured, detailed process for developing a coordinated emergency response plan for local communities.

APELL ensures not only a better level of preparedness by local emergency services but also an understanding by local people of how to react to an emergency if one should occur in their neighbourhood. This is achieved through a meaningful dialogue between industry, local authorities and local community leaders. APELL creates a structured forum to communicate the potential hazards and risks to which a community is exposed. The raising of public awareness is critical in helping real prevention measures to be taken.

APELL is designed to achieve prevention of and preparedness for accidents. The output is a contingency plan that defines the roles of response agencies in case of a future accident. The APELL process is a managerial tool to build a multi-stakeholder group that subsequently develops a contingency plan ahead of any foreseeable disaster. This plan means that damage from a potential disaster is reduced. Indirectly, such a plan also results in risk-reduction measures being taken. If an accident does occur, the response actions are already defined in the contingency plan.

The *APELL Handbook* sets out a ten-step process for the development of an integrated and functional emergency response plan involving local communities, governments, emergency responders and others. This process creates an awareness of hazards in communities close to industrial facilities, encourages risk reduction and mitigation and develops preparedness for emergency response.

The key steps of the APELL process are:

- Identify key players in vulnerable communities.
- Examine risk scenarios and possible consequences.
- Suggest prevention and preparedness measures to be implemented.
- Work through existing institutions and mechanisms for action.
- Monitor progress and test the plan.
- Revise the contingency plan as necessary.

APELL was originally developed to cover risks arising from fixed installations, but it has also been adapted for specific applications: *APELL for Port Areas* was released in 1996, *TransAPELL: Guidance for Dangerous Goods Transport: Emergency Planning in a Local Community* was published in 2000, and *APELL for Mining* released in 2001.

A number of industrial complexes in developing countries have introduced APELL (Argentina, Brazil, Colombia and Thailand) and some countries have adopted APELL concepts in legislation (Croatia and India). India and Brazil are creating APELL centres. The mining sector is currently making APELL a priority work programme through the International Council on Mining and Metals (ICMM). Regional cooperation on the Barents Sea is also based on APELL.

FURTHER INFORMATION

United Nations Environment Program (UNEP), Awareness and Preparedness for Emergencies at a Local Level (APELL) website: www.uneptie.org/apell

APELL IN SÃO SEBASTIÃO, BRAZIL: PETROBRAS

ONE GOOD EXAMPLE OF APELL (AWARENESS and Preparedness for Emergencies at a Local Level) implementation is found at São Sebastião in Brazil. São Sebastião is one of the major ports in Brazil, responsible for the movement of approximately 50% of the nation's crude oil. Petrobras has in the area a terminal called Terminal Almirante Barroso that is completely encroached by the surrounding population.

The mayor of São Sebastião decided in the late 1990s that implementing APELL was a priority to raise awareness in the population and to increase the safety of the area. He worked with Petrobras and the community to implement APELL. In 2001 the first full-scale drill was carried out. The mayor and the city decided to promulgate a municipal decree in 2000 defining an 'Alert Day' during which a full-scale drill will be performed every year, on the third Saturday of October. In 2002 the 'Alert Day' had the participation of some 900 people.

Several issues have contributed to the success of this initiative, namely:

- The full support of the three major partners (industry [Petrobras], local authorities [city mayor and civil defence] and the community)
- Extensive preparation for and information on the APELL programme before its implementation and before each full-scale drill
- Financial support from local industry
- The development of a mechanism of continuity (Alert Day)

The experience confirmed that involving the local community in emergency prevention and preparedness programmes is one of the most important features of the APELL programme.

The cost of the APELL process can vary; the example here cost Petrobras nearly US$40,000 overall up to 2003. Petrobras budgeted that an APELL implementation at any of their sites would cost around R$100,000. It is a variable number that depends on the level of risk identification already in place in a given community.

FURTHER INFORMATION

United Nations Environment Programme (UNEP), Awareness and Preparedness for Emergencies at a Local Level (APELL) website: www.uneptie.org/apell

Petrobras website: www.petrobras.com.br

TOOL

CHILD LABOUR MONITORING SYSTEM

International Labour Organisation, International Programme on the Elimination of Child Labour

RECENTLY DEVELOPED BY THE INTERNATIONAL Programme on the Elimination of Child Labour (IPEC) of the International Labour Organisation (ILO), the Child Labour Monitoring (CLM) system encourages companies to partner with other societal stakeholders to combat child labour. For individual businesses, it can help to identify the various local and national actors working to combat child labour, allowing them to take constructive action on Principle 5 of the UN Global Compact. The CLM system is coordinated at the national level (for availability in individual countries consult the ILO), where a focal point identifies and organises the different groups according to the relevant mandates, competences and access for monitoring.

For many years, monitoring has been part of the routine tasks of government, labour, factory, school and health inspectors. Trade unions and employers have also paid attention to underage workers as part of their regular activities. In addition, parents, teachers and community members have kept a watchful eye on children to ensure that they stay in school and do not undertake dangerous activities. The CLM system is designed to bring these various groups together to combat child labour in the most effective way possible. The CLM system is:

- A programme to assist companies and other stakeholders to help and provide appropriate alternatives for children working in dangerous conditions
- A national and local framework that enables partners with complementary resources to work together efficiently
- A means of gathering and sharing information on child workers
- An adjunct to the formal inspection services of governments that are ultimately responsible in ensuring there are no children in hazardous work

At the local level, it works through the following means:

- **Inspection:** regular observation to identify children in the workplace
- **Assessment:** checking to see what hazards children may be exposed to and whether these risks are being managed properly
- **Removal or referral:** withdrawing children from hazardous work immediately if they are at serious risk, and creating a system of referral and an action chain
- **Verification:** a means of checking if children have actually moved from hazardous work to school (or another alternative)

Each of these activities, at the local level as well as at the national level, should help to get children out of danger and also produce information. The CLM system ensures that this information is collected in a consistent fashion, sent to a central point and then shared with those who need it to undertake further action.

CLM works best through partnerships because it is virtually impossible for one agency or company to do everything alone. Most importantly, CLM should not occur unless the chain of action is in place, so that, once a child in hazardous work is identified and removed, a service is already arranged to receive the child.

This programme is interesting for businesses because they can use the local or national information gathered to improve their working conditions, to the benefit of all workers. In addition, it may allow the companies to differentiate themselves by signalling to consumers the information that will ultimately determine whether those consumers purchase the goods produced in that company's sector or country.

FURTHER INFORMATION

International Labour Organisation (ILO), International Programme on the Elimination of Child Labour (IPEC) website: www.ilo.org/public/english/standards/ipec/index.htm

FROM THE PLANTATION TO SCHOOL: ABOLITION OF CHILD LABOUR AT SOTIK TEA COMPANY

SOTIK TEA COMPANY LTD, FOUNDED IN 1945, is situated in the highlands of Sotik, 400 km from Nairobi, Kenya. The company manages the Sotik Highlands Tea Estates, where its tea plantation occupies 1,800 hectares (ha), and another 850 ha is fuel-wood plantation. Close to 96% of its tea is exported to Europe and the Middle East, leaving only 4% for local markets.

There are 4,500 employees. Of this number, 2,078 are housed in company premises, the rest commuting from their own homes. In total, an estimated 6,729 live in company housing units, with 3.4 people per unit, where children account for 45% of the total number of inhabitants. The Kenya Plantation and Agricultural Workers Union (KPAWU) represents the workers.

Child labour has emerged as one of the most intolerable forms of child exploitation and abuse in some parts of the world. In Kenya, the history of child labour dates back to pre-independence days when Africans on the periphery of white settlements sent their children to work in the farms and homes of settlers as a source of income. To date, information available indicates that child labour is widespread and the escalating number of children subjected to it in rural and urban areas is a threat to the social and economic fabric of the economy.

According to a Child Labour Module Survey conducted between December 1998 and January 1999, there were 1.9 million working children aged 5–17 years in Kenya. Of these, 984,000 were boys and 910,000 girls. The Employment Act CAP 226, Part IV on Employment of Women and Juveniles, discourages the employment of children.

In 1995, Sotik Tea became obliged by shareholders and overseas buyers to set employment criteria. The buyers required that no child labour be used in picking tea or for any form of work within the estate. The requirement was part of the campaign to ensure that multinational companies participated in efforts to eliminate child labour as part of their corporate citizenry. At the time, the company was told 'any product that will be deemed to have been manufactured or produced with the services of children shall face a boycott in the international markets'.

After becoming aware of the importance of eliminating child labour, the company decided to take a more proactive approach to combat the issue instead of waiting for it to become a serious problem. As a first step, the company appointed one of its senior managers to coordinate campaigns against child labour within the company. The coordinator's key tasks were to:

- Liaise with the Federation of Kenya Employers (FKE), the International Labour Organisation (ILO) and the programme manager of the International Programme on the Elimination of Child Labour (IPEC) on the implementation of activities at enterprise level

- Hold frequent workshops to sensitise workers and the community to the negative consequences of child labour

- Prepare posters and other training materials on the elimination of child labour

- Advise management on appropriate strategies to eliminate child labour

- Seek advice from local people and convene meetings with village elders

The company is also continuously evaluating auxiliary programmes to combat child labour. These include a school bursary fund, a benevolent fund, a saving and credit cooperative scheme and strategic alliances to support educational materials for workers' children. The company's management is participating in the IPEC programme, which is nationally administered in Kenya. In addition, the FKE has been implementing a programme that targets employers in the plantation sector, through which guidelines on the elimination of child labour are provided. On 4th June 1999 a workshop in Nakuru, organised by the FKE under the IPEC programme, provided for the management of Sotik Tea a roadmap on the programme approach.

As a result of all these actions, Sotik Tea is one of the companies in Kenya where child labour no longer exists. Its efforts to find partners for educational materials and scholarships, along with a zero tolerance of child labour at the estate, have contributed to a significant increase in the enrolment rate at the local school. Sotik Tea has also adopted an open policy towards social audits, including surveillance audits on child labour. As a result, the company has fully complied with the Tea Sourcing Partnership (TSP) requirements on juvenile employment. This is monitored annually by TSP.

The collaboration between Sotik Tea and FKE has been a success story. All workers and the community are well informed on the ills of child labour. The company is committed to sustaining these campaigns. Future plans include extending the current campaign to cover house helpers, continuing to provide new posters, preparing 'role model' audio visual aides, organising company festival events and soliciting more support from outside stakeholders.

FURTHER INFORMATION

International Labour Organisation (ILO) website: www.ilo.org/multi

Tea Sourcing Partnership (TSP) website: www.teasourcingpartnership.org.uk

A FORUM AGAINST HUMAN TRAFFICKING IN THE MANILA PORTS: WG&A

THE PHILIPPINE PORTS AUTHORITY IS A government corporation specifically charged with the financing, management and operation of public ports throughout the Philippines archipelago. The corporation manages the Manila Ports, the largest in the country, with 3–5 million people transiting the Northern Manila Harbour every year. A percentage of the authority's revenue is placed in a programme that carries out various developmental activities in cooperation with non-governmental organisations (NGOs) and government departments.

William Gothong & Aboitiz Inc. (WG&A) is the largest shipping company in the Philippines. It is engaged in passenger transport and cargo liner services on most major routes in the Philippines archipelago. The company has helped to create jobs through the expansion of its business activities and is also engaged in many corporate social responsibility (CSR) initiatives, from recycling programmes, to support for governmental immunisation efforts through its Super Garantisadong Pambata programme, to support for local schools through the donation of textbooks.

In the Philippines a significant number of adults and children are trafficked domestically from poorer areas to urban centres for the commercial sex industry and domestic work.[4] These people are often promised good working conditions and a way out of poverty only to be disappointed and forced into situations that are far worse for them than before. For example, several years before this case study, the number of child prostitutes in Metro Manila was estimated to be at least 20,000[5] with the majority originating from the poorer areas of the Philippines.

Visayan Forum, a Philippine NGO that provides specialised care for migrants and children in situations of domestic work and trafficking, undertook a situational analysis in 2000 of victims of trafficking transiting through Manila North Harbour. It found two groups of women and children who were at risk. The first of these are groups of people recruited in their home provinces by local recruiters working for traffickers. The second group were independent travellers who come to Manila looking for work or to live with families and who are prey to illegal recruiters who wait for them at the port.

Field research has allowed local groups to identify a pattern whereby recruiters convince parents to allow their children to travel to Manila with the promise of a job in domestic work. During transport, recruiters instruct children to declare false names and ages or to claim that they are relatives. At other times children travel alone hoping to join family or friends in Manila, who do not pick them up at the port. These children are at risk of falling victim to recruiters who wait at the docks to find workers for prospective employers.

Dealing with the problem of trafficking at the North Manila Port was something that no one company or organisation could take on alone. After a series of consultative meetings between local firms, the Port Authority, the Federation of Free Workers[6] and the Visayan Forum, it was recognised and agreed on that intervention from a variety of groups was necessary to combat trafficking and forced labour in this context.

continued opposite →

---

4   US Department of State, 'Trafficking in Persons Report', 12 July 2001.
5   NGO Coalition for Monitoring the CRC (UN Committee on Rights of the Child), 'Supplementary Report on the Implementation of CRC', submission to the UN CRC, January 1995.

---

6   A trade union comprised of stevedores, porters, cargo handlers and vendors.

A FORUM AGAINST HUMAN TRAFFICKING IN THE MANILA PORTS: WG&A

→ *from previous page*

The specific roles that the different actors now play are outlined below.

The Visayan Forum:

- Provides training to port police under the authority of the Manila Port Authority in issues of trafficking and cooperates with shipping companies and the police to identify victims and those at risk of trafficking
- Runs a halfway house called Balay Silungan sa Daungan in front of Pier 8, which provides 24 hour services for trafficking victims, including:
  - Emergency temporary shelter before reintegration
  - Informational assistance about travel, employment and support networks
  - Quick referral of cases, including legal remediation
  - Telephone hotline counselling

The WG&A shipping company:[7]

---

7 It should be noted that other companies actively cooperate in this programme.

- Now refers cases to the halfway house and gives the halfway house contact information to children and young persons on the voyage; this kind of help provides useful information to children so they can avoid abuse and exploitation at their destination
- Arranges for general orientations of their shipping crew on the issue of trafficking
- Offers free or discounted repatriation rates to children
- Offers safe custody during travel of repatriated children and personally turns over the children to local social workers

The Federation of Free Workers:

- Refers stranded children or those who escaped from their employers
- Maintains food staples for children's consumption in the centre

The Manila Port Authority

- Provides the Visayan Forum's halfway house and also provides funds for expenses for administrative purposes and building maintenance

- Instructs its staff to refer children and other stranded passengers to the halfway house
- Instructs the port police and coast guard routinely to check suspected traffickers once a ferry has docked

In 2001 the Visayan Forum project reported to have removed 500 victims or people at risk of trafficking and provided assistance to them. Many of these people have either been repatriated or placed with employers in Manila. The project has been such a success that it is currently being expanded to other ports in the Philippines.

FURTHER INFORMATION

International Labour Organisation (ILO) website:
www.ilo.org/multi

Visayan Forum website: www.visayanforum.org

STRENGTHENING LOCAL INSTITUTIONS FOR THE RIGHTS OF SIX MILLION CHILDREN: TELEMIG CELULAR

TELEMIG CELULAR, A CELLULAR SERVICE

provider in the Brazilian telecommunications sector in the State of Minas Gerais, looked for a programme that would contribute to projects for the improvement of citizens' life. At the beginning of 2001 its Instituto Telemig Celular (Telemig Cell Phone Institute) launched the Pro-Committee Programme, aiming to strengthen the existing municipal committees for the Rights of Children and Adolescents and the committees on the Rights of the Child in the State of Minas Gerais and to encourage the establishment of such committees where they are not present. A federal law requires each city to have its own committee, but so far implementation of the law has been patchy, depending on the motivation and competence of the various municipalities. One of the main goals of the Pro-Committee Programme was the creation of an integrated network for the protection of the rights of children and adolescents within the State, to involve local governments, the private sector and non-governmental organisations (NGOs).

Encompassing the 853 municipalities of the State of Minas Gerais, the programme includes ten projects; their implementation phase should end on December 2004. To enable its success, the Pro-Committee Programme was designed and introduced gradually. First, partners were identified and strategies defined to conduct baseline research — titled 'Getting to Know the Reality', a detailed study of the structure and the working conditions of the municipal committees for the rights of children and adolescents and of the committees on the

rights of the child of all municipalities of the state of Minas Gerais.

A total of 12 seminars, held throughout the State, sealed the programme's start. Then, over 40 representatives of municipalities formed a Group for Strategic Actions, including several active partners for the enforcement of the rights of children and adolescents. This Group organised quarterly meetings to analyse goals, action patterns and the methodology for evaluating results. For each project, Instituto Telemig Celular searched for specific partners and sponsors, identifying public or private institutions the missions of which showed synergy with the purpose of the project. Strategies were designed to stimulate interaction with the legislative and the judicial branches of the municipalities, directly involving the mayors in the process, to build awareness and to give absolute priority to children and adolescent issues.

The major beneficiary of the programme was the population of six million young citizen under 17 years old in the State. The State now has stronger and more structured committees. Thus, the municipalities will be in a better condition to enforce the rights of these young people and to implement public policies that will take action on the problems that afflict this age group. The municipalities also drew up guidelines more consistent with local needs.

The mobilisation achieved through the programme was an extremely positive result. Over 680 committees were created from August 2001 to December 2003, now reaching 80% of all State municipalities. Its network of

regional support groups mobilised 360 volunteers, 292 public promoters and 10,000 counsellors throughout the State of Minas Gerais, able to offer consultation and support to district attorneys, mayors and local communities.

Telemig Celular managed to engage about 89 of its authorised dealers in the Friendly Cellular project to provide cellular phones for 200 committees and 100% of the municipalities in the area covered by Telemig. The company also mobilised its suppliers and other private institutions in an annual campaign inviting companies and citizens to contribute to the Child and Adolescents' Rights Fund, which until that time had been practically unknown. The number of companies participating in that fund increased almost 300% in two years, and the participation of citizens increased by around 180% over the same period.

Internal successes were meaningful, too. The partnerships contributed to consolidating the enthusiasm, the self-confidence and the credibility of Telemig Celular staff regarding the work performed. The Pro-Committee Programme helped the development of better practices applicable to the management of committees. The programme did not replace the administrative structure but improved its operation in terms of implementing public policy.

FURTHER INFORMATION

Instituto Telemig Celular (Telemig Cell Phone Institute) website: www.telemigcelular.com.br

CONFLICT IMPACT ASSESSMENT AND RISK MANAGEMENT

United Nations Global Compact Office

THIS BUSINESS GUIDE ON CONFLICT IMPACT

Assessment and Risk Management is intended to aid companies in the development of strategies that minimise the negative effects and maximise the positive effects of investing in areas of conflict or potential conflict. In this sense, it can assist corporations, including small and medium-sized enterprises (SMEs), in promoting the basic conditions for successful investment such as transparency, sociopolitical stability, the rule of law and respect for all stakeholders involved in corporate activities. It can also help managers determine when underlying tensions and conflicts might escalate to violent confrontations between groups or communities and ensure that their actions and decisions do not exacerbate them. Even in areas with great potential for business growth, mismanagement of actual or possible conflict situations can undermine a company's licence to operate, damage its corporate reputation, threaten its investment and place its personnel and facilities at risk. The ultimate aim of this Business Guide is to help companies contribute to a sustainable business environment in their countries of operation and to contribute positively to conflict prevention and peace-building.

The experience of many corporations and others involved in the drafting of this Guide is that corporations operating in the global arena need a new type of risk assessment and management guide. Existing types include political risk assessment and management (outlining how the political and social context can affect the development and operation of proposed investments) and financial risk assessment and management (focusing on specific issues related to financial liabilities). This Business Guide develops a new type of risk assessment and management, one that goes beyond the ambit of the prior two types. By providing a series of questions a manager might consider, this Guide assists companies in developing conflict impact risk strategies at two critical stages:

- At the pre-investment and pre-operational stage
- At the operational stage

To this end:

- It contains an introduction to and a matrix of risk assessment and management questions to be asked, and decisions to be made, during the above two stages. This matrix focuses on key areas of concern, including governance, economics, labour, security and environment.

- It contains a detailed stakeholder analysis designed to identify key stakeholders, their interests and their relation to the company and suggests types of activity the company could develop to engage these stakeholders.

- It includes impact assessments in the areas of human rights, international humanitarian law, labour and the environment.

The tool is designed as a practical guide that companies can use to assess and manage risk in conflict and conflict-prone contexts and thereby promote a positive business, social and political environment. However, it does not offer an exhaustive quantitative political or social risk strategy related to conflict situations. By placing a focus on asking the right questions, it aims at a qualitative assessment for appropriate business actions and decisions in challenging contexts.

FURTHER INFORMATION

United Nations Global Compact Office website:
www.unglobalcompact.org

Corruption Perception Index

Type of resource: index

Source organisation: Transparency International

Frequency of publication: annual

First published in 1995 the Transparency International Corruption Perceptions Index (CPI) is a composite index that ranks countries in order of the degree to which corruption is perceived to exist among public officials and politicians. The 2003 survey ranked 133 countries and drew on 17 different polls of surveys from 13 independent institutions carried out among business people and country analysts, including surveys of residents, both local and expatriate.

Since no methodology exists to collect meaningful hard data on actual levels of corruption, the CPI collects what is available — that is, the perceptions of decision-makers in the areas of investment and trade. It is a valuable tool for building public awareness of the corruption issues while drawing the attention of governments to the negative image of their nation that low rankings in the CPI reflect, adding a further reason for them to address the problem.

FURTHER INFORMATION

Transparency International website:
www.transparency.org

Business and Social Initiatives Database

Type of resource: database

Source organisation: International Labour Organisation

Frequency of updates: periodic

Business and Social Initiatives (BASI) is a searchable database on business and social initiatives that includes comprehensive information on private-sector initiatives that address labour and social conditions in the workplace and in the community where enterprises operate. The database features corporate policies and reports, codes of conduct, accreditation and certification criteria and labelling and other programmes.

FURTHER INFORMATION

International Labour Organisation (ILO),
Business and Social Initiatives (BASI)
Database website: www.ilo.org/basi

The Business of Peace: The Private Sector as a Partner in Conflict Prevention and Resolution

Type of resource: publication

Author organisation: The Prince of Wales International Business Leaders Forum and International Alert

Year of publication: 2000

Violent conflict continues to affect the lives of millions of people, undermining human progress and economic development. This has important implications for the private sector, which has become an influential player in many conflict-prone or conflict-ridden countries. This publication provides a comprehensive and practical overview of the linkages between business and conflict.

To support company managers in making decisions relating to activities in insecure areas, the publication lists five principles of corporate engagement in conflict prevention and resolution (and contains many examples of how they can be implemented):

- Strategic commitment (i.e. provide CEO and board-level leadership and establish policies, guidelines and operating standards that make explicit mention of, for example, human rights)
- Risk and impact analysis
- Dialogue and consultation (i.e. identify and engage with key stakeholders)
- Partnership and collective action
- Evaluation and accountability

The publication includes many illustrations and examples and a list of 12 key management challenges in conflict zones.

FURTHER INFORMATION

The Prince of Wales International Business Leaders Forum website: www.iblf.org

International Alert website: www.international-alert.org

Vision

Leadership

Empowerment

Resources

Policies and strategy

Processes and inovation

Impact on employees

Impact on society

Impact on value chain

Reporting

CHAPTER FOURTEEN

COMMUNICATION OF PROGRESS AND RESULTS

COMPANIES STARTED TO REPORT ON THEIR environmental performance in the early 1990s. By the end of that decade the metaphor of the triple bottom line changed the nature of such reports; they now also include the company's main social and environmental impacts in order to provide a comprehensive view of efforts and contributions towards sustainable development. From only a handful in 1991 (Norsk Hydro, Dow, ICI and Monsanto were early movers), the number of company reports inflated to several hundred in 2002 according to a survey by KPMG and the University of Amsterdam.[1] This survey of the 1,928 largest companies in the world found that 478, about 25%, published an environmental or sustainability report. But even at this level that only covers a tiny fraction[2] of the companies that could publish such a report.

Should they? A general frustration expressed by those who make the effort of reporting is that 'few read them and fewer believe them'. The few who read them are employees, some non-governmental organisations (NGOs) with an interest in analysing companies' progress,[3] and a number of financial services and consultants who publish performance indices and reporting league tables. They are engaged and knowledgeable readers whose views and comments stimulate a drive for excellence and clearly influence the practice of reporting. Still, are such 'beauty contests' and 'benchmarks' worth the effort to produce a document that only catches the interest of this elite?

We will build the case for reporting from three differing perspectives (see Figure 20). The first perspective is a commitment to the UN Global Compact. This includes an explicit commitment to communicate on progress. One of the strengths of the Global Compact is its voluntary nature and its recognition of the value of continuous improvement. We have stressed this point at many

---

1 KPMG and University of Amsterdam, 'International Survey of Corporate Sustainability Reporting 2002'; KPMG Global Sustainability Services, De Meern, the Netherlands, 2002, www.kpmg.com.

2 There are about 50,000 listed companies; see World Bank, *World Development Indicators* (Washington, DC: World Bank, 2003, www.worldbank.org).

3 Ecodurable, 'Survey of French NGOs' (2003), www.man-com.com.

places in this book. But a voluntary approach loses all integrity and credibility if it cannot demonstrate progress. A failure to communicate regularly on activities and results would make it hard to believe that the Global Compact is more than what has been called by some activists as 'bluewash', using the UN as a flag of convenience for the benefit of public relations.

The Global Compact requires,[4] therefore, a yearly communication on progress, with at least three elements:

- A general statement by the CEO (or an equivalent senior person) of the company's activities in support of the Global Compact

- A description of how these activities have, in the past year, integrated the Global Compact principles into company practice, including highlights of key outcomes and evidence of progress

- As a company may not deal with all principles at once, it should also provide its plans to address those remaining.

This guidance leaves a lot of flexibility. The communication can be included in the annual reports for shareholders; it can be part of a public report on sustainable development; it can be paper-based or published on the Internet. Companies are encouraged to use existing indicators such as those developed by the Global Reporting Initiative

---

4 For the guidance note, see www.unglobalcompact.org.

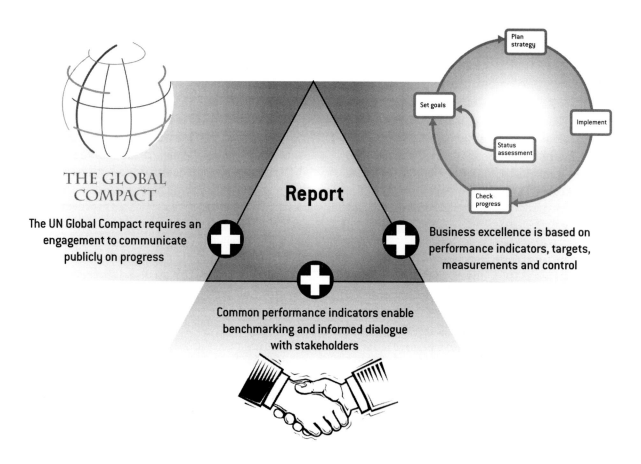

Figure 20 THREE PERSPECTIVES TO GUIDE THE DESIGN OF A PUBLIC REPORT

(GRI).[5] But compliance is not optional. Failure to communicate on progress after more than a year would de facto disrespect the genuine engagement of others and break the company's commitment.

The second perspective is consistent with the performance model and the 'check' phase of the Deming cycle[6] — 'You improve only what you measure'. At this stage of the performance model it is thus normal to assume that a company knows what it wants; it has already decided on the best performance variables to monitor progress towards its vision and strategic objectives (as covered in Part 2 of this book, Chapters 5–10). This choice took into account the need to have a set of variables that are *necessary and sufficient* to enable progress to be reliably judged, and to move to the next phase, the 'act' phase, in the Deming cycle, where the corrective or further improvement decisions are made.

This 'materiality' test is crucial, not only for performance management but also, as we will see later, for disclosure and public credibility. It is important to have clarity about the operational definition of each performance variable; it is one thing to declare a 'zero-accident' safety performance target, but how do you define 'accidents' so that the organisation can accurately measure and communicate progress and results in a way that remains consistent and comparable over time?

Following this work on choice and definition of performance variables the company should have further clarified its processes, its organisation and the role of the employees involved. Finally, it should have assessed its current level of performance and set quantitative targets. The targets define where the company should be to be satisfied with its progress in accordance with the vision and strategy. The next step now is implementation, with regular measurement of the performance variables. Whether this is recorded in the form of a time chart, a control chart, a checksheet or a Pareto diagram or any other statistical quality tools, it is also a performance report. It is a performance report for those managing the processes and organisation that influence the variables in question. Short of public disclosure, it is the meaningful communication on progress that is needed by all employees and managers who share the ambition and responsibility for progress.

The next decision, then, is about the extent of public disclosure. The performance model suggests the need for an internal report with at least two essential qualities: materiality and targets. The ideal report concentrates on the variables that drive the underlying processes that generate change and value. It is explicit about where leadership is taking the company in the short to medium term. It is the control panel that enables the leadership to steer efficiently towards its vision.

The Global Compact expects the company to communicate progress to the public. The perspectives to be covered as outlined above create, therefore, a strong argument to disclose all or part of the internal performance reporting. By sharing the real performance management system the company creates credibility and trust on several counts: it is an act of transparency, it displays managerial competence and the published targets express the company's commitment to create a better future. Reports without targets are only looking backwards; they are six to nine months out of date by the time they reach the readers. There is, however, more than this to credibility. Although transparency, professional competence and targets go a long way to creating credibility and trust, a fourth quality — responsiveness — is also required, and we will address this aspect later in this chapter.

Not every report has followed those principles. Many current publications exhibit the reverse of the iceberg phenomenon: the majority of their substance is on the surface; they have lots of text, stories and slick photography but little to measure any progress against. In the report from the United Nations Environment Programme (UNEP) and SustainAbility, *Trust Us: The Global Reporters 2002 Survey of Corporate Sustainability Reporting*,[7] such reports are dubbed 'the 21st century, triple bottom line version of "greenwash" . . . the focus is on looking good, too often regardless of the underlying performance'. But beware of the other extreme — the 'carpet bombing' syndrome — described in *The Global Reporters 2002* as 'inundating readers with information, presumably in the hope that readers

---

5   For details of the GRI, see www.globalreporting.org.
6   On the Deming cycle, see Chapter 3, page 57.

7   UNEP (United Nations Environment Programme) and SustainAbility, *Trust Us: The Global Reporters 2002 Survey of Corporate Sustainability Reporting* (2002), www.sustainability.com.

will be able to find what they are looking for' (however, for UNEP and SustainAbility's 'Magnificent Seven' reports, and for companies receiving awards for their reports from the Association of Chartered Certified Accountants, see Table 11).

A separate supporting argument for reporting is that some of the data are required, directly or in some aggregated form, in the non-financial information that is essential for the company's supervisory bodies to properly execute their governance function; some are also legally required by public authorities and shareholders statutes. Facilitating access to a broader public only enhances the profile of openness and responsibility of the company.

Another common frustration on the part of companies producing sustainability reports is that 'there is no evidence that they improve performance'. We believe that the right approach is therefore to *start* from the need to improve performance and build a report that serves foremost this purpose of performance management. That is the report's primary value. Whether or not it fascinates outside readers or wins a design award is only a secondary objective. It is noteworthy that the 'most famous' reports actually attract interest precisely by their insights into their authors' strategy, dilemmas, policies and search for the best performance indicators and drivers of value.

There is a further perspective to a broader communication of performance. How does the company measure up to others in business and to the expectations of business observers and stakeholders? Benchmarking is important and useful in the context of the performance model. It is important that a company's indicators of performance measure its own progress and that they also determine where it stands relative to the performance of others in its field. It is important to identify which area of sustainability has been overlooked and which indicators of performance would improve the balance of approach

and allow the company to respond better to stakeholder expectations.

When it comes to sustainability reporting, the debates have advanced sufficiently to offer a common framework of indicators and reporting guidelines. This perspective is served by the work of the GRI and its guidelines. The GRI was convened in 1997 by UNEP and the Coalition for Environmental Responsible Economies (CERES) to elevate environmental and sustainability reporting practices to a par with financial reporting. The Guidelines (see pages 202-207), last revised in 2002, are the result of a long, open and broad debate among company experts, social and environmental NGOs, accountancy organisations, trade unions, financial analysts and other interested stakeholders. The GRI Guidelines support all the principles in the Global Compact with a number of appropriate performance indicators. By 2004 over 400 companies were already referring to the Guidelines when they produced their public performance reports.

With 50 'core indicators' and a further 47 indicators, the 2002 Guidelines are comprehensive. But they can be daunting for a first-time reporter. This is why the best approach for a company leader is to first define those indicators that are most useful in driving performance and measuring change in their company. Then it is useful and important to test this set of indicators against the GRI operational definitions and its guidance for presentation and disclosure. This helps to attune the company's essential indicators to those proposed by the GRI, if there is any difference at all. The 2002

Table 11 **THE 'BEST OF 2002' SUSTAINABILITY REPORTS**

The 'Magnificent Seven'	ACCA awards
● The Co-operative Bank	● Europe: The Co-operative Bank
● Novo Nordisk	● Europe SME: Neumarkter Lammsbräu
● British Airports Authority	● North America: Ben & Jerry
● British Telecom	● North America: Chiquita
● Rio Tinto	● Australia: City West Water
● Shell	*Source:* www.accaglobal.com/sustainability/awards
● British Petroleum	

Source: UNEP (United Nations Environment Programme) and SustainAbility, *Trust Us: The Global Reporters 2002 Survey of Corporate Sustainability Reporting* (2002), www.sustainability.com

Guidelines recognise the need for incremental application and advise how first-time reporters can develop an approach that gets the benefits of benchmarking and of the collective experience wired into the Guidelines.

Once a company has decided to disclose its performance data it should also consider the credibility of these data to outside readers. The efforts invested in ensuring materiality and accuracy for internal managerial needs have surely covered, to a large extent, the needs of external audiences. Nevertheless, some reporters increasingly seek independent assurance or verification and certification. According to the KPMG 2002 survey mentioned above, about 150 reports out of 478 were reviewed by outside verifiers. The Volkswagen 2001/2002 environmental report[8] describes the details of such a process before presenting the auditors' report. A verification process is fairly time-consuming and expensive. Typically it results in a small-print document of careful statements such as: 'nothing has come to our attention that causes us not to believe that management has not done its best to be reasonably effective in avoiding . . .', etc. The language does little justice to the thorough and competent feedback actually provided by the audit team during the verification process. But such assurance statements will contribute to a report's credibility only moderately, if at all. Their absence raises questions and even suspicion, but their presence is taken for granted and rapidly discounted.

A stronger factor of credibility and trust is how a company responds to stakeholder needs and how it seeks their comments and feedback. There may be a number of issues that will be of greater interest to external observers than they will be to the company's staff. As discussed in Part 1 (Chapters 1–4), this process of dialogue should start long before reporting, at the stage of vision and leadership priorities (Chapters 5 and 6). This principle of responsiveness receives due attention in the only framework that addresses the issues of accountability and assurance in the domain of sustainability and social responsibility — the AA1000 Framework developed by the UK-based professional institute AccountAbility.[9] This framework positions multi-stakeholder processes as key links in the overall assurance process.

In line with the Global Compact and the performance model, it seems that the best approach to communicating progress should be based mainly on the sustainability performance indicators and targets that serve management, directors and shareholders. The GRI has developed a rich inventory of ready options for consideration. An open and serious dialogue with key stakeholders strengthens the strategy and uses the communication on progress as a shared basis for taking the dialogue forward and identifying additional indicators of performance and progress.

It is advisable to let the strategy shape the reporting rather than let external reporting guidelines shape the strategy. The Deming cycle works clockwise, 'plan' and 'do' come first. Rio Tinto's Sir Robert Wilson, speaking at the Conference on Corporate Social Responsibility at the Royal Institute of International Affairs, sums it up:[10]

> From a company's perspective, reporting and verification are *not* the next step after pronouncement of a policy. After policy development comes implementation; next, comes training where it is required and then internal reporting systems. External reporting and verification [are] the final step for those of us in the world of converting words into action.

Yet through stakeholder dialogue the final step again becomes the first in completing the cycle of continual improvement.

This chapter presents several reporting and assurance frameworks. They should help round up the performance model with a set of indicators that serves company progress towards more complete application of the Global Compact principles.

---

8 VW (Volkswagen AG), 'Environmental Report 2001/2002'; VW, 38436 Wolfsburg, Germany, www.volkswagen-environment.de.

9 See www.accountability.org.uk; see also pages 208-209.

10 R. Wilson, 'Corporate Social Responsibility: Putting the Words into Action', speech made at the Conference on Corporate Social Responsibility, Royal Institute of International Affairs, Chatham House, London, 16 October 2001; quoted in the World Business Council for Sustainable Development (WBCSD) book published by Greenleaf Publishing: C.O. Holliday, Jr, S. Schmidheiny and P. Watts, *Walking the Talk: The Business Case for Sustainable Development* (Sheffield, UK: Greenleaf Publishing, 2002): 140.

THE 2002 SUSTAINABILITY REPORTING GUIDELINES

Global Reporting Initiative

THE GLOBAL REPORTING INITIATIVE (GRI)

Sustainability Reporting Guidelines are the ideal tool to use when reporting on how an organisation has progressed with Global Compact principles and on sustainability in general. GRI's broadly accepted, globally applicable, common reporting framework provides the basis for gauging progress, benchmarking and identifying opportunities for internal management improvements. The GRI Guidelines were developed, and are continually improved, in a global multi-stakeholder manner, engaging thousands of experts from every continent and constituency.

The Guidelines present reporting principles and specific content indicators to guide sustainability reporting at the organisational level. The reporting principles help ensure that reports produced with use of the framework present a balanced and reasonable account of sustainability performance, facilitate comparison over time and across organisations and credibly address issues of concern to stakeholders. The principles are grouped into four clusters:

- **Forming the overall framework:** transparency, inclusiveness, auditability
- **Choosing what to report:** completeness, relevance, sustainability context
- **Ensuring quality and reliability:** accuracy, neutrality, comparability
- **How readers will access the report:** clarity, timeliness

The GRI indicators organise sustainability reporting in terms of economic, environmental and social performance. The indicators are divided into two categories:

- Core indicators are those that have been judged applicable to most reporting organisations and of interest to most stakeholders.
- Additional indicators are those that may be of high importance to reporters or stakeholders in certain sectors or regions.

Through a process of stakeholder engagement, and by applying the GRI reporting principles, organisations determine which indicators they will report on. An organisation that has endorsed the Global Compact principles may refer to the Global Compact principles (listed on page 9) or to Table 16 of the GRI Guidelines (Table 12 in this book, pages 204-207) in order to choose a selection of GRI indicators that will demonstrate the organisation's commitment and progress on the Global Compact principles.

Depending on the goals and objectives of the reporting organisation, it may choose to apply an incremental approach (referred to here as 'incremental reports') or aim to be fully 'in accordance' with the GRI Guidelines (referred to here as 'in-accordance' reports). To be fully in accordance with the Guidelines the reporting organisation must respond to each core indicator and include a statement signed by the CEO or board of directors, among other items (see page 13 of the 2002 Guidelines). When linking an incremental report or an in-accordance report to the Guidelines the inclusion of a GRI content index is the most important tool for the reporter

continued opposite →

THE 2002 SUSTAINABILITY REPORTING GUIDELINES

Global Reporting Initiative

→ *from previous page*

and the report user. This index directs readers quickly and conveniently to the location of GRI information in the report (see page 86 of the 2002 Guidelines).

GRI recognises that sector-specific guidance must be developed to supplement the general information elicited in the Guidelines. Sector Supplements are designed to be used in addition to the Guidelines, not as a replacement, and are available for the following industries:

- Automotives
- Financial Services
- Mining and Metals
- Tour operators
- Telecommunications
- Public Agencies

The GRI process also includes the development of resource documents and technical protocols to assist organisations with reporting on special topics and indicators. Working groups have developed a resource document on HIV/AIDS as

well as protocols on energy, water, child labour and health and safety. The GRI has produced a draft protocol on child labour to help reporters with definitions based on the International Labour Organisation (ILO) Conventions.[11]

The GRI Guidelines do not provide instruction for designing an organisation's internal data management and reporting systems. Nor do the Guidelines offer methodologies for preparing reports or for the monitoring and assurance of such reports.

By its very nature, triple-bottom-line reporting requires information-gathering across the entirety of the organisation; also, sustainability reporting is a key stakeholder engagement and communications tool. Cooperation among various departments on setting objectives for the report may also be necessary. Since the GRI indicators have been aligned with major international agreements, many organisations collect data on these already, but there may be a need for new data-gathering systems to be put in place. The overall costs of preparing a

sustainability report — including stakeholder engagement, data collection, assurance, publishing and distribution — differs widely across organisations.

GRI indicators for progress on the UN Global Compact

Table 12 lists a selection of core performance indicators from the 2002 Global Reporting Initiative (GRI) Sustainability Reporting Guidelines. This selection covers the nine Global Compact principles.

It is not intended to form a comprehensive comparison. Table 12 does not include, for example, some GRI disclosure elements found in the Guidelines under Report Content (Sections 1–3).

FURTHER INFORMATION
Global Reporting Initiative (GRI) website:
www.globalreporting.org

---

11 On the ILO Conventions, see www.ilo.org.

GLOBAL COMPACT PRINCIPLES	GRI CORE INDICATORS: REPORT CONTENT		
	CATEGORY	INDICATOR #	INDICATOR
Human rights			
1. Businesses are asked to support and respect the protection of international human rights within their sphere of influence;	Social Indicators: Human Rights *Strategy and Management*	HR1	Description of policies, guidelines, corporate structure, and procedures to deal with all aspects of human rights relevant to operations, including monitoring mechanisms and results.
		HR2	Evidence of consideration of human rights impacts as part of investment and procurement decisions, including selection of suppliers/contractors.
		HR3	Description of policies and procedures to evaluate and address human rights performance within the supply chain and contractors, including monitoring systems and results of monitoring.
	Social Indicators: Human Rights *Non-discrimination*	HR4	Description of global policy and procedures/programmes preventing all forms of discrimination in operations, including monitoring systems and results of monitoring.
2. Make sure their own corporations are not complicit in human rights abuses.	Social Indicators: Human Rights *Strategy and Management*	HR2	Evidence of consideration of human rights impacts as part of investment and procurement decisions, including selection of suppliers/contractors.
		HR3	Description of policies and procedures to evaluate and address human rights performance within the supply chain and contractors, including monitoring systems and results of monitoring.
Labour			
3. Businesses are asked to uphold the freedom of association and the effective recognition of the right to collective bargaining;	Social Indicators: Human Rights *Freedom of Association and Collective Bargaining*	HR5	Description of freedom of association policy and extent to which this policy is universally applied independent of local laws, as well as description of procedures/programmes to address this issue.
	Social Indicators: Labour Practices and Decent Work *Labour/Management Relations*	LA3	Percentage of employees represented by independent trade union organisations or other bona fide employee representatives broken down geographically OR percentage of employees covered by collective bargaining agreements broken down by region/country.
		LA4	Policy and procedures involving information, consultation, and negotiation with employees over changes in the reporting organisation's operations (e.g. restructuring)

Table 12 **GLOBAL REPORTING INITIATIVE (GRI) INDICATORS RELATED TO THE NINE UN GLOBAL COMPACT PRINCIPLES** (continued opposite)

GLOBAL COMPACT PRINCIPLES	GRI CORE INDICATORS: REPORT CONTENT		
	CATEGORY	INDICATOR #	INDICATOR
Labour (cont.)			
4. The elimination of all forms of forced and compulsory labour;	Social Indicators: Human Rights *Forced and Compulsory Labour*	HR7	Description of policy to prevent forced and compulsory labour and extent to which this policy is visibly stated and applied as well as description of procedures/programmes to address this issues, including monitoring systems and results of monitoring.
5. The effective abolition of child labour;	Social Indicators: Human Rights *Child Labour*	HR6	Description of policy excluding child labour as defined by the ILO Convention 138 and extent to which this policy is visibly stated and applied, as well as description of procedures/programmes to address this issue, including monitoring systems and results of monitoring.
			See GRI draft Child Labour Protocol
6. The elimination of discrimination in respect of employment and occupation.	Social Indicators: Human Rights *Non-discrimination*	HR4	Description of global policy and procedures/programmes preventing all forms of discrimination in operations, including monitoring systems and results of monitoring.
	Social Indicators: Labour Practices and Decent Work *Diversity and Opportunity*	LA10	Description of equal opportunity policies or programmes, as well as monitoring systems to ensure compliance and results of monitoring.
		LA11	Composition of senior management and corporate governance bodies (including the board of directors, including female/male ratio and other indicators of diversity as culturally appropriate.
Environment			
7. Businesses are asked to support a precautionary approach to environmental challenges;	Governance Structure and Management Systems *Overarching Policies and Management Systems*	3.13	Explanation of whether and how the precautionary approach or principle is addressed by the organisation.

Table 12 (from previous page; continued over)

GLOBAL COMPACT PRINCIPLES	GRI CORE INDICATORS: REPORT CONTENT		
	CATEGORY	INDICATOR #	INDICATOR
Environment (cont.)			
8. Undertake initiatives to promote grater environmental responsibility;	Environmental Indicators: Materials	**EN1**	Total materials use other than water, by type.
		EN2	Percentage of materials used that are wastes (processed or unprocessed) from sources external to the reporting organisation.
	Environmental Indicators: Energy	**EN3**	Direct energy use segmented by primary source.
		EN4	Indirect energy use.
			See GRI Energy Protocol
	Environmental Indicators: Water	**EN5**	Total water use.
			See GRI Water Protocol
	Environmental Indicators: Biodiversity	**EN6**	Location and size of land owned, leased, or managed in biodiversity-rich habitats.
		EN7	Description of the major impacts on biodiversity associated with activities and/or products and services in terrestrial, freshwater and marine environments.
	Environmental Indicators: Emissions, Effluents, and Waste:	**EN8**	Greenhouse gas emissions.
		EN9	Use and emissions of ozone-depleting substances.
		EN10	NO_x, SO_x, and other significant air emissions by type.
		EN11	Total amount of waste by type and destination.
		EN12	Significant discharges to water by type.
		EN13	Significant spills of chemicals, oils, and fuels in terms of total number and total volume.

Table 12 (from previous page; continued opposite)

GLOBAL COMPACT PRINCIPLES	GRI CORE INDICATORS: REPORT CONTENT		
	CATEGORY	INDICATOR #	INDICATOR
Environment (cont.)			
8. Undertake initiatives to promote grater environmental responsibility;	Environmental Indicators: Products and Services	**EN14**	Significant environmental impacts of principal products and services.
		EN15	Percentage of the weight of products sold that is reclaimable at the end of the products' useful life and percentage that is actually reclaimed.
	Environmental Indicators: Compliance	**EN16**	Incidents of and fines for non-compliance with all applicable international declarations/conventions/treaties, and national, sub-national, regional, and local regulations associated with environmental issues.
	Vision and Strategy	**1.1**	Statement of the organisation's vision and strategy regarding its contribution to sustainable development.
9. Encourage the development and diffusion of environmentally friendly technologies.	Environmental Indicators: Energy *(additional indicator, by example)*	**EN17**	Initiatives to use renewable energy sources and to increase energy efficiency.

Table 12 (continued)

ACCOUNTABILITY 1000 (AA1000) FRAMEWORK

AccountAbility

THE ACCOUNTABILITY 1000 (AA1000)

Framework, including standards, guidelines and professional development, provides a systematic stakeholder-based approach to organisational accountability. The AA1000 Framework offers guidance on how to establish accountability processes that generate indicators, targets and communications systems. These systems impact on decisions, activities and overall organisational performance. Its principles and process standards for planning, accounting, auditing and reporting have been used by businesses, non-profit organisations and public bodies internationally.

The AA1000 Framework covers a process, from agreeing on the terms of engagement with stakeholders through to reporting and assurance. It is a foundation standard, and can be used in two ways:

- As a common currency to underpin the quality of specialised accountability standards, existing and emergent

- As a stand-alone system and process for managing and communicating social and ethical accountability and performance

The AA1000 principles are:

- **Materiality:** knowing what is important to you and your stakeholders

- **Completeness:** knowing your impact and what people think of you

- **Responsiveness:** demonstrating response to people's concerns

The principles and process standards are underpinned by the principle of accountability to and inclusiveness of stakeholders.

The AA1000 Framework process model works as follows (see also Figure 21):

- Planning:
  - P1: Establish commitment and governance procedures
  - P2: Identify stakeholders
  - P3: Define or review values

- Accounting:
  - P4: Identify issues
  - P5: Determine process scope
  - P6: Identify indicators
  - P7: Collect information
  - P8: Analyse information, set targets and develop an improvement plan

- Auditing and reporting:
  - P9: Prepare report(s)
  - P10: Audit report(s)
  - P11: Communicate report(s) and obtain feedback

- Embedding:
  - P12: Establish and embed systems

Figure 21 THE ACCOUNTABILITY 1000 (AA1000) FRAMEWORK PROCESS MODEL

Use of the AA1000 Framework process model contributes to the following:

- **Accountability and performance.** The AA1000 Framework links the definition and embedding of an organisation's values to the development of performance targets and to the assessment and communication of organisational performance. By focusing around the organisation's engagement with

continued opposite →

ACCOUNTABILITY 1000 (AA1000) FRAMEWORK

AccountAbility

→ *from previous page*

stakeholders, AA1000 ties social and ethical issues into the organisation's strategic management and operations.

- **Improving performance.** There are a variety of dimensions along which the AA1000 Framework can be used to improve organisational accountability and performance. The following is not a complete list, but illustrates the possible applications of the AA1000 Framework to the benefit of an organisation and its stakeholders:

  - **Measurement.** The AA1000 Framework outlines a process by which key performance indicators are identified through engagement with stakeholders.

  - **Quality management.** By measuring, communicating and obtaining feedback on social and ethical performance an organisation will be better placed to understand and respond to the needs and aspirations of its stakeholders, and to manage these alongside (and as part of) its objectives and targets.

  - **External stakeholder engagement.** The AA1000 Framework can play a key role in building an organisation's relationships with its external stakeholders, which will then provide more accurate information on which to base decisions,

and a climate of increased trust in which to implement them.

  - **Partnership.** The AA1000 Framework can support the deepening of value-based relations along an organisation's supply chain and in other partnership processes.

  - **Risk management.** The AA1000 Framework can enable an organisation to identify, evaluate and better manage the risks arising from its impacts on and relationships with its stakeholders. These may include risks to reputation and brand, and from customer and employee liability suits.

  - **Investors.** The AA1000 Framework can provide clear and verifiable information about social and ethical performance and stakeholder perceptions and expectations, which provides a valuable reference point for investor assessment of the quality of management and the market positioning of an organisation.

  - **Governance.** The AA1000 Framework feeds into the organisation's control process by which the Framework ensures the alignment of company values and strategy with company behaviour and outcomes of activities.

  - **Government and regulatory relations.** The adoption of the AA1000 Framework can play a part in encouraging governments to acknowledge self-regulating processes that

organisations are following to improve accountability and performance.

  - **Training.** The AA1000 Framework facilitates the training and the identification of qualified and experienced service providers.

As well as being used with existing management systems, the AA1000 Framework, as a process standard, was designed to work in parallel with other social accountability tools. No social accountability standard can give comprehensive guidance. Indeed, use of the AA1000 Framework is common alongside other well-established standards. Organisations take what they can from the AA1000 Framework and look elsewhere to fill the gaps. ISO 14001 (see page 140) and the OECD Guidelines for Multinational Enterprises (see page 41) are often used in conjunction with the AA1000 Framework — but by far the most commonly cited is the Global Reporting Initiative (GRI; see pages 202-207). Companies have also used the AA1000 Framework along with the Social Accountability 8000 (SA8000) standard system (see page 136), the Ethical Trading Initiative (ETI) (see page 177) and the OECD Guidelines, which also apply to the UN Global Compact.

FURTHER INFORMATION

AA1000 Framework: www.accountability.org.uk
(available for free download)

TOOL

ACCOUNTABILITY 1000 (AA1000) ASSURANCE STANDARD

AccountAbility

THE ACCOUNTABILITY 1000 (AA1000)

Assurance Standard was launched in March 2003 following an international stakeholder engagement process as a generally applicable standard for assessing, attesting to and strengthening the credibility and quality of organisations' sustainability reporting and their underlying processes, systems and competences.

The AA1000 Assurance Standard is designed to improve accountability and performance by learning through stakeholder engagement. It can provide risk management by acting as an early warning system and it can improve performance by signalling new market opportunities, for example. It provides guidance on key elements of the assurance process.

The AA1000 principles are:

- **Materiality:** knowing what is important to you and your stakeholders

- **Completeness:** knowing your impact and what people think of you

- **Responsiveness:** demonstrating response to people's concerns

The AA1000 Assurance Standard's key characteristics are that it:

- Covers the full range of organisational performance (i.e. sustainability performance)

- Focuses on the materiality of subject matter to stakeholders as well as on its accuracy

- Examines the completeness of an organisation's understanding of its own performance and impacts and associated stakeholder views

- Assesses reporting organisations' responsiveness to stakeholders and in doing so interprets reporting as part of an ongoing engagement with those stakeholders

- Provides a forward-looking approach that indicates how able an organisation is to carry out stated policies and goals as well as to meet future standards and expectations

- Establishes the basis for public assurance statements that build the credibility of public sustainability reports

- Supports and integrates approaches to assurance by using multiple providers, approaches and standards, including specific compatibility with the Global Reporting Initiative (GRI) Sustainability Reporting Guidelines (see page 202)

- Applies to different types and sizes of organisations and assurance providers from diverse geographical, cultural and social backgrounds

- Requires disclosure by assurance providers covering their competences and relationships with the reporting organisation (i.e. their client)

The AA1000 Assurance Standard is primarily intended for use by assurance providers in guiding the manner in which their assurance assignments are designed and implemented. In addition, the AA1000 assurance standard should inform the way that:

- Reporting organisations assess, plan, describe and oversee the implementation of their assurance (including internal assurance), as well as guide directors and boards in overseeing non-financial disclosures

- Reporting organisations' stakeholders query and assess the quality of assurance and associated reporting

- Standards bodies and policy-makers develop private, voluntary standards as well as voluntary and statutory aspects of organisational accountability, particularly reporting and assurance

- Professional development and training practitioners build professional competences in assurance and overall organisational accountability

All AA1000 'principles' must be applied in any assurance assignment. In addition, the AA1000 Assurance Standard should be used as a basis for continual improvement.

FURTHER INFORMATION

AA1000 Assurance Standard: www.accountability.org.uk
(available for free download)

PERFORMANCE BEYOND THE WALLS AT VANCITY

FOUNDED IN 1946, VANCOUVER CITY SAVINGS Credit Union (VanCity) is a democratic, ethical and innovative provider of financial services to its members.

VanCity is committed to doing business in a way that strengthens its own long-term success while contributing to the social, economic and environmental well-being of the community. Members have a say in the future of the credit union, but they also share in its earnings.

VanCity is Canada's largest credit union, with Can$8.2 billion in assets, 289,000 members and 40 branches throughout Greater Vancouver, the Fraser Valley and Victoria. VanCity owns Citizens Bank of Canada, serving members across the country by telephone, ATM (automatic teller machine) and the Internet. Both VanCity and Citizens Bank are guided by a commitment to corporate social responsibility and to improve the quality of life in the communities where employees live and work.

VanCity looked to the AccountAbility 1000 (AA1000) Framework to assist the company in building a values-based culture rather than a compliance-based culture. The AA1000 Framework helped VanCity come to terms with

who we are and how the different parts fit together; what is our purpose and how are we doing . . . we had become a complex organisation and there was no place to understand all the

missions and visions and so on — this [AA1000 Framework] was really helpful in doing that. The stakeholder model really does give a better understanding of what is important (Priscilla Boucher, Manager of Corporate Social Responsibility, VanCity).

VanCity simply drew on AA1000 principles in developing its approach to social accountability and stakeholder engagement. By effectively engaging with those that it impacts, and those who in return impact on it, VanCity went from intention to result by identifying its stakeholders, developing a process for engaging them and then developing a coherent system of response to that feedback, by, for example, incorporating their concerns into key performance indicators. Information from reporting against these key performance indicators offered valuable insight into how VanCity could improve its performance.

As time passed and the organisation became more experienced, accountability increasingly affected strategy. The information collected from VanCity's first social audit was presented to the executive and board and a number of commitments resulted, but this process was outside of the normal business planning cycle. Since then, the company has worked to gradually align its social auditing with wider business planning procedures.

VanCity is now in its third cycle of social auditing and reporting and, by using key performance indicators, it

has attempted to identify possible new business initiatives by feeding them into the business planning process. Where stakeholder engagement has influenced the company's strategic approach, the importance of target setting on the back of performance indicators for improvement has focused minds, stimulated action and driven these issues up the corporate agenda and into the strategic consideration. VanCity's experience is that, with each cycle of auditing and reporting, social accountability became more integrated into the organisation.

The AA1000 Framework has not only encouraged a more systematic approach to engaging in stakeholder dialogue in whatever form (forums, questionnaires and so on) it has also changed the nature of these exchanges. The conversations VanCity holds with its stakeholders now take in a wider vista and are much more concerned with the relationship, rather than on specific business initiatives, as in the past. A stakeholder model such as the one set out in the AA1000 Framework forces an organisation to report its performance in areas it would not otherwise do — 'it expands beyond the walls of the corporation' (Priscilla Boucher, VanCity).

FURTHER INFORMATION

Vancouver City Savings Credit Union: www.vancity.com

AccountAbility: www.accountability.org.uk

TOOL

MANUAL ON ECO-EFFICIENCY INDICATORS

United Nations Conference on Trade and Development

THIS MANUAL ON ECO-EFFICIENCY INDICATORS, including accounting framework and guidelines on eco-efficiency indicators which a company can use in reporting, enables enterprises to provide information on environmental performance *vis-à-vis* financial performance in a systematic and consistent manner over periods of time. So far, every company measures its environmental impact and its eco-efficiency (environmental item in relation to a financial item) in a different way, thus making it impossible to benchmark performance in this area. Correctly linking environmental variables with financial variables will also be useful in investor relations and mergers and acquisitions.

The manual helps management to benchmark, set efficiency targets and report performance to stakeholders on a consistent basis. Using the guideline, companies can report their eco-efficiency performance by using environmental performance indicators for the five elements: water use, energy use, global warming contribution, ozone-depleting substances and waste. In addition, the guidelines present the accounting treatment of financial items used for the calculation of eco-efficiency indicators. It also deals with issues of consolidation of financial information that can guide the consolidation of environmental data.

The manual is general and can be adapted to company circumstances. It can serve as a guide in preparing company, industry or region-specific reports. It follows closely the logic of the widely accepted International Accounting Standards. As such, it is rigorous in its accounting treatment of enterprises' environmental impact, and 'speaks' to business people and investors accustomed to 'straight' financial accounting

The application of the guideline goes in three steps:

- Step 1: gather data on raw environmental consumption and production.
- Step 2: aggregate this data into meaningful and simple indicators and ratios.
- Step 3: include the indicators in the enterprise's financial and environmental reports.

Most of the data needed are commonly gathered by enterprises either in their accounting or production planning system or in a specific environmental management system.

The accounting department takes over steps 2 and 3. The calculation of the indicators is described in detail in the manual, as are the methods (disclosure and consolidation) to integrate them in the company's financial and environmental reports.

For first-time users, the manual is supported by a long-distance learning website hosted by the University of Geneva in Switzerland, and experts can be contacted through UNCTAD.

For those companies that have an environmental and an accounting unit, the production of these indicators should not incur any additional cost in the long run. It might be necessary to provide the staff involved with a half-day training course, which can be accessed through the distance-learning programme of the University of Geneva. UNCTAD experts and consultants can deliver company-specific or sector-specific training to interested companies. They have already held regional workshops and trained over 1,000 financial and environmental officers. The electronic copy of the training manual is available free of charge at the websites listed below.

The manual is very thorough, and can be used by the largest companies. Small and medium-sized enterprises (SMEs) may find it daunting at first sight. A second look reveals that large parts can be skipped either because they are not applicable to the specific industry or country of operations or just because the diversity of resources used is much narrower than what is covered by the manual.

FURTHER INFORMATION

United Nations Conference on Trade and Development (UNCTAD) website: www.unctad.org/isar

Document: *A Manual for the Preparers and Users of Eco-efficiency Indicators*: www.unctad.org/en/docs//iteipc20037_en.pdf

University of Geneva distance-learning website: http://supprem.unige.ch/cours/welcome.php

THE CIBA EXPERIENCE

CIBA SPECIALTY CHEMICALS IS A LEADING global specialty chemicals producer, with 60 production sites in 23 countries. In 2002 Ciba employed 19,007 people and generated sales of US$5.6 billion.

For many years, Ciba has been using a system that allows the production sites to report their environmental, health and safety (EH&S) performance as well as their energy consumption.

The company produced its first EH&S report in 1992. In 2001, the company made its first attempt to integrate reporting of its EH&S performance with its financial performance. One major challenge was to make EH&S data understandable to the financial world. In its 2001 report, the company published figures relating its energy usage, water usage and

carbon dioxide emissions to its gross profit and production volume.

Shortly after producing its 2002 report, the EH&S team received the United Nations Conference on Trade and Development (UNCTAD) eco-efficiency manual. The manual fitted the team's objective of relating EH&S performance to financial performance. Its advantage is that it provides a standardised method of consolidating the data into eco-efficiency indicators and can be applied by all companies, regardless of which sector they are active in. It allows meaningful comparisons to be made between companies in the same sector. The team found the manual very detailed and appreciated its step-by-step approach with good examples to show how data has to be consolidated.

Ciba's concern was to ensure that this new methodology was consistent with the one it had used previously. The manual was tested with use of raw data over several years. As expected, although the absolute figures were different, the trends were similar. Different calculation methods always give different results — this is why environmental data produced today by companies is seldom comparable. The crucial result of this test was that the trends derived from the two methods were very similar. The decision was therefore made to use the UNCTAD guidelines for the 2003 EH&S report.

FURTHER INFORMATION
Ciba Specialty Chemicals website: www.cibasc.com

THE EFFICIENT ENTREPRENEUR CALENDAR

United Nations Environment Programme and Wuppertal Institute

THE WUPPERTAL INSTITUTE'S SUSTAINABLE

Production and Consumption and the United Nations Environment Programme (UNEP) Division of Technology, Industry and Economics (DTIE) have jointly developed the Efficient Entrepreneur Calendar for small and medium-sized enterprises (SMEs).

In combination with an additional booklet (*The Efficient Entrepreneur Assistant*) and a website, the calendar provides assistance and guidance on how to measure and improve eco-efficiency performance and stakeholder relations. It charts a month-by-month programme that ends with an 'efficient entrepreneur report'. The methodological concept underlying the programme proved to be a successful approach to reach SMEs worldwide. The calendar and its assistant cover 12 months (Figure 22) and are divided into three parts.

- **Part 1: January and February.** The year starts with introducing 'what' the company will achieve month by month and explains 'why' improving environmental performance is a good idea. A description is given on how to start up, organise and supervise an environmental project in a company. The Calendar recommends that the project team start with a qualitative review to 'get an overall picture'. This first part is intended to help the team coordinator to motivate and inform top management, as well as the employees of the company, resulting in commitment and active involvement in the Efficient Entrepreneur project.

- **Part 2: March to September.** Following the maxim of 'only what's measured gets done', the Calendar introduces self-assessment questions, checklists and indicators to review and measure environmental performances and related costs, and supplier relations (emphasising the life cycle perspective and product stewardship issues) and community relations are introduced. These measures help to take a look at the current situation and to identify efficiency improvement opportunities. Each 'environmental performance month' combines a short awareness-raising story, explains why the company should measure its performance in this area and how to do so and suggests simple tips for action. The project team is asked to identify inefficiency problems and opportunities to solve these problems. An evaluation of which improvement opportunity has priority can be carried out by examining a few given parameters (in the form of a simple economic, environmental and technical evaluation). The development of action plans to keep track of projects (the implementation of improvement opportunities), deadlines, responsibilities, funding and so on is suggested. Simple and no-cost improvement opportunities should be implemented right away to ensure continued interest and commitment to the project. Further practical help in the form of checklists, questions, work sheets, diagrams and evaluation methodologies is supplied by the *Efficient Entrepreneur Assistant*.

- **Part 3: October to December.** At the end of the year the user is asked to monitor and evaluate the success of the implemented options, to communicate efficiency improvements and responsibilities to people inside and outside the company (e.g. using the 'Efficient Entrepreneur' reporting form included) and to integrate the experiences and results gained during the year in a continued preventative 'Efficient Entrepreneur' management system. Furthermore, success should be celebrated within the company and rewarded by applying to award programmes at the local, regional or national level. In the annexes to the Assistant, references to environmental performance affairs, award programmes, reporting and supporting organisations, both international and national, can be found.

Since 2000 The Efficient Entrepreneur Calendar has been published in various languages (English, French, Spanish, Italian, German and Dutch). It is relevant to any firm that considers itself to be a SME-type firm or,

continued over →

THE EFFICIENT ENTREPRENEUR CALENDAR

United Nations Environment Programme and Wuppertal Institute

➜ *from previous page*

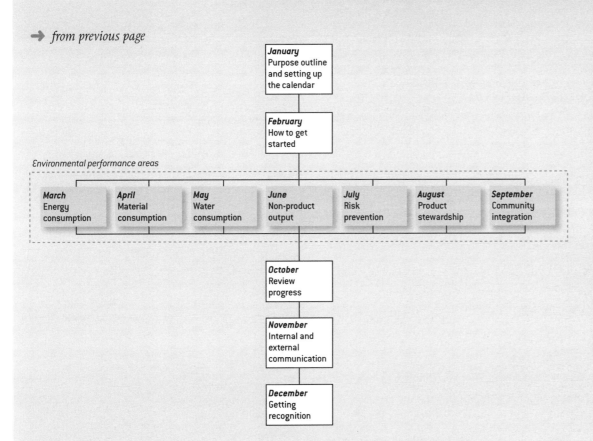

Environmental performance areas

January
Purpose outline
and setting up
the calendar

February
How to get
started

March
Energy
consumption

April
Material
consumption

May
Water
consumption

June
Non-product
output

July
Risk
prevention

August
Product
stewardship

September
Community
integration

October
Review
progress

November
Internal and
external
communication

December
Getting
recognition

Figure 22 **THE STRUCTURE OF THE EFFICIENT ENTREPRENEUR CALENDAR**

indeed, to any firm that requires an introduction to environmental performance measurement and communication (e.g. in preparation for the ISO 14001 or Eco-Management and Audit Scheme [EMAS] implementation process).

Currently, the Efficient Entrepreneur Calendar is expanded to cover additional sustainability aspects and to enhance it to guide SMEs on social aspects as well. In an expanded partnership the United Nations Environment Programme (UNEP), the Global Reporting Initiative (GRI), the Wuppertal Institute, InWEnt (Internationale Weiterbildung und Entwicklung gemeinnützige GmbH) and CSR Europe are developing a triple-bottom-line (TBL) performance toolkit that will help SMEs to measure and improve TBL performance and their transparency and accountability worldwide. The toolkit will be called 'The SMART Entrepreneur' (SMART = Sustainability for the Small and Medium-sized enterprise committed to Accountability, Responsibility and Transparency). This diary and electronic guide will be available as of the end of 2005.

FURTHER INFORMATION

Calendar website: www.uneptie.org/outreach/business/calendar.htm

United Nations Environment Programme (UNEP) Division of Technology, Industry and Economics (DTIE) website: www.uneptie.org

Wuppertal Institute website: www.wupperinst.org

Measuring and Reporting on Company Human Rights Performance

Type of resource: publication

Author organisations: CSR Europe and Business for Social Responsibility

Year of publication: 2001

Over the past five years, companies have begun to address human rights at a greatly accelerated pace. In this report, Business for Social Responsibility (BSR) and CSR Europe outline some of the most important efforts to date to develop human rights measures and address some of the questions these two organisations see as central in promoting further discussion and progress on human rights measures. This report, the first joint product of a partnership between the organisations' programmes on business and human rights, will serve as a useful catalogue of these efforts and is a useful contribution to the debate on human rights metrics.

The tool catalogues the various initiatives designed to help companies develop and implement metrics to assess and report on their human rights policies and practices. It can be used by companies to review the various tools available to them in this fast-changing area of corporate social responsibility. Companies that have not yet begun to measure and report on their human rights performance, or those that have not yet developed or implemented human rights policies, can use this tool to develop metrics that will be relevant to their company and industry sector.

The primary limitation of the tool is that it was written in 2001, and some of the metrics that are referenced in the document have been updated since publication.

The resources needed to use this tool are limited and are mainly dependent on the degree to which companies seek to develop comprehensive methods for measuring and reporting on human rights performance.

FURTHER INFORMATION

Business for Social Responsibility (BSR) website: www.bsr.org/humanrights

CSR Europe website: www.csreurope.org

AA1000 Conversations: Lessons from the Early Years (1999–2001)

Type of resource: publication

Author organisation: AccountAbility

Year of publication: 2001

This report explores different ways in which the AccountAbility 1000 (AA1000) Framework is used and its influence on the way organisations really work. It describes the results of in-depth interviews carried out in ten organisations.

FURTHER INFORMATION

AccountAbility website: www.accountability.org.uk

The State of Sustainability Assurance

Type of resource: publication

Author organisation: AccountAbility

Year of publication: annual

This annual report seeks to promote effective sustainability assurance by describing some of the most important assurance trends and by providing highlights of emerging practices. Perspectives from accountancy bodies, assurance providers, businesses, the investment community and standards bodies have been gathered to assess the current state of sustainability assurance.

FURTHER INFORMATION

AccountAbility website: www.accountability.org.uk

Sustainable Development Reporting Portal

Type of resource: website

Author organisation: World Business Council on Sustainable Development

The World Business Council on Sustainable Development (WBCSD) Sustainable Development Reporting Portal offers quick access to information detailing which member company is reporting, on what, and when. It features a list of electronic reports in four categories:

- Environment
- Health, safety and environment
- Social responsibility
- Sustainable development

In addition to the list of electronic reports, the portal showcases reporting practices from almost 50 companies, representing 14 business sectors, and provides a step-by-step guide to help companies to develop or improve their sustainable development reports.

FURTHER INFORMATION

Web address: www.sdportal.org

World Business Council for Sustainable Development (WBCSD) website: www.wbcsd.org

Sustainable Development Reporting: Striking the Balance

Type of resource: publication

Author organisation: World Business Council for Sustainable Development

Year of publication: 2002

This report answers the worldwide call to companies for greater accountability and transparency. It does this by explaining why and how reporting can help turn the recent wave of boardroom scandals into renewed boardroom trust. It is both a guide to help companies produce reports and a policy document offering insights into the reporting standardisation debate.

The report's main purpose is to help companies to understand the added value that reporting can bring to them. It also provides guidance, to the initiated and the uninitiated, on how to report, thus complementing other initiatives guiding companies on reporting.

FURTHER INFORMATION

World Business Council for Sustainable Development (WBCSD) website: www.wbcsd.org

Yardsticks for Workers' Rights: Learning from Experience

Type of resource: online database

Author organisation: Human Rights First

This analysis is a detailed look the problem of how to measure compliance with workers' rights standards in factories around the world. It is linked to a free, online database showing 2,900 units of measurement currently in use.

It looks at the questions:

- How is respect for workers' rights actually being measured in workplaces around the world?
- What exactly are the facts to collect?
- What are the questions to ask?
- What are the indicators to look to?

Different participants in this field are using very different sets of yardsticks, which vary widely in terms of the type, scope, level of detail and precision of the measurements they produce. Not surprisingly, the different yardsticks also vary widely in their ability to pinpoint issues and problems. The lack of consistent, comprehensive sets of measurements has been a major obstacle to effective accountability.

This analysis, available online, offers as complete a picture as possible of current practice, topic by topic, in eight major areas of labour standards and workers' rights. It shows the strengths and weaknesses of current practice and offers extensive, detailed suggestions for improvements, topic by topic.

FURTHER INFORMATION

Web address: www.workersrights.humanrightsfirst.org

Human Rights First (formerly the Lawyers Committee for Human Rights) website: www.humanrightsfirst.org

PERFORMANCE AND VALUE CREATION

Claude Fussler
World Business Council for Sustainable Development

YOU HAVE NOW COME FULL CIRCLE, FROM vision to results, from the first letter to support the UN Global Compact, to the first progress report, via a comprehensive model of implementation that is both effective and efficient. Again and again this book has implied that the performance model is not only for the benefit of society but also will produce tangible business results. In other words, it believes the 'business case' for supporting the Global Compact to be true and that the performance model is a way to secure its financial benefits. Can this be proven?

Much has been written in recent years about the business case. New stock market indices such as the FTSE4Good or the Dow Jones Sustainability Index have focused attention on the business case, and much has been written about it. The list of business benefits is well summarised in the developing value matrix tool of Chapter 6 (pages 87-88), as shown in Table 13.

Such a list always creates the impression that there are no limits and no downsides to this business case. Every business should be doing this! So, what is still holding up so many? Two things —

both of which we have already described in several places. First, the Global Compact performance model requires a will to change and a wilful coordination of practices and resources to enable that change. The majority of people prefer to ride the waves. They change only under pressure or because of a great inspiration. Second, there are a number of discouraging market conditions and institutional

AREA	BENEFIT
Revenue growth and market access	Product and service innovation, a new-ventures approach to the huge potential of basic-needs and low-purchasing-power markets to create new growth.
Cost savings and productivity	Eco-efficiency programmes and process control reduce the consumption of energy, water and raw materials and save waste and emissions costs.
Access to capital	A convincing spectrum of risk management policies and a high brand reputation attract investors and reassure bankers.
Risk management and licence to operate	By going beyond the obvious risks and setting radical reduction goals, business disruptions are reduced. Frequent information and consultation with stakeholders avoid delays in building and operation permits.
Human capital	It is easier to attract and retain talented people. Motivation, creativity and focus run high in the company.
Brand value and reputation	A proactive social responsibility and sustainability strategy opens many doors: to public authorities and procurement, green consumers and the press.

Table 13 **BUSINESS BENEFITS OF SUPPORTING THE UN GLOBAL COMPACT**

failures that raise the uncertainty of success and demand even greater courage and creativity to take the step and 'lean out of the window'.

However, on balance, the advantages are convincing when one analyses the performance of those who have mustered this courage, taken the step and declared their commitment to the Global Compact and now allow the public to track their progress on social responsibility and sustainability. To get the facts, we turned to the research team at SAM Sustainable Asset Management. SAM produces, from its Zürich base, the Dow Jones Sustainability Index, which enables many financial institutions to create equity funds on the basis of a sustainability filter. With SAM we asked ourselves how the group of Global Compact supporters that are included in the SAM database (listed in Table 15 on page 223) scored on a number of criteria. We then also asked how a fund, solely based on Global Compact supporters, would reward its investors compared with a fund of non-supporters. We were curious to see if it would make a noticeable difference. We were even apprehensive that it could turn out to be worse; it would be out of character to cover up the evidence, but certainly awkward to explain in a text written to show companies how to implement the Global Compact! Fortunately, the analysis shows rather robust advantages.

SAM has developed a thorough process to evaluate companies through a comprehensive set of criteria based on sustainability. The proprietary process filters out sustainability leaders and creates a group of companies that can be tracked for

performance in the form of an index. The founders of SAM started their work in 1995 as asset managers at the early stage of the socially responsible investment wave that in the meantime has grown to a US$2,000 billion business worldwide. Their methodology to screen and select a distinct portfolio of companies proved successful and robust. They could demonstrate that this selection consistently outperformed the Morgan Stanley Capital Index (MSCI) which tracks a similar but much larger group of stocks. The selected stocks presented a positive risk–value profile. This was one of the strongest pieces of research into the objective correlation between shareholder value and a sustainability strategy. At last the advocates of the business case were vindicated by this clear difference in performance between the peaks and troughs of two stock market charts. In 1999 the SAM selection was adopted into the Dow Jones family as the Dow Jones Sustainability Index (DJSI). It is now the basis for a number of specific variations and facilitates the design and delivery of customised financial products based on equities screened for sustainability.[1]

Every year SAM takes the largest 2,500 companies, by market capitalisation, from the Dow Jones Global Index. In order to avoid comparing a mining company with a bank or a food producer, it sorts the companies into market groups by their respective major activity. Although all companies

are invited to take part in the evaluation, 487 responded to a detailed questionnaire in 2003. Another 284 were evaluated from publicly available data. The SAM evaluation competes for time with more and more questionnaires from other rating agencies. Invariably, such questionnaires land on the desk of the same person who may already be grappling with the internal process of the company's own sustainability report. This is not likely to change. There are ever more analysts looking for insights on the social responsibility side. Companies have far more staff to cultivate the traditional financial analysts through yearly group briefings, monthly conference calls, special interviews and continuous news lines. It may be time to think about the opportunity for their investor relations staff to master the issues of sustainability.

The SAM questionnaire details most of the performance aspects we have presented and discussed in the performance model; it is also tailored to each market sector. It probes for key performance elements in the environmental, social and economic domains under the aspects of risk and opportunity management. This questionnaire is practically SAM's version of a yearly performance report, as comprehensive as the Global Reporting Initiative (GRI) guidelines in several aspects but also more focused on elements that have a material impact on the financial bottom line. SAM carefully scores each element of the questionnaire for each company in each market sector. It also assesses the information from other sources for complementary

---

1 For the latest DJSI charts, consult www.sustainability-index.com.

evidence of performance. As a result it gets a league table of companies ranked by scores; it retains in each sector the leader and the top 10% or more, with the aim of including at least 20% of the market capitalisation of that sector.

In the 2004 vintage, 317 companies qualified for the index, with a leader in each of the 18 market sectors (see Table 14). Some have maintained a lead obtained in previous years, whereas others have lost or gained in a remarkable new race to the top.

The yearly SAM corporate sustainability assessment includes a good number of Global Compact supporters. There were 99 in the 2003 assessment, and 76 made it to the index (see Table 15 on page 223). This is a good sample but represents only large market capitalisation companies that are included in the Dow Jones and STOXX markets. Small companies, privately held companies or state companies are, of course, not included. With this limitation in mind we found that the group of 76 signatories — let's call it the GCS76 — clearly outperformed the mainstream Morgan Stanley Capital World Index (MSCI) by 3.4% over the period between January 2002 and January 2004 analysed in terms of US dollars (Figure 23).

Furthermore, the DJSI also outperformed by 0.5% points the mainstream market, as measured by MSCI World in US dollars, over the period between January 2001 and January 2004 (Figure 24). Colin le Duc, former Head of Research Operations at SAM Sustainable Asset Management, points out that:

SECTOR	YEAR		
	2001	*2002*	*2003*
Automobiles	Volkswagen	Volkswagen	Toyota
Banks	UBS	Westpac	Westpac
Basic resources	Dofasco	Dofasco	Dofasco
Chemicals	Dow Chemical	DuPont	DuPont
Construction	Skanska	Lafarge	CRH
Cyclical goods and services	Sony	Teijin	Philips Electronics
Energy	Shell	Shell	BP
Financial services	ING	Land Lease	British Land
Food and beverage	Unilever	Unilever	Unilever
Healthcare	Bristol-Myers Squibb	Novozymes	Novozymes
Industrial goods and services	3M	3M	3M
Insurance	Swiss Re	Swiss Re	Swiss Re
Media	Granada Media	Pearson	Pearson
Non-cyclical goods and services	Procter & Gamble	Procter & Gamble	Procter & Gamble
Retail	Ito Yokado	Marks & Spencer	Marks & Spencer
Technology	Intel	Intel	Intel
Telecommunications	British Telecom	British Telecom	British Telecom
Utilities	Severn Trent	Severn Trent	Severn Trent

Table 14 **DOW JONES SUSTAINABILITY INDEX LEADERS, BY MARKET SECTOR**

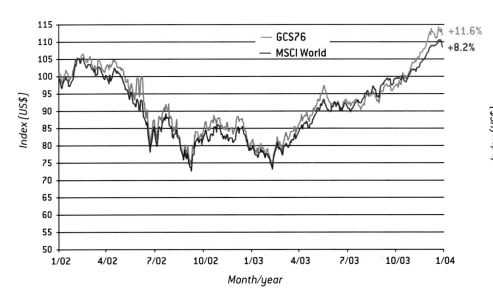

Figure 23 TWO-YEAR STOCK PERFORMANCE OF THE 76 GLOBAL COMPACT SIGNATORIES COMPARED TO THE MORGAN STANLEY CAPITAL INDEX

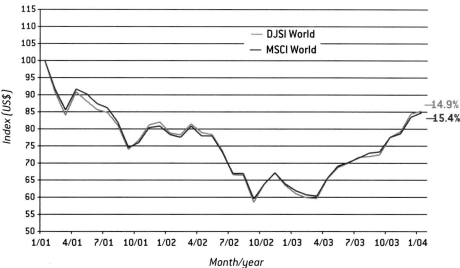

Figure 24 THREE-YEAR PERFORMANCE OF THE DOW JONES SUSTAINABILITY INDEX COMPARED TO THE MORGAN STANLEY CAPITAL INDEX

Furthermore, the risk [the degree of uncertainty of return on equity] was 26.43% for the GCS76 compared to 20.99% for the MSCI. This is an extremely interesting risk profile for an investor. Excess return is achieved at relatively low risk, even though only 76 companies are part of the GCS76, compared to approximately 1,500 companies in the MSCI. One would usually expect a much higher risk for such a small selection of companies. Thus, a broad conclusion is that Global Compact Signatories and members of the DJSI create premium shareholder value at acceptable risk

levels. They definitely do not carry a handicap for shareholders relative to the mainstream market.[2]

In theory, an investor takes more risk in reducing investment options to a portfolio that covers only a fraction of the market opportunities, but the experience shows that a sustainability criterion is an efficient method to pick investments. It produces rewards that clearly outweigh the risks. Of course, it

is not the only method to pick a winning group of stocks. Warren Buffet's focused Berkshire Hathaway portfolio is a resounding example.[3] Nor is the sustainability portfolio failsafe; in 2000 the sharp simultaneous fall of Dell, Intel, AOL and Lucent stock values was such that it caused the whole DJSI to underperform the market average for several

2 Personal communication.

3 R.G. Hagstrom, *The Warren Buffet Portfolio* (New York: John Wiley, 1999).

months before rebounding into the lead. The sustainability premium goes only so far.

Can we really speak of a Global Compact market premium? It is a fact that if we had bought the 76 shares of the GCS76 in October 2001 instead of the 1,500 shares of the larger MSCI group we would be 3.4% better off at the end of January 2004 (in the context of a declining market). As a group, the Global Compact signatories created more value. We have yet to understand why. The first possible answer is that over that period there were more bidders than sellers for their shares and that the bidders were prepared to offer a premium so that sellers let go of their shares. This is why markets move up — the bulls outnumber the bears. Why did the bidders behave like this? Obviously, they felt that this purchase was a safe use of their money and they speculated that it would return more than inflation, treasury bonds or whatever else they could use it for. They expected the companies in that group to do better in the future. One always buys shares for future returns, in the short or long term.

What did the Global Compact bring to this speculative move? Is it a magic wand that boosts stock appeal? Of all investors trading in and out of those equities none is likely to trade purely on the basis of a Global Compact criterion, or even know anything about it. A significant few, the socially responsible investors, definitely select shares on the basis of principles that include human rights, corruption, labour standards and environmental responsibility. They have leverage but not to the extent of pushing this kind of premium in the highly traded, large market capitalisation stocks of the group of 76.

So, why is there a premium? The more realistic influence on this premium lies finally in the overall quality of each company that composes this group. It is their credibility as paragons of management excellence and responsibility and the resultant portent of future returns that draws the investors to these companies. This same responsible excellence opens and moves the leadership of those companies to support the Global Compact and use it to trigger and focus further improvements. Engagement with the Global Compact is an effect of responsible excellence with the potential to become another key driver through the performance model and other means of strategic integration.

We need to temper these conclusions with a reminder of the uncertainties, or risk profile, of such a comparison. Beside the assumed value of the sustainability commitment of the GCS76 there are a number of other biases, such as geography, currency and market mix, in the comparison with the MSCI. These could well be the main cause for the value differential, but we lean toward the sustainability explanation for two reasons. One is the growing body of research in this area, in particular a recent study by Claudia Volk and Hendrik Graz of WestLB; in *More Gain than Pain*[4] they clearly establish the value of a sustainability investment style, giving a detailed discussion of its

risk profile and statistical confidence for various traditional investment categories. The second reason is that, when it comes to a large number of managerial practices that are driving business excellence, the group of Global Compact signatories demonstrate a clear difference from non-signatories. This discovery of a difference was actually the first objective of our inquiry. It was only after we found such a clear difference that we assumed our readers would also wonder about a stock value correlation; it is a simple way to check the business case and to catch the attention of business readers.

Let's therefore look at this first inquiry. We 'mined' the SAM database for details of company practices in as many elements of the performance model we could find collected data (see Table 16). We could extract a number of indicators for a reliable comparison between two groups of companies — those 99 companies that have signed the Global Compact and the 436 that had not. We could also include in the comparison the 308 companies that made it to the 2004 DJSI. This index actually includes 76 of the Global Compact signatories. The other 23 signatories (see Table 15) have still some way to go to move into the index — a proof, if needed, that support for the Global Compact is not a magic wand to performance but the start of an interesting journey. But all three groups are already remarkable for the fact that they qualified for the SAM corporate sustainability assessment. The differences therefore become a clear sign of leadership and excellence. They provide further evidence that it is possible to live up to the

---

4 H. Garz and C. Volk, *Update: More Gain than Pain* (London: WestLB AG, October 2003; www.westlb.com).

THE GCS76 INCLUDED IN THE MARKET VALUATION (FIGURE 24)

- ABB Ltd
- Accor
- AGF
- Allianz AG
- Asahi Breweries Ltd
- Aventis
- Aviva plc
- Banca Monte Dei Paschi Di Siena
- Banco Bilbao Vizcaya Argentaria
- Banco Itaú Holding Financeira SA
- BASF AG
- Bayer AG
- Bayerische Motoren Werke AG (BMW)

- Bhp Billiton Ltd
- Bnp Paribas
- BP plc
- BT Group plc
- Carrefour
- Coloplast
- Credit Suisse Group
- Danisco A/S
- Deutsche Bank AG
- Deutsche Lufthansa AG
- Deutsche Telekom AG
- Dexia
- Diageo plc
- Du Pont De Nemours & Co.
- Electrolux AB
- Endesa SA

- Groupe Danone
- Groupe Société Générale
- Grupo Ferrovial SA
- Grupo Iberdrola
- Grupo Santander Central Hispano
- Henkel KGaA
- Hennes & Mauritz AB
- Hewlett-Packard Co.
- Holcim
- HSBC Holdings plc
- Inditex SA
- ISS A/S
- L.M. Ericsson
- Lafarge
- Li & Fung Ltd
- Nestlé SA

- Nexen Inc.
- Nike Inc.
- Nokia Corp.
- Norsk Hydro ASA
- Novartis AG
- Novo Nordisk A/S
- Novozymes A/S
- Pearson plc
- Pfizer Inc.
- Reed Elsevier plc
- Ricoh Co.
- Rio Tinto plc
- Royal Dutch/Shell Group of Companies
- Saint-Gobain
- SAP AG Pfd
- Schneider Electric Sa

- Serono
- ST Microelectronics
- Statoil ASA
- Stora Enso Oyi
- Storebrand ASA
- Suez
- Technip-Coflexip
- Telenor ASA
- UBS Group
- Unilever
- UPM-Kymmene Oy
- Veolia Environnement
- Volkswagen AG
- Volvo AB
- Westpac Banking Corporation

OTHER COMPONENTS OF GCS99 INCLUDED IN TABLE 16

- Air France
- Aracruz Celulose
- AXA
- Cisco Systems Inc.
- DaimlerChrysler AG

- EPCOS AG
- France Telecom
- ICI
- L'Oreal
- LVMH Moet Hennessy

- Norske Skogsindustrier Free
- Rabobank
- Renault
- San Paolo-IMI

- Sanofi-Synthelabo
- Sasol
- Skanska AB
- Sodexho Alliance SA
- Telecom Italia Mobile

- Telecom Italia SPA
- Telefonica SA
- Titan Cement Co.
- TotalFinaElf

Table 15 **GLOBAL COMPACT SIGNATORIES INCLUDED IN THE 2004 SAM CORPORATE SUSTAINABILITY ASSESSMENT™**

recommendations made in this performance model without an economic penalty but, on the contrary, a market value premium. It must be noted that 90% of the Global Compact sample have headquarters in Europe.

For instance, when the leaders take a stand on the boundaries and the scope of responsibility they clearly influence the behaviour of their suppliers and contractors; they show a stronger customer orientation and their engagement with stakeholders has moved beyond communication and dialogue to partnerships on projects (2 out of 3 companies [64%]). Their investment in employee skills and knowledge and satisfaction is deeper — as a result, more than 1 of 3 (38%) could measure progress in employee satisfaction. Every second company has set public environmental targets (56%) and 2 out of 5 have greenhouse gas reduction objectives (40%). One out of 3 gets its sustainability report certified 36%). When it comes to codes of conduct, all companies in the assessment score high. The differentiation may be in implementation.

Are such differences enough to create value? The answer is: not on their own, but they evolve from a broader base of value drivers. There is no simple equation or a mathematical model that enables one to calculate the market value of the soft dimensions of performance such as having a diversity target, the certification of a sustainability report or even the more tangible targets of waste and emission reductions. A few logical chains, however, link social and environmental responsibility to financial value. It is easier to argue the links to the value of traded

PARAMETER	PERCENTAGE OF		
	SAM436	DJSI308	GCS99
Have guidelines for suppliers on:			
Human rights	28	43	65
Environment	68	82	90
Labour practices	46	58	68
Occupational health and safety	53	63	73
Audit suppliers performance	36	40	39
Corporate environmental policy covers impacts of:			
Products and services	77	84	95
Suppliers and service providers	66	75	83
Other business partners	23	28	26
Measure customers' satisfaction	28	33	37
Engagement with external stakeholders:			
Engage with shared project teams	36	50	64
Key stakeholders are prioritised	51	55	67
Seek feedback from stakeholders	52	56	58
Provide regular briefings	75	81	75
Spend more than 1% of EBIT for social investments and philanthropy	23	29	31
Employee survey show a trend for:			
Higher satisfaction	20	28	38
Constant satisfaction	26	24	20
Lower satisfaction	3	3	1

PARAMETER	PERCENTAGE OF		
	SAM436	DJSI308	GCS99
Specific job training covers 90–100% of employees	23	28	35
Over 80% of employees covered by knowledge management system	38	43	44
Long-term success of human resources policies is measured	84	86	95
Performance indicators are used and published for			
Diversity	25	38	54
Environment, health and safety	40	49	66
Layoffs	9	14	24
Discrimination	11	16	25
Freedom of association	6	9	17
Forced labour	10	11	8
Child labour	12	13	9
A certified environmental management system for over 90% of business	22	24	20
Publish a certified sustainability report with strong social component	14	23	36
Publish corporate environmental targets	41	52	56
Have set a greenhouse gas reduction target	37	52	40
Have a greenhouse gas inventory for over 80% of operations	66	80	72
Have a corporate governance policy	74	80	84
The code of conduct covers			
Environment, health and safety	85	92	92
Discrimination	84	90	90
Corruption and bribery	84	89	83

SAM436: have not signed the Global Compact   **GCS99: have signed the Global Compact**   **DJSI308: are selected for the Dow Jones Sustainability Index 2004**

Table 16 **SAM CORPORATE SUSTAINABILITY ASSESSMENT™: SELECTED EVALUATION**

shares, but this should not leave out all those companies that are not publicly traded. At some point of time state companies could be offered to public investors, private companies acquire, merge, pass to successors or secure credit lines; they too need to be concerned about value and how to enhance it for the long run.

Share value is a reflection of a company's worth through a complex prism — the economy at large, the news, the cash flows of investors, the situation of the company's sector and the investors' reading of the relative risks and opportunities of all the other choices in the market, to name a few. The market is a real-time approximation of the company's worth and, as many painful corrections have shown, its own dynamics can carry it away. The market actually does not create value like a product or service business. It creates value through arbitrage between investors who have different views and expectations about the value of the titles they are prepared to sell or buy. But what finally counts in the long run is the quality of earnings of the company behind the traded security.

What creates a premium is the expectation of excess returns compared with other options to invest money. These excess returns depend on the competitive advantage of the company and, particularly, on the sustainability of its competitive advantage over time. Thousands of financial analysts continuously screen the universe of companies to assess company strategies and future earnings in relation to the companies' current market value. Are companies undervalued in relation to their business opportunities? Are they overvalued in relation to their business risks? Alois Flatz, head of SAM Research, observes that:[5]

> Investors are once again looking for returns in excess of a general risk premium caused by exceptional costs that the economy must absorb. While throughout the '90s the economy benefited from the peace dividends of the end of the Cold War, we had to cope in the few past years with the costs of ecological disasters of a new magnitude, anti-terrorism, pre-emptive wars, country reconstruction and major corporate failures. In many ways the lack of sustainability raises the hurdle or risk premium that earnings must exceed to reward investors in absolute terms and create real financial value.

This financial value premium is based on strategy — hardly big news but sometimes taken lightly in the more extreme moods of the stock market. As highlighted in Part 2 of this book, strategy is the effective and efficient combination of resources and business processes, employee creativity and empowerment towards a shared vision, in ways that are difficult to imitate by competition.

Are the Global Compact signatories, then, better at strategy than others? We think so; at least we believe that they continue to be better than many others. Business excellence is fostered by the goals of sustainability, the challenges of social responsibility and leaders who are inspired by principles higher than the profit motive; this argument has been presented over and over in this book and by many business thinkers before. The Global Compact brings an additional aspect: a voluntary public exposure. The majority of business leaders shy away from such an exposure because they just hate to admit that they don't quite have their act together on all issues. An engagement with the Global Compact is therefore a strong indication of confidence by a company in its own performance. It is even a bet that, for a certain number of issues, it is more interesting to get one's act together through public exposure and stakeholder dialogues rather than behind closed doors with like-minded, or like-confused, colleagues. As Professor Gary Hamel has written:[6]

> If a company is interested in understanding the future, most of what it needs to learn about the future it is going to learn outside of its own industry.

Plain signs of this confidence to interact on sustainability issues can be read from our SAM Corporate Sustainability Assessment table (Table 16): they are the companies with the highest proportion of reporters, verification, public improvement targets and depth of interaction with selected stakeholders.

5 Alois Flatz, private note to the authors; paper to be published in 2004.

6 G. Hamel, 'Reinventing the Basis for Competition', in Rowan Gibson (ed.), *Rethinking the Future: Rethinking Business, Principles, Competition, Control, Leadership, Markets and the World* (London: Nicholas Brealey, 1998): 82.

Managing plantations, drilling platforms, extruders, clean rooms, warehouses, truck fleets, computers and bank accounts is one thing — and complex enough. If that were the only source of value a good accountant would quickly establish book value: end of story. Yet companies are valued at several multiples of their book value. The difference is 'goodwill' made of many layers of 'intangible' assets — intangible but essential to generate earnings, starting with the strategic savvy, the managerial competence and the know-how, creativity and motivation of the personnel. Goodwill is also the art of relationships, of building credibility, commitment and loyalty, not only with commercial partners but also with public authorities, communities or new consumers, such as the poor, who have needs that no one has yet cared to satisfy adequately. We are back in the area of the Global Compact and sustainable development. And we are at a major source of the future cash flows and the excess returns investors are looking for. Brand strength and reputation are all about this art of relationships and vision.

Ivo Knoepfel, founder of OnValues, an investment research expert, has a view:[7]

> Many of the Global Compact signatories are the 'supertankers' of their industries, they take (or are forced to take) a leadership role in their industries because of sheer size. These companies typically also take the lead in industry associations and push the agenda on standardisation, transparency and excellence in their industry. What comes first, the chicken or the egg, success or leadership, success or engagement for sustainability? Nobody really knows; these dimensions are probably intertwined.

In the long run we believe that strategies and actions consistent with the principles of the Global Compact exercise and enhance a number of intangible assets that drive value. Although causality is hard to prove it may be just as well to believe it and manage accordingly. Investors expect excess returns, and it is for managers to make them happen. This brings the management of intangible assets into focus and the necessity to understand how they drive value.

As society recognises the vital role of business in wealth creation and economic development, transparency and accountability have come to the forefront of the qualities expected from business management. The Global Compact performance model is part of the answer. Those who embrace it beyond the declarations and token documentation, to effectively drive progress towards sustainable development, do not lose out. On the contrary, the evidence grows that they also do well on the financial scorecard.

The metaphor of the triple bottom line is now popular to describe how value is a composite of economic, social and environmental performance. Beware of the simplistic maths: it is not a sum; social and environmental progress will not offset an economic loss. Milton Friedman was justified in his claim that the primary social responsibility of business is to make profits; he should not have stopped there, however. We need some higher maths to better encapsulate how responsible excellence drives value. An appropriate formula may be:[8]

$$P = me^i$$

The share's market price, P — and hence the market capitalisation — is the multiple, m, of expected earnings per share, e; the exponent i stands for an important cluster of **impacts** (social and environmental), **innovation** and the **intangible** drivers of reputation discussed above. The power of this index will enhance value when it is positive and growing, but, as algebra and business life has taught us, when it turns negative it slashes value with a vengeance. The power of i rises from vision, leadership and a wilful, creative coordination of the elements of responsible excellence.

It comes to this: think hard how you can make your contribution to a better society *and* how you drive value. Then don't stop improving and don't be satisfied with only small change. The Global Compact performance model can be a rewarding way to start the journey.

---

7 I. Knoepfel, written comments to Claude Fussler during peer review of Chapter 15, 2003; see also www.onvalues.ch.

8 Proposed by Claude Fussler in a keynote at the launch of the EDF Sustainability Chair of Ecole Polytechnique de Paris, February 2003; see also C. Fussler, 'Responsible Excellence Pays', in M. McIntosh, G. Kell and S. Waddock (eds.), *Learning to Talk: Corporate Citizenship and the Development of the UN Global Compact* (Sheffield, UK: Greenleaf Publishing, 2004): 276-88.

Further reading

The editorial team recommend the following:

Collins, J., *Good to Great* (New York: Harper Collins, 2001).

Elkington, J., *Cannibals with Forks: The Triple Bottom Line of 21st Century Business* (Oxford, UK: Capstone Publishing, 1997).

Elkington, J., *The Chrysalis Economy: How Citizen CEOs and Corporations can Fuse Values and Value Creation* (Oxford, UK: Capstone Publishing, 2003).

Holliday, C.O., Jr, S. Schmidheiny and P. Watts, *Walking the Talk: The Business Case for Sustainable Development* (Sheffield, UK: Greenleaf Publishing, 2002).

Kazazian, T., *Il y aura l'âge des choses légères* (Paris: Editions Victoires, 2003).

Leipziger, D., *The Corporate Responsibility Code Book* (Sheffield, UK: Greenleaf Publishing, 2003).

McIntosh, M., G. Kell and S. Waddock (eds.), *Learning to Talk: Corporate Citizenship and the Development of the UN Global Compact* (Sheffield, UK: Greenleaf Publishing, 2004).

Sullivan, R. (ed.), *Business and Human Rights: Dilemmas and Solutions* (Foreword by Mary Robinson; Sheffield, UK: Greenleaf Publishing, 2003).

Von Weizsäcker, E.U., A. Lovins and L.H. Lovins, *Factor Four: Doubling Wealth, Halving Resource Use* (London: Earthscan Publications, 1997)

INDEX